Finding Your Passion

by Dr. Noeline Kirabo

for dummies®
A Wiley Brand

Finding Your Passion For Dummies®

Contents at a Glance

Contents at a Glance

Table of Contents

Introduction

What is passion, and why should you find yours? Passion is more than a mere emotion; it's the essence of your authentic self. It's your heart-beat, the pulsating rhythm that propels you forward with a sense of purpose and fervor. It's the magnetism that draws you toward activities and pursuits that resonate with the core of your being. Imagine it as the North Star, the guiding light illuminating the path of self-discovery and purposeful living.

In the vast cosmos of human existence, the pursuit of passion emerges as a sacred journey that beckons you to delve deep into the recesses of your being to unearth the treasures hidden within. In the narrative of your life, passion guides your course, offering a profound sense of purpose and fulfillment. As you embark upon this odyssey, you discover who you are and explore the profound significance of passion — a force that can revolutionize your very existence.

Beyond the surface allure of passion lies a nuanced landscape, a terrain rich with self-expression, joy, and meaning. It's an intimate dance between your desires and the world, a dialogue with your innermost longings that, when heeded, can transform the mundane into the extraordinary. Passion manifests in the strokes of an artist's brush, the words of a storyteller, the precision of a scientist, and the compassion of a caregiver. It's as diverse as the human experience itself, waiting to be uncovered.

About This Book

I wrote this guide not merely as a compendium of wisdom but as a treasure map to navigating the labyrinth of your own passions. It's an invitation to embark on a profound journey of self-discovery, where the compass is your passion, and the destination is a life infused with purpose and fulfillment. Through insightful reflections, practical strategies, and a wealth of inspiration, this guide is a road-map to unraveling the layers of your authentic self.

How does the discovery and pursuit of your passion ripple through the various dimensions of life, creating a revolution of the soul? Imagine a life where every pursuit is an artistic expression, where the mundane is transformed into the extraordinary, and where each day becomes a canvas upon which the strokes of passion paint a masterpiece. This is the promise that passion holds — an invitation to transcend the mundane and embrace a life of profound significance.

In the professional realm, aligning your career with passion is akin to finding a vocation rather than merely a job. It transforms the concept of work from a means of survival to a medium of self-expression and contribution. When passion is the driving force, the boundaries between work and personal fulfillment blur, creating a seamless integration of purpose and profession. The result isn't just a successful career but a calling — a journey that transcends the pursuit of success to embrace a holistic and meaningful contribution to society.

In relationships, the impact of passion is equally transformative. When you're connected with your passions, you bring a vibrancy and authenticity to your interactions with others. Shared passions become the glue that binds your relationships, creating a deeper and more meaningful connection. And when you're fulfilled in your personal pursuits, you're better equipped to contribute positively to your relationships, fostering an environment of mutual support and growth.

Yet, the revolution of passion extends beyond you and your immediate circles. As a passionate individual, you often become the catalyst for societal change because your authenticity and dedication inspire others to seek purpose and meaning in their lives. Thus, the pursuit of passion creates a ripple effect, contributing to a cultural shift toward a more fulfilled and purpose-driven existence.

Dear reader, it's time to embark on this transformative expedition. Turn the page to delve into the recesses of your passions, unravel the brilliance within, and chart a course toward a life that resonates with your truest self. The adventure awaits.

Foolish Assumptions

Every author must make a few assumptions about their audience, and I've made a few assumptions about you.

- » You're a person who wants to feel more passionate about life.
- » You want to focus your time, energy, and talents to a pursuit you really care about.
- » You want clear, actionable advice on how to map your path to success.

>> You're ready to explore new avenues, people, and experiences to discover your passion.

If this sounds like you, welcome to *Finding Your Passion For Dummies*.

Icons Used in This Book

Here and there, sprinkled in the margins of the book, are small pictures that point to important parts of the text. Here are the icons I used and what they mean.

TIP

These nuggets of advice can save you valuable time or prevent headaches in the future.

WARNING

Think of these warnings as flags that a minesweeper has placed in the field before you so you know where you can safely step and where you definitely can't.

REMEMBER

File these things away in your mind because, somewhere down the road, you'll be glad you did.

Beyond the Book

In addition to the pages you're reading right now, this book comes with a free, access-anywhere online Cheat Sheet that summarizes some of our key advice at a glance. To access this Cheat Sheet, go to www.dummies.com and type **finding your passion cheat sheet** in the search box.

Where to Go from Here

If you want to read about all aspects of the pursuit of passion, you can read this book straight through. But you don't have to read cover to cover to meet your needs.

Depending on where you are on your path to realizing your passion, different sections of the book may be of more interest to you. If you're just starting to think about what direction to take, you can read about navigating your passion pursuit — including self-discovery and how to begin exploring new or long-dormant interests in the chapters of Part 1.

For information on pursuing education or other types of training, adopting a mindset for success, or even launching your own entrepreneurial pursuit, Parts 2 and 3 have a wealth of information to guide you. To better understand the ways in which you can practice self-care or manage disappointment and other setbacks to maintain your well-being, head over to Part 4. Tips for jumpstarting and maintaining your energy for passion pursuit are the subject of Part 5.

However you read this book, it's intended to serve you and give you the information you need to navigate your passion pursuit.

1

Figuring Out What You're Passionate About

Understand the role that passion plays in your life.

Use self-discovery to discover your passion.

Identify and overcome obstacles that stand in your way.

Be open to exploring different areas of interest.

Chapter 1

What It Means to Find Your Passion

The term *passion*, although familiar to most, is often overused, which masks its true depth and significance. What does it mean to have or find your passion? Can you only have one passion, and is it something you're born with or something you can discover over time?

At its heart, passion represents an intense enthusiasm or desire that drives you toward certain pursuits, acting as the lifeblood of dreams and aspirations. However, it's crucial to differentiate genuine passion from transient interests or fleeting infatuations that often are conflated under the same label.

True passion is a strong and intense feeling that you have toward something that you deeply care about. It's a driving force that motivates and inspires you to pursue your interests and goals with dedication, enthusiasm, and persistence.

Passion can come in many forms and can be related to a variety of activities or interests, such as sports, music, art, science, and social causes. It's often characterized by a sense of excitement, joy, and fulfillment and can bring a great deal of meaning and purpose to your life.

Passion isn't just a passing interest or hobby, but rather a deep-rooted and persistent desire to pursue a particular activity or cause. The journey of pursuing your passions can be deeply rewarding and transformative.

WARNING

Although passion can be a powerful force for personal growth and development, it's not a guarantee of success or happiness. Pursuing your passion often involves hard work, dedication, and overcoming obstacles and setbacks — all of which I cover later in this book.

Your passion serves as a guiding star, providing direction and purpose, and instilling resilience in the face of challenges. When you align your life with your passions, you transition from mere existence to a state of thriving, experiencing heightened joy, fulfillment, and overall life satisfaction. This alignment not only enriches personal experiences but also leaves indelible marks on communities and societies by inspiring and igniting the same fire in others.

This book explores what passion is (and isn't), why it's important in your personal and professional life, and how its pursuit benefits you. These pages guide your thinking about your life, your goals, and your interests to help you find your own passion. This chapter starts by looking at what passion is and what myths surround it.

How Passion Affects Your General Well-Being

Pursuing your passion can give you a sense of control and autonomy over your life. This can be particularly important if you feel stuck or uncertain in a certain area. By engaging in activities that you enjoy and feel passionate about, you can regain a sense of agency and empowerment.

Furthermore, pursuing your passion can make you feel accomplished and raise your self-esteem. As you develop skills and knowledge in your areas of interest, you may experience a greater sense of confidence and competence, which can improve your overall mental health. It can bring about a feeling of community and connection.

A growing body of research indicates that finding and pursuing your passion can have positive effects on well-being. Although the causal relationship can be complex and multidimensional, several studies have provided empirical evidence supporting this connection. Here are some key findings from the literature:

>> **Positive psychological well-being:** Harmonious passion, where you freely engage in your passion without external contingencies, is related to higher levels of well-being. In contrast, obsessive passion, driven by internal and external pressures, can sometimes be detrimental.

>> **Physical health:** Engaging in passionate activities often leads to increased physical activity, which has innumerable health benefits. For example, if you're passionate about dancing, hiking, or playing a sport, you're more likely to be physically active, which is linked to a host of health benefits, from improved cardiovascular health to better mental well-being.

>> **Neurological effects:** Engaging in activities you're passionate about releases dopamine, a neurotransmitter associated with pleasure and motivation. This not only makes the activity enjoyable but also energizes and motivates you, leading to increased determination and resilience.

>> **Social connections:** Engaging in passionate pursuits often connects you with like-minded peers, leading to increased social interaction and community-building. Social connections have been consistently linked to improved mental health and longevity.

>> **Cognitive benefits:** Pursuing your passion often involves learning new skills and knowledge. This can keep the brain active and protect against cognitive decline. Engaging in cognitively stimulating activities has been linked to decreased risks of neurodegenerative diseases like Alzheimer's.

>> **Improved mental health:** Engaging in activities that you're passionate about can have a positive impact on your mental health. Pursuing your passions can give you a sense of purpose and direction, which can combat feelings of anxiety, depression, and loneliness. Additionally, engaging in activities that you enjoy can boost your mood and increase your overall sense of well-being.

>> **Increased happiness and life satisfaction:** Pursuing your passions can increase your overall happiness and life satisfaction. When you're engaged in activities that you enjoy, you're more likely to experience positive emotions and feel a sense of accomplishment. This can lead to a greater sense of overall well-being and fulfillment.

>> **Reduced stress and anxiety:** Pursuing your passions can be an effective way to reduce stress and anxiety. When you're engaged in activities you love, you're more likely to experience a state of flow, which can reduce stress and anxiety. Additionally, pursuing your passions can bring about a sense of control and predictability, which can reduce feelings of stress and anxiety.

>> **Improved physical health:** Pursuing your passions can also have a positive impact on your physical health. Engaging in physical activities that you take delight in, such as hiking or dancing, can improve your cardiovascular health and overall fitness level. It can also reduce your risk of developing chronic health conditions such as obesity, diabetes, and heart disease.

» **Increased energy and motivation:** Pursuing your passions can increase your energy and motivation levels. You're more likely to experience excitement and enthusiasm, which can boost your energy and motivation levels. This increased energy and motivation can carry over into other areas of your life, helping you be more productive and successful.

Defining Passion in Your Life and Work

In the vast tapestry of life, passion stands out as the vibrant thread that weaves moments of significance, color, and brilliance. In your personal journey, passion becomes the heartbeat that syncs your dreams with your actions, transforming mere existence into a dance of purpose and fulfillment.

Everyone yearns for moments of transcendence, where the mundanity of daily routines gives way to pursuits that invigorate the soul. It's passion that provides this gateway, turning the prosaic into poetic, the ordinary into the extraordinary. When you embrace your passions, you live with a fervor and zest that infuses your days with meaning, making every sunrise a promise of possibilities and every sunset a reflection of purpose realized.

In the professional realm, passion is the catalyst that propels innovation, perseverance, and excellence. If you're a passionate professional, you don't merely work; you craft, innovate, and transcend. The challenges that might deter others become mere steppingstones if you're fueled by passion. You view your career not as a series of tasks, but as a mission, a calling that you're destined to fulfill.

Your enthusiasm becomes infectious, inspiring colleagues, lifting team morale, and often leading to breakthroughs that redefine industries. As a passionate professional, you also have an uncanny ability to see beyond the horizon, to envision futures that others might deem impossible. You're the visionary, the trailblazer, the one who leaves indelible marks on your fields of endeavor.

However, you need to understand that passion isn't a mere emotion; it's a commitment. It demands dedication, continuous learning, and often, sacrifices. But the fruits it bears, both in personal joy and professional accolades, are unparalleled. Passion bridges the chasm between mediocrity and greatness, between living and thriving. In a world inundated with choices, distractions, and challenges, let passion be your compass, guiding you toward a life of significance, impact, and profound fulfillment.

Passion bestows upon you numerous gifts that elevate the quality and essence of your existence. Among the greatest of these is the gift of purpose. With passion as your guide, your life begins to unravel with a newfound direction, enveloped in a sense of purpose. This not only infuses your days with profound meaning but grants you a sense of fulfillment that transcends the ordinary.

But the gifts of passion don't end there. Passion beckons you onto a path of self-discovery, acting as a mirror reflecting your deepest desires and values. As you tread this path, you find yourself evolving, understanding your intrinsic nature, and embracing personal growth. Such introspection invariably leads to heightened self-awareness, allowing you to grasp the nuances of your character and aspirations more clearly. Furthermore, passion becomes the wellspring of creativity and innovation. It ignites the flames of imagination, giving birth to ideas and perspectives that have the power to redefine and enrich your personal world.

Your mental sanctuary, too, finds solace in the embrace of passion. In today's fast-paced world, stress has become an unwelcome companion for many. Yet, diving deep into your passions offers a haven, a respite where relaxation meets rejuvenation. This not only fortifies your mental health but uplifts your overall well-being, creating ripples of positivity in your life. Additionally, passions forge bonds, acting as threads that weave you into the fabric of communities. When you engage in activities that resonate with your heart's true calling, you inevitably find others who share your zeal. These shared pursuits cultivate social connections, giving rise to communities bound by shared interests and mutual admiration.

On the ladder of personal growth, every rung climbed while pursuing your passions imbues you with a sense of accomplishment. Each goal achieved, each milestone reached in alignment with your passions, swells your heart with pride. This not only amplifies your self-esteem but fortifies your confidence, making you more resilient and determined in the face of life's challenges. The journey of passion is also one of relentless growth and evolution. As you navigate its pathways, you're constantly challenged, prompting you to acquire new skills, adapt to fresh perspectives, and thus mature in your personal and professional spheres.

In the grand balancing act of life, where work and personal pursuits often vie for your attention, passion ensures equilibrium. It encourages you to find that coveted work-life balance, ensuring that you lead a life that's not just productive, but deeply fulfilling. In doing so, it promotes a holistic sense of well-being, reminding you that life, in all its complexity, is a symphony that's best enjoyed when all its notes are in harmony.

Passion is a crucial aspect of personal and professional fulfillment. It offers a sense of purpose and meaning in your life and motivates you to work toward your goals and dreams. When you're passionate about something, you're more likely to invest your time and energy into it, and you're willing to overcome obstacles and challenges to pursue your passions.

Passion in your personal life

Here are some of the important ways that passion can influence your personal life:

» **Provides a sense of purpose and meaning:** Pursuing your passions gives you a sense of purpose and direction in your life, which can bring a greater sense of meaning and fulfillment.

» **Encourages self-discovery:** Exploring your passions can help you learn more about yourself and what you value, leading to greater self-awareness and personal growth.

» **Fosters creativity and innovation:** Passionate pursuits can spark creativity and innovation, leading to new ideas and perspectives that can enrich your world.

» **Promotes mental health and well-being:** Pursuing your passions can be an outlet for stress relief and relaxation, which can be good for your mental health and overall well-being.

» **Offers a way to connect with others:** Pursuing shared passions can be a way to connect with others who share similar interests, fostering social connections and a sense of community.

» **Offers a sense of accomplishment and pride:** Achieving goals related to your passions can bring a sense of accomplishment and pride, boosting self-esteem and confidence.

» **Promotes personal growth and development:** Pursuing your passions can challenge you to learn new skills and gain new perspectives, leading to personal growth and development.

» **Encourages a healthy work-life balance:** Balancing work and personal passions can lead to a more fulfilling and well-rounded life, promoting overall health and well-being.

Passion in your professional life

In your professional life, passion can be a key factor in career success and satisfaction. When you're passionate about your work, you're more likely to excel in your job and be recognized for your contributions. Passion can also lead to new opportunities and career advancement, as well as a sense of purpose and fulfillment in your professional endeavors.

Here are some of the important ways that passion can affect your professional life:

>> **Increases job satisfaction:** When you're passionate about your work, you're more likely to feel satisfied with your job and find meaning in your work.

>> **Boosts productivity:** As a passionate employee, you tend to be more productive and engaged in your work, leading to better performance and results.

>> **Enhances creativity and innovation:** You're more likely to think outside the box and come up with creative solutions to problems, driving innovation and growth.

>> **Attracts new opportunities:** You're often sought after by employers and may have more opportunities for career advancement and development.

>> **Builds strong professional networks:** You're more likely to network with others in their field, building strong relationships that can lead to new opportunities and collaborations.

>> **Improves job performance:** You tend to be more committed to your work and may go above and beyond to ensure quality and success in your roles.

>> **Fosters leadership qualities:** You may demonstrate strong leadership qualities and inspire others to achieve their goals and pursue their passions.

>> **Contributes to a positive work environment:** You create a positive work environment, boosting morale and inspiring others to be their best selves.

Overall, passion can play a critical role in your professional life, contributing to job satisfaction, productivity, innovation, and career success. By pursuing your passions and finding meaning in your work, you can build a fulfilling career that contributes to your overall well-being and success.

The Value of Finding Your Passion

The relentless pursuit of passion is often likened to chasing the North Star, a guiding light that leads you through life's twists and turns. Embracing passion, whether as a life's calling or a momentary interest, can unleash a cascade of benefits that touch nearly every facet of your existence:

>> **A directional compass:** First and foremost, passion points to a clear direction. In a world where distractions abound and choices can be overwhelming, knowing

your passion can serve as a beacon, illuminating the path forward. It offers a roadmap, delineating the journey between where you are and where you yearn to be, making your decisions more intentional and your goals more attainable.

» **Elevation of well-being:** Physical, emotional, and psychological well-being often see an uplift when you're immersed in your passion. Activities you pursue with genuine interest can be both cathartic and therapeutic. They act as an outlet, channeling your energies positively and keeping negative stressors at bay. The joy derived from doing what you love has a direct impact on your mental health, staving off feelings of despair and despondency.

» **A forge for resilience:** Challenges and setbacks are a part and parcel of life. However, the vigor that stems from passion arms you with resilience. It makes the hurdles seem surmountable and failures just pit stops in the longer journey. Your commitment to your passion gives you the grit and determination to rise from setbacks, learn from them, and move forward with renewed zest.

» **Catalyst for personal growth:** Passion has a transformative power. As you delve deeper into your interests, you invariably find yourself on a path of continuous learning. This not only broadens your skill set but expands your horizons, leading to overall personal development. Moreover, passion fuels creativity, making you think outside the box and approach challenges with innovative solutions.

» **Stronger social bonds:** Shared passions pave the way for meaningful connections. Engaging in group activities or communities centered around common interests can foster deep, lasting relationships. These relationships, built on mutual respect and shared excitement often enrich your social life and foster a sense of belonging.

» **Self-identity boost:** Knowing and pursuing your passion contributes significantly to your sense of identity. It gives you a clearer understanding of who you are, what you value, and what drives you. This clarity and self-awareness can be instrumental in building self-esteem and confidence.

» **Enhanced productivity and satisfaction:** Engaging in tasks you're passionate about naturally increases your efficiency and productivity. When work aligns with passion, it ceases to be a mere chore. Instead, it transforms into a labor of love, resulting in higher quality outputs and greater personal satisfaction.

The act of identifying and pursuing your passions isn't just a fanciful endeavor. It's a powerful commitment to yourself, a journey that promises manifold returns — from personal happiness to professional excellence. In the grand tapestry of life, passion is the thread that adds vibrancy, purpose, and depth, making each day a masterpiece in its own right.

Common Myths and Misconceptions about Passion

Finding your passion can be a challenging journey, filled with uncertainty and self-doubt. Unfortunately, many myths and misconceptions surrounding the pursuit of passion can make the journey even more difficult. This section explores some of the most common myths and misconceptions about finding passion and sets the record straight.

Myth 1: You should follow your passion at any cost

One of the most pervasive myths about finding passion is that you should follow it at any cost. Although it's important to pursue what you love and find meaningful, blindly following your passion without considering the practicalities can have negative consequences. For example, quitting your job to pursue a passion without a plan or financial stability can result in financial difficulties and other challenges.

It's important to strike a balance between passion and practicality. Pursuing your passion in a way that's financially sustainable and aligns with your personal and professional goals can lead to a fulfilling and successful career.

This myth is often perpetuated by the idea that if you love what you do, you'll never work a day in your life. Although there's some truth to the idea that finding work that you love can lead to greater job satisfaction and fulfillment, it's important to balance this with practical considerations.

Consider the reality of the situation when pursuing your passion. You might have a passion for something that doesn't pay well or where jobs are scarce. In these cases, you may need to find ways to supplement your income or pursue a related career that still allows you to utilize your passion. If you have other responsibilities, such as family, it's important to consider their needs as well.

Myth 2: Passion is something you're born with and can't develop

Another common myth is that passion is something you're born with and can't develop. Although some people may naturally gravitate toward certain interests or activities, passion isn't a fixed trait. You can cultivate and develop it over time through exploration, practice, and persistence.

Approach passion with a growth mindset, recognizing that you can develop it and nurture it over time. By exploring different interests and investing time and effort into pursuing them, you can develop a passion for something that you never thought possible. Passion isn't something that just happens to you. You create it through your own efforts. While some people may naturally have a strong inclination toward certain activities or interests, you can develop passion over time through experience, exposure, and deliberate practice.

Passion is often fueled by a sense of purpose or meaning, which you can develop by exploring different areas of interest and finding activities or causes that resonate with you on a deeper level. This exploration can involve trying out different hobbies, volunteering for organizations that align with your values, or pursuing education or career paths that allow you to make a meaningful impact.

Deliberate practice is also important in developing passion. This involves setting goals, seeking feedback, and consistently working toward improving your skills and knowledge in a particular area. As you become more skilled and knowledgeable, you may find that your passion for the activity or topic grows stronger.

Passion isn't a fixed trait; it can change and evolve over time. By actively seeking out experiences and opportunities that align with your interests and values, and by putting in the effort to develop your skills and knowledge, you can cultivate passion and find fulfillment in your pursuits.

Myth 3: Pursuing passion is selfish

Another myth about pursuing passion is that it's a selfish pursuit that ignores the needs of others. Although it's important to consider the impact of your decisions on others, pursuing your passions can also benefit those around you.

Passion can inspire others, bring people together, and lead to positive change in the world. By pursuing your passions, you may also find ways to give back to others and contribute to your community. For example, a passion for volunteering can lead to opportunities to make a positive impact in your community.

Some may view the pursuit of passion as a self-indulgent or frivolous pursuit, but in reality, following your passion can be a deeply meaningful and purposeful endeavor that benefits not only you, but those around you.

When you're passionate about something, you're often driven to pursue it with dedication and enthusiasm. This can lead to the development of skills and knowledge that you can apply in many different areas of life, including relationships, work, and community involvement.

Additionally, pursuing your passion can lead to personal fulfillment and happiness, which can have positive ripple effects in many areas of life. When you're fulfilled and happy, you're more likely to be kind, compassionate, and generous to others.

Furthermore, following your passion can often lead to the creation of new ideas, products, or services that benefit society as a whole. Many of the world's most significant advancements and innovations have come from individuals who were passionate about their work and committed to pursuing their ideas.

In short, pursuing your passion isn't a selfish pursuit. Instead, it can be a deeply purposeful and meaningful endeavor that benefits both you and those around you.

Myth 4: Passionate people are always happy

It's a common misconception that passionate people are always happy and fulfilled. Although pursuing your passion can bring a sense of purpose and fulfillment, it's not a guarantee of happiness. Like any pursuit, the pursuit of passion can be challenging and comes with its own set of ups and downs.

It's important to approach passion with a realistic perspective, recognizing that it's not a panacea for all of life's challenges. Even passionate people experience sadness, frustration, and disappointment. But by cultivating resilience and a positive mindset, you can navigate the challenges of pursuing your passion and find fulfillment even in difficult times.

In fact, sometimes passionate people may experience negative emotions more intensely than others because their investment in their passions can make them more vulnerable to setbacks or failures. This can be particularly true if you're pursuing creative or entrepreneurial endeavors because these fields often involve a great deal of risk-taking and uncertainty.

Passion isn't a constant state, and it can wax and wane over time. Even if you're deeply passionate about your work or hobbies, you may experience periods of burnout or disillusionment.

That being said, passion can provide a sense of purpose and direction that can help you weather difficult times and find meaning in your struggles. As a passionate person, you're more likely to bounce back from setbacks or failures because your drive and commitment can help you stay focused on your goals and maintain a positive outlook.

So even though passion can bring a great deal of joy and fulfillment, it's not a guarantee of constant happiness. Like all emotions, it can fluctuate over time. You can experience a range of feelings as a passionate person.

Myth 5: Finding passion is easy

Finally, one of the most damaging myths about finding passion is that it's easy and straightforward. In reality, finding your passion can be a long and winding journey that requires patience, persistence, and self-reflection.

It's important to approach the pursuit of passion with an open mind and a willingness to try new things. By exploring different interests and activities, you may discover a passion that you never knew existed.

Some individuals may discover their passions early in life or stumble upon them by chance, but for many people, the process of finding passion can be a long and challenging journey.

Finding your passion often requires a great deal of self-reflection and exploration. It may involve trying out different hobbies, pursuing education or career opportunities in different fields, or engaging in personal growth and development activities such as therapy or self-help.

In some cases, finding your passion may also require overcoming fears or limiting beliefs that have held you back from pursuing your true interests and aspirations. This can involve taking risks, stepping out of your comfort zone, and pushing through self-doubt and uncertainty.

Furthermore, the process of finding your passion isn't always linear. It may involve many twists and turns, and individuals may discover that their passions change or evolve over time as they grow and change.

Although finding your passion may not be easy, it can be a deeply rewarding and transformative process. By committing to the journey of self-discovery and exploration, you can find a sense of purpose and fulfillment that can bring greater meaning and joy to your life.

The pursuit of passion is an important journey that can bring fulfillment and meaning to your personal and professional life. By dispelling these common myths and misconceptions, you can approach the pursuit of passion with a realistic and empowered perspective, leading to a more fulfilling and successful life.

Getting Started Identifying Your Passion

Although the remainder of this book delves more deeply into strategies for identifying your passion and understanding the benefits it can have across your life, Figures 1-1 and 1-2 give you a starting point, with questions to get you started in your self-evaluation to discover what your passion — or passions — are and how you can cultivate and put them into practice in your life.

Instructions: For each question, rate your level of agreement on a scale from 1 to 5, with 1 being strongly disagree and 5 being strongly agree.

I feel most alive when I'm doing something I love._____

I'm willing to make sacrifices to pursue my passion. _____

I often lose track of time when I'm engaged in an activity I enjoy. _____

I'm motivated to learn and improve in areas that I'm passionate about. _____

I feel a sense of purpose and fulfillment when I'm pursuing my passions. _____

I'm willing to take risks and step outside my comfort zone to pursue my passions. _____

I'm willing to invest time, money, and effort into my passions. _____

I'm able to clearly articulate what I'm passionate about to others. _____

I feel a sense of excitement and energy when I think about pursuing my passions. _____

I believe that pursuing my passions can lead to a fulfilling and meaningful life. _____

Scoring: Add up your scores for each question to get a total out of 50. The higher your score, the more aligned you are with your passions.

Score:

FIGURE 1-1: Self-assessment: Understanding your passion.

Instructions: Using a calendar or a time-tracking app, keep track of how you spend your time for one week. Categorize your activities into the following types: work, leisure, socializing, hobbies/interests, and other. At the end of the week, answer the following questions:

Which activities did you enjoy the most? Why?

Which activities did you dread or find unfulfilling? Why?

Did you spend more time on work or leisure activities? Why?

Were there any activities that you wish you had more time for? Why?

Did you spend any time pursuing hobbies or interests? If so, how much time did you spend on these activities?

Did you spend any time socializing with friends or family? If so, how much time did you spend on these activities?

Did you feel a sense of purpose or fulfillment from any of the activities you engaged in?

Activity categories:

Work: _____

Leisure: _____

Socializing: _____

Hobbies/interests: _____

Other:

_____

Total time allocated to each category every week:

Work   _____

Leisure   _____

Socializing   _____

Hobbies   _____

Others   _____

Total Time: _____

IN THIS CHAPTER

» Taking stock of your values,
weaknesses, and strengths

» Assessing your own personality

» Looking at which interests can grow
into passions

Chapter 2

Looking Inward: Self-Discovery

Few journeys are as profound, challenging, and ultimately rewarding as the voyage inward. It's easy for the modern world to pull attention outward. You're conditioned to seek validation, happiness, and meaning in external accolades, possessions, and social metrics. But true fulfillment, as countless philosophers, poets, and thinkers have proposed, lies not outside but within. It's in the silent moments of introspection, the quiet reflection of a serene evening, and the intense focus of meditation that you often stumble upon your most profound revelations.

Truly knowing yourself, delving deep into the caverns of your own psyche and spirit, is both an art and a science. This chapter invites you on such a pilgrimage — a quest not to foreign lands, but to the uncharted territories of your own soul. Self-discovery isn't a linear process with a defined start and finish. It's cyclical, evolving as you grow and change. With every challenge you face, every dream you chase, and every loss you endure, you gain a deeper understanding of who you truly are and what you stand for.

This chapter aims to be your guide on this introspective journey. It explores various avenues and tools for self-discovery, from age-old meditation techniques to modern-day psychological tests. It benchmarks examples of individuals who have embarked on this journey, gleaning insights from their challenges and triumphs. And, most importantly, it has strategies and exercises to help you tune out the noise of the outside world and home in on your innermost thoughts, feelings, and desires.

So, as you turn the page, take a deep breath. You're about to embark on the most important expedition of all — one that leads to the very core of your being.

Understanding Your Values, Strengths, and Weaknesses

Like a unique piece of art, you're a blend of contrasts and harmonies, strengths and vulnerabilities, passions and reluctances. Before you can embark on a fulfilling journey of self-discovery or personal growth, there lies a foundational step — understanding your intrinsic values, recognizing innate strengths, and acknowledging inherent weaknesses. This isn't merely a process of self-assessment; it's a profound venture into self-awareness.

At the heart of every choice you make and every dream you chase are your core values — those unwavering principles that guide your actions and decisions, serving as the moral compass of your life. They shape your perceptions, influence your reactions, and define your character. To know your values is to have a roadmap to purpose and meaning.

Parallelly, recognizing your strengths allows you to harness your potential, channeling your energy into avenues where you can shine and excel. It's about aligning with your natural inclinations, celebrating your unique talents, and optimizing your potential for success. Conversely, understanding your weaknesses isn't about self-critique but self-growth. It's an invitation to develop, learn, and evolve, turning perceived shortcomings into opportunities for growth.

This section covers the processes and tools that assist in this introspective journey. Through thoughtful exercises, reflective questions, and insightful anecdotes, it guides you in unearthing your core values, leveraging your strengths, and addressing your weaknesses. The goal? To lay the foundation for a life lived authentically, aligning actions with values and aspirations with capabilities.

Prepare to embark on a transformative exploration, one that promises clarity, self-affirmation, and a deeper connection to your authentic self.

Understanding your values, strengths, and weaknesses is a crucial step in finding your passion and pursuing a fulfilling life. Are you ready?

The importance of understanding your values

Your values are the principles and beliefs that guide your decision-making and behavior. When you understand your values, you can align your actions and goals with what's truly important to you. This can lead to greater satisfaction and fulfillment in both your personal and your professional life.

Understanding your values is crucial to finding and pursuing your passion because your values are the things that matter most to you. Your values are the principles, beliefs, and ideals that guide your behavior and decision-making. They're what you hold dear, that give your life meaning, and that you're willing to fight for.

By understanding your values, you can identify the types of activities and pursuits that align with your core beliefs and provide a sense of purpose and fulfillment. For example, if one of your core values is creativity, you may find that pursuing a career in the arts or design provides a sense of meaning and fulfillment that other careers may not.

Similarly, if one of your core values is social justice, you may find that volunteering for a non-profit organization or pursuing a career in advocacy gives you a sense of purpose and fulfillment that other careers may not.

In addition to helping you identify potential areas of passion, understanding your values can help you make better decisions and prioritize your time and resources. When you understand what's most important to you, you can make choices that align with your values and avoid wasting time and energy on what doesn't.

Finally, understanding your values can help you navigate challenges and setbacks. When you face difficult decisions or challenges, you can turn to your values for guidance and direction so that you stay true to what matters the most to you.

Overall, understanding your values is crucial to finding and pursuing your passion because it helps you identify the types of activities and pursuits that align with your core beliefs and bring you purpose and fulfillment. By prioritizing your values and aligning your choices with what's most important to you, you can lead a more meaningful and fulfilling life.

Identifying your core values

To identify your core values, ask yourself what motivates you, what you stand for, and what principles you live by.

Some common values include integrity, compassion, creativity, and honesty. Once you've identified your core values, you can use them to guide your decision-making and pursue opportunities that align with those values.

Overall, identifying your core values is an important step in finding and pursuing your passion. By taking the time to reflect on your life experiences, motivations, role models, strengths and weaknesses, and potential values, you can identify the things that matter most to you and use this knowledge to guide your choices and pursuits.

Identifying your core values is an important step in finding and pursuing your passion. Read on for how to identify your core values.

Reflect on your life experiences

Take some time to reflect on your life experiences and consider what's been most important to you in your life. What have been the defining moments or experiences that have shaped who you are and what you value?

Consider what motivates and inspires you

Think about the activities or pursuits that motivate and inspire you. What are the common themes or values that underlie these activities or pursuits?

Identify your role models

Consider the people you admire and look up to. What values do they embody that resonate with you?

Consider your strengths and weaknesses

Your values are often closely tied to your strengths and weaknesses. What values are reflected in the activities or pursuits where you excel? Conversely, what values are reflected in the areas where you struggle or need improvement?

Write a list of potential values

Based on your reflections and considerations, make a list of potential values that are important to you. Some examples of values include creativity, compassion, justice, loyalty, and honesty.

Narrow down your list

Review your list of potential values and identify your most important ones. Aim to narrow your list to around five core values.

Test your values

Once you've identified your core values, test them out by making choices and decisions that align with them. See how it feels to live in alignment with your values, and make adjustments as needed.

Steps to help you define your values

The following list can help you zero in on your values and guide your passion pursuit. Figure 2-1 can lead you through this deep thinking.

1. **Reflect on your life:** Think about the moments in your life where you felt most fulfilled and satisfied. What were you doing? Who were you with? What values were present in those experiences?

2. **Identify your values:** Based on your reflections, list the values that were present in those moments. Examples might include compassion, honesty, creativity, and resilience.

3. **Narrow down your list:** Look at your list and identify your most important values. If you could choose only three values to guide your life, what would they be?

4. **Prioritize your values:** Once you've identified your top values, prioritize them. Which value is most important to you? The second most important? And so on.

5. **Use your values to guide your decisions:** With your core values in mind, think about how you can use them to guide your decisions and actions. For example, if one of your core values is honesty, you might ask yourself, "Is this decision aligned with my value of honesty?"

6. **Review and update your values:** Your core values may shift and change over time. It's important to review them regularly and adjust them as needed.

Taking stock of your strengths and weaknesses

In the vast landscape of personal growth, few endeavors hold as much transformative power as the act of assessing your strengths and weaknesses. But why is this introspective evaluation so crucial? At its core, the journey of self-assessment is less about scrutiny and more about enlightenment; it's about gaining a clearer vision of yourself to navigate the complexities of life with greater purpose, efficacy, and self-awareness.

Reflect on your life: Think about the moments in your life where you felt most fulfilled and satisfied. What were you doing? Who were you with? What values were present in those experiences?

Sample answer: When I volunteered at the local animal shelter, I felt a sense of compassion and empathy for the animals.

When I completed a challenging project at work, I felt a sense of pride in my work and my ability to overcome obstacles.

When I spent time with my family, I felt a sense of love and connection.

Identify your values: Based on your reflections, list the values that were present in those moments.

Compassion

Empathy

Pride

Hard work

Love

Connection

Narrow down your list: Look at your list and identify your most important values. Ask yourself, "If I could choose only three values to guide my life, what would they be?"

Compassion

Hard work

Connection

FIGURE 2-1:
A guide to finding your values.

Prioritize your values: Once you've identified your top values, prioritize them. Which value is the most important to you? The second most important? And so on.

Compassion

Connection

Hard work

Use your values to guide your decisions: With your core values in mind, think about how you can use them to guide your decisions and actions.

If I'm deciding whether or not to donate money to a charity, I'll consider my value of compassion.

If I'm deciding whether or not to take on a new project at work, I'll consider my value of hard work.

If I'm deciding how to spend my free time, I'll consider my value of connection.

Review and update your values: Your core values may shift and change over time. Review them regularly and adjust them as needed.

FIGURE 2-1:
Continued

The need to assess your strengths and weaknesses isn't a mere exercise in introspection — it's a fundamental step toward creating a life of purpose, growth, and genuine fulfillment. By understanding where you shine and where you need to grow, you position yourself to make the most of every opportunity, challenge, and experience that comes your way.

Your strengths are the skills and qualities that you excel in, and your weaknesses are areas where you may struggle or need improvement. Identifying your strengths and weaknesses can help you make better career and life choices and set more realistic goals.

Empowerment through recognition

Understanding your strengths is like uncovering hidden treasures within you. When you identify and acknowledge what you excel at, you empower yourself to harness these assets, channeling them into your personal and professional life. This recognition can be the catalyst for self-confidence, paving the way for you to take on challenges with gusto and achieve your goals with a reinforced sense of purpose.

Growth through acknowledgment

Addressing your weaknesses, on the other hand, isn't an exercise in self-doubt but rather one in growth potential. By pinpointing areas of improvement, you're not magnifying your flaws but illuminating opportunities for development. Every recognized weakness becomes a path to learning, an avenue for personal development, and a steppingstone to a more holistic version of yourself.

Informed decision-making

With a lucid understanding of your strengths and weaknesses, your decision-making process becomes more informed and aligned with your true capabilities. You become better equipped to choose roles, tasks, and challenges that align with your strengths while seeking support, education, or tools in areas you're looking to develop.

Authentic relationships

An honest self-assessment not only affects your relationship with yourself but also with others. When you're transparent about your strengths and limitations, you foster trust, encourage genuine connections, and build more authentic relationships, both personally and professionally.

Identifying your strengths and weaknesses

What follows can help you recognize your strengths and weaknesses. Figure 2-2 can guide your assessment.

List your accomplishments: Think about the times in your life when you've felt successful or accomplished. What did you do? What skills did you use? Write down at least five accomplishments.

Identify the skills you used: Look at each accomplishment and identify the skills you used to achieve it. For example, if you received a promotion at work, the skills you used might include leadership, communication, and problem-solving.

Ask for feedback: Ask friends, family, or colleagues for honest feedback about your strengths and weaknesses. Ask them to identify what they think you do well and what you could improve upon.

Take a personality assessment: Consider taking a personality assessment, such as the Myers–Briggs Type Indicator or the Big Five personality traits. These assessments can help you better understand your personality and identify your strengths and weaknesses.

Identify areas for improvement: Based on your accomplishments, feedback from others, and personality assessment results, identify areas where you could improve. These might include specific skills or aspects of your personality.

Create an action plan: Once you've identified your strengths and weaknesses, create an action plan to improve in the areas where you need it most. This might include taking a class, seeking out a mentor, or practicing a skill.

List your accomplishments:

Received a promotion at work

Completed a marathon

Learned to speak a second language

Organized a successful fundraiser

Completed a challenging project on time

Identify the skills you used:

Leadership, communication, problem-solving (promotion at work)

Endurance, discipline, goal-setting (completed a marathon)

Language learning, cultural awareness (learned a second language)

Event planning, marketing, communication (organized a successful fundraiser)

Time management, organization, attention to detail (completed a challenging project on time)

Ask for feedback:

Strengths: Leadership, organization, attention to detail

Weaknesses: Public speaking, delegation

FIGURE 2-2:
Assessing your strengths and weaknesses: Sample answers.

Take a personality assessment:

Personality type after taking the Myers-Briggs: ENFJ (extroverted, intuitive, feeling, judging)

Strengths: Excellent people skills, ability to inspire and motivate others

Weaknesses: Tendency to be overly sensitive to criticism, difficulty making tough decisions

Identify areas for improvement:

Public speaking

Delegation

Decision-making

Create an action plan:

Take a public speaking class

Seek out a mentor who's skilled at delegation

Practice decision-making by making a small decision every day

FIGURE 2-2:
Continued

Empowering yourself by finding your weak spots

Life, in its essence, is a journey, not a destination. And just as every journey has its terrains to navigate, life offers you myriad opportunities for self-betterment. Identifying areas of improvement is akin to charting out the next waypoints on this journey, ensuring that you're always progressing, evolving, and growing. But why is the act of pinpointing these areas so pivotal, and how does it shape your trajectory?

Identifying areas of improvement isn't about magnifying your shortcomings. Instead, it's about spotlighting opportunities, paving the way for continued growth and resilience. It's about ensuring that the journey of life, with all its twists and turns, remains one of perpetual evolution and enrichment.

Self-awareness as a catalyst

At the heart of personal growth lies an acute sense of self-awareness. Recognizing areas that require enhancement isn't a sign of inadequacy, but a testament to your self-awareness and eagerness to evolve. It's the initial step in acknowledging that even though you're proficient in many spheres, there's always room to expand, learn, and refine.

Targeted growth

By clearly identifying areas of improvement, your growth becomes targeted. Rather than attempting to grow in all directions, you can channel your energy, resources, and time into specific facets, ensuring that your efforts yield maximal results. This targeted approach not only boosts your efficiency but enhances the likelihood of tangible improvement.

Building resilience

Embracing your imperfections and actively seeking areas to better yourself often leads to a more resilient mindset. When you're open to feedback and willing to adapt, you become more resistant to setbacks. Instead of perceiving them as failures, they transform into learning opportunities, allowing you to bounce back even stronger.

Enriched relationships and collaborations

In both personal and professional spheres, acknowledging your areas of improvement fosters an environment of humility and openness. By being candid about where you seek growth, you invite constructive feedback, encourage collaborations, and cultivate relationships grounded in authenticity and mutual respect.

Lifelong learning

Embracing the need for improvement solidifies a commitment to lifelong learning. It establishes a mindset that treasures growth over perfection, valuing the journey and the lessons it brings over the illusion of a final, flawless destination.

Deciding on areas for improvement

Once you've identified your strengths and weaknesses (Figure 2-3 can help you do so), you can develop a plan to improve in areas where you may be lacking. For example, if you struggle with public speaking, you may seek out opportunities to practice and improve your skills. Here are the steps you should take to improve on your weaknesses:

1. **Identify the areas of your life that you want to improve:** This could be related to your career, relationships, health, personal growth, or any other area that you feel needs development.

2. **Assess your current state:** Take some time to assess your current state in each area. What's working well for you? What needs improvement?

3. **Set specific goals:** Based on your assessment, set specific goals for each area that you want to improve. Make sure your goals are measurable, achievable, relevant, and time-bound.

4. **Create an action plan:** Once you've set your goals, create an action plan for each one. What steps do you need to take to achieve your goals? Who can help you achieve them? What obstacles might you face, and how can you overcome them?

5. **Monitor your progress:** Keep track of your progress toward your goals. This helps you stay motivated and make adjustments to your action plan as needed.

6. **Celebrate your successes:** Celebrate your successes along the way, no matter how small they may seem. This keeps you motivated and builds momentum toward achieving your goals.

Identify the areas of your life you want to improve.

Career: I want to improve my time management skills to be more productive at work.

Relationships: I want to improve my communication skills to better connect with my partner.

Health: I want to improve my fitness level and develop healthier eating habits.

Personal growth: I want to learn a new skill or hobby to broaden my horizons.

Assess your current state.

Career: I often feel overwhelmed and struggle to prioritize my tasks.

Relationships: I tend to avoid difficult conversations and struggle to express my emotions.

Health: I often skip workouts and struggle to stick to a healthy eating plan.

Personal growth: I haven't explored new hobbies or interests in a while.

Set specific goals.

Career: I'll develop a daily schedule to prioritize my tasks and manage my time more efficiently.

Relationships: I'll practice active listening and express my emotions more openly in conversations with my partner.

Health: I'll commit to working out three times per week and meal-prepping healthy lunches for work.

Personal growth: I'll take a cooking class to learn new healthy recipes and develop my culinary skills.

Create an action plan.

Career: I'll create a daily schedule each morning and use a time-management app to track my progress.

Relationships: I'll read a book on effective communication skills and practice active listening with my partner each week.

Health: I'll join a gym, schedule my workouts on my calendar, and research healthy meal-prep recipes to make on Sundays.

Personal growth: I'll research local cooking classes and sign up for one that fits my schedule.

FIGURE 2-3:
Seeking areas for improvement.

Monitor your progress.

Career: Each week, I'll evaluate my progress toward completing my daily tasks and adjust my schedule as needed.

Relationships: I'll track the number of times I practice active listening each week and note any improvements in my conversations with my partner.

Health: I'll track my workouts and meals in a fitness app and monitor my progress toward my fitness goals.

Personal growth: I'll attend the cooking class and track my progress in learning new recipes and cooking techniques.

Celebrate your successes

Career: When I successfully complete all my daily tasks for the week, I'll treat myself to a relaxing activity, like a massage or a movie night.

Relationships: When I have a successful conversation with my partner, I'll plan a special date night to celebrate our improved communication.

Health: When I reach a fitness milestone, like running a 5k, I'll reward myself with a new pair of sneakers.

FIGURE 2-3:
Continued

Assessing Your Personality and Interests

In the vast mosaic of human experience, you stand out as a unique tile, characterized by specific hues of personality and patterns of interest. Understanding these intrinsic attributes — your personality traits and the passions that ignite your spirit — is more than just a quest for self-awareness; it's a key to unlocking a life of authenticity, fulfillment, and alignment.

In essence, assessing your personality and interests is the cornerstone of living authentically. It's about resonating with your true self, making choices that reflect your genuine nature, and navigating the world with a clear sense of who you are and what ignites your spirit. This journey of self-assessment promises not just self-awareness but a life lived with purpose, passion, and profound alignment.

Assessing your personality and interests is an important step in finding your passion. Understanding your personality can help you identify the activities and work that best align with your strengths and values. Additionally, identifying your interests can help you find the areas of work or activities that you enjoy and are most likely to lead to long-term satisfaction.

Discovering your unique blueprint

Your personality, that intricate combination of traits, behaviors, and temperaments, shapes your reactions, decisions, and interactions. Assessing your personality is akin to exploring the unique blueprint that dictates how you engage with the world around you. It's a deep dive into understanding your inherent nature, motivations, and inclinations.

Alignment with passions

Beyond the contours of personality lies the realm of interests — the things that excite you, inspire you, and drive you. Recognizing and honoring these interests is paramount to crafting a life infused with joy and passion. Whether it's a hobby, a professional pursuit, or a casual inclination, your interests are the compass points that guide you toward genuine satisfaction.

Informed choices and direction

With a clear grasp of your personality and interests, decision-making becomes more intuitive and aligned. Whether choosing a career path, seeking out hobbies, or forging relationships, this understanding is a roadmap that resonates with your true self, ensuring that your choices are in harmony with your innate tendencies and passions.

Enhanced interpersonal relationships

Recognizing your personality traits helps you navigate the intricate dynamics of interpersonal relationships. It offers insights into your communication styles, conflict resolution techniques, and collaboration methods, making you more empathetic and effective in your interactions with others.

Lifelong self-exploration

The endeavor to assess your personality and interests isn't a one-time task but a continuous journey of self-exploration. As you evolve, so do your traits and inclinations. Revisiting and reassessing them periodically ensures that you remain in tune with your evolving self, always aligned with your authentic core.

Understanding different personality types

A personality type is a set of enduring characteristics and traits that shape an individual's patterns of thinking, feeling, and behaving. It's often assessed through personality assessments like the Myers-Briggs Type Indicator (MBTI), the Big Five Personality Traits, or other similar tools. Each person falls along a spectrum in various personality dimensions, and these assessments categorize individuals into specific types or traits based on their dominant characteristics.

The models for categorizing personality types are many, each with its own unique set of traits and characteristics. Three popular models follow:

The Myers-Briggs Type Indicator (MBTI)

This model, based on the work of psychologist Carl Jung, categorizes individuals into 16 personality types based on four dichotomies:

Extraversion (E) vs. Introversion (I): Extraverts tend to be outgoing and sociable, whereas introverts tend to be more reserved and reflective.

Sensing (S) vs. Intuition (N): Sensors tend to focus on concrete, sensory information, whereas intuitives tend to focus on abstract concepts and patterns.

Thinking (T) vs. Feeling (F): Thinkers tend to prioritize logic and reason, whereas feelers tend to prioritize empathy and emotional considerations.

Judging (J) vs. Perceiving (P): Judgers tend to be organized and structured, whereas perceivers tend to be more flexible and adaptable.

The Big Five Personality Traits

This model categorizes individuals based on five broad personality dimensions:

Openness to Experience: This trait reflects a person's level of imagination, creativity, and openness to new experiences.

Conscientiousness: This trait reflects a person's level of organization, responsibility, and dependability.

Extraversion: This trait reflects a person's level of sociability, assertiveness, and enthusiasm.

Agreeableness: This trait reflects a person's level of kindness, empathy, and cooperativeness.

Neuroticism: This trait reflects a person's level of emotional instability, anxiety, and moodiness.

The Enneagram

This model categorizes individuals into nine personality types based on their core motivations and fears:

Type 1: The Perfectionist: Motivated by a desire for perfection and fear of being wrong or bad.

Type 2: The Helper: Motivated by a desire to be needed and fear of being unloved or rejected.

Type 3: The Achiever: Motivated by a desire for success and fear of failure or being worthless.

Type 4: The Individualist: Motivated by a desire for uniqueness and fear of being ordinary or mundane.

Type 5: The Investigator: Motivated by a desire for knowledge and fear of being ignorant or overwhelmed.

Type 6: The Loyalist: Motivated by a desire for security and fear of being without support or guidance.

Type 7: The Enthusiast: Motivated by a desire for adventure and fear of being limited or deprived.

Type 8: The Challenger: Motivated by a desire for control and fear of being weak or vulnerable.

Type 9: The Peacemaker: Motivated by a desire for harmony and fear of conflict or disruption.

Keep in mind that these models aren't perfect and shouldn't be used to label or categorize individuals. They can, however, be helpful tools for gaining insight into your own personality and the personalities of others.

Identifying your own personality type

The relationship between personality type and passion finding lies in the alignment of personal preferences, strengths, and inclinations with activities or pursuits that resonate with those preferences.

While understanding your personality type is a valuable tool, it's important to note that it's not a rigid determinant. People are complex, and individual differences exist within each personality type. Additionally, passions can evolve over time, influenced by experiences and personal growth. Therefore, using personality type as a guide rather than a strict rule can contribute significantly to the process of finding and nurturing one's passion.

Here's how personality type contributes to the process of discovering and pursuing one's passion:

Certain personality types may be naturally inclined towards specific strengths. For example, an extroverted person might find passion in roles that involve social interactions, while an introverted person might excel in more solitary pursuits.

Identifying personal strengths helps individuals focus on activities that leverage their innate abilities, making the pursuit of passion more rewarding. This is also valuable in guiding career choices.

>> **Myers-Briggs Type Indicator (MBTI):** The MBTI, one of the most well-known personality assessments, is based on the work of Carl Jung. It categorizes individuals into 16 personality types based on four dichotomies: extraversion vs. introversion, sensing vs. intuition, thinking vs. feeling, and judging vs. perceiving. www.16personalities.com/free-personality-test

>> **Big Five Personality Traits:** The Big Five Personality Traits, also known as the Five Factor Model, categorize individuals based on five broad traits: openness, conscientiousness, extraversion, agreeableness, and neuroticism. www.truity.com/test/big-five-personality-test

>> **Enneagram:** The Enneagram is a personality assessment that categorizes individuals into nine different personality types based on their motivations and core fears. www.truity.com/test/enneagram-personality-test

>> **DISC Assessment:** The DISC Assessment categorizes individuals into four different personality types based on their behavior styles: dominance, influence, steadiness, and conscientiousness. www.123test.com/disc-personality-test/

>> **CliftonStrengths:** The CliftonStrengths assessment categorizes individuals into 34 different strengths based on their talents, skills, and abilities. www.gallup.com/cliftonstrengths/en/strengthsfinder.aspx

Taking these assessments can help you gain a deeper understanding of your personality type and how it influences your interests, strengths, and weaknesses. This knowledge can help you identify potential areas of passion and pursue them in a way that aligns with your unique personality type.

Although these assessments can be helpful, they're not definitive and should be used as a starting point for self-exploration and growth. Ultimately, the most important thing is to stay open-minded and willing to explore different interests and pursuits to find what resonates with you and brings you a sense of fulfillment and purpose. Once you know your type, you can better understand your strengths and weaknesses and identify the types of activities and work that will be most fulfilling for you.

Figure 2-4 provides a worksheet to help you conduct your own personality assessment.

REMEMBER

This is just a simple example of a personality assessment worksheet. Many different types of personality assessments are available, and it may be helpful to consult with a qualified professional to determine which assessment is best suited to your needs.

Name: _____

Date: _____

Instructions: For each question, choose the statement that best describes you. Be as honest and accurate as possible.

1. When meeting new people, I prefer:

    a) Large groups and social events

    b) One-on-one conversations

2. I am more:

    a) Detail-oriented

    b) Big-picture focused

3. When making decisions, I rely more on:

    a) Logic and reason

    b) Intuition and feelings

4. I am more:

    a) Structured and organized

    b) Flexible and spontaneous

5. In my free time, I prefer:

    a) Being around people and socializing

    b) Spending time alone or with a few close friends

6. I am more:

    a) Task-oriented and goal-focused

    b) Relationship-oriented and people-focused

FIGURE 2-4:
Personality
assessment.

FIGURE 2-4:
Continued

7. When faced with a challenge, I am more likely to:

   a) Take a step back and analyze the situation

   b) Take action and jump in immediately

8. I am more:

   a) Practical and realistic

   b) Idealistic and imaginative

Scoring:

For questions 1, 2, 3, 4, 5, and 7, give yourself 1 point for every (a) answer and 2 points for every (b) answer.

For questions 6 and 8, give yourself 2 points for every (a) answer and 1 point for every (b) answer.

Add up your points and use the following chart to identify your personality type:

8–10 points: Extroverted, detail-oriented, logical, structured, people-oriented, analytical, practical

11–14 points: Balanced, adaptable, intuitive, flexible, relationship-oriented, action-oriented, realistic

15–16 points: Introverted, big-picture focused, intuitive, spontaneous, task-oriented, imaginative, idealistic

The role of interests in finding passion

Your interests are the things you enjoy doing in your free time. They can include hobbies, sports, or other activities. It's important to consider your interests when looking for your passion because pursuing something you enjoy doing can lead to greater fulfillment and happiness in your life.

Interests can play an important role in finding passion because they provide clues about the types of activities and pursuits you find enjoyable and fulfilling. Your interests are the things you're naturally drawn to and enjoy doing, whether it's reading, playing music, gardening, or something else entirely.

By exploring your interests, you can begin to identify potential areas of passion and pursue them in a way that aligns with your core beliefs and abilities. This can involve trying out new hobbies, attending workshops or classes, or exploring different career paths to see what resonates with your interests.

Furthermore, your interests can be opportunities for personal growth and development. By pursuing activities that you're interested in, you can develop new skills and knowledge that you can apply in other areas of your life. For example, if you have an interest in photography, you may develop skills in composition, lighting, and editing that you can apply to other areas of your life or to your career.

Finally, your interests can give you a sense of fulfillment and satisfaction in your life. When you engage in activities that you're interested in, you often experience a sense of flow, where you become completely absorbed in the activity and lose track of time. This can be a source of fulfillment and satisfaction that can be difficult to achieve through other means.

Your interests can supply clues about the types of activities and pursuits that you find enjoyable and fulfilling, leading to opportunities for personal growth and development, and providing a sense of fulfillment and satisfaction. By exploring your interests and pursuing activities that you're passionate about, you can lead a more meaningful and fulfilling life.

Take some time to reflect on the things that you enjoy doing in your free time. Consider what activities you're naturally drawn to and what gives you a sense of satisfaction. Write down your interests and passions, and use them as a starting point for exploring different career paths and activities that align with your personality and values.

Identifying your interests and passions is an important step in finding fulfillment and purpose. You can identify your interests and passions in several ways.

First, you can reflect on your hobbies and activities. What do you like to do in your free time? What activities make you feel most alive and engaged?

Second, consider your childhood interests and what you enjoyed doing then. Do any activities or interests from that period still hold a special place in your heart?

Third, explore new hobbies and activities. Try out some that you may not have considered before. Attend workshops or classes in different areas of interest to see what resonates with you.

Fourth, think about your values. Consider your core values and what's most important to you. What activities and pursuits align with these values?

Fifth, pay attention to what excites and energizes you. What topics or activities do you find yourself drawn to naturally?

Sixth, ask friends and family for feedback on what they see as your strengths and passions. Sometimes others may see things in you that you don't see in yourself.

Finally, try different things, and don't be afraid to take risks. You may discover a passion that you never knew existed!

Overall, identifying your interests and passions takes time and self-reflection. By exploring different hobbies and activities, considering your values, paying attention to what excites you, and trying new things, you can begin to identify potential areas of passion and pursue them in a way that aligns with your core beliefs and abilities.

Figure 2-5 is a worksheet for identifying your interests and passions.

Review the following list of interests and passions. Circle the ones that resonate with you.

Rank your top five interests and passions in order of importance:

Interests:

Sports

Music

Art

Reading

Writing

Traveling

Cooking

Gardening

Volunteering

Gaming

Dancing

Fashion

Film

Photography

Hiking

Meditation

Yoga

Technology

Politics

Science

History

FIGURE 2-5: Identifying interest and passions.

Passions:

- Helping others
- Learning new things
- Making a difference in the world
- Creativity
- Innovation
- Personal growth and development
- Relationships
- Adventure
- Nature
- Entrepreneurship
- Health and wellness
- Social justice
- Animals
- Education
- Community involvement
- Family
- Sportsmanship
- Leadership
- Travel
- Artistic expression

Rank your top five interests and passions in order of importance. For example, if you're an introvert who enjoys spending time alone, you may be more suited to a career that allows you to work independently, such as freelance writing or software development. On the other hand, if you're an extrovert who enjoys being around people, you may be more suited to a career in sales or customer service.

FIGURE 2-5:
Continued

Identifying Your Natural Talents and Skills

You possess your own unique set of talents and skills that define, distinguish, and direct you. These innate abilities and acquired proficiencies are the pillars upon which you build your aspirations, achievements, and sense of self-worth. Recognizing them is crucial not just for personal growth but for carving a life that resonates with purpose and potential.

You're born with a specific set of natural talents, those spontaneous inclinations and abilities that seem to flow effortlessly. Whether it's a creative knack, an analytical mindset, or an inherent ability to lead and inspire, these talents are the raw materials that, with nurturing, can transform into powerful tools for success and fulfillment.

Identifying your natural talents and skills is a crucial step toward finding your passion and pursuing a fulfilling career. Although talents and skills are often used interchangeably, they're actually two distinct concepts.

Talents refer to innate abilities that you're born with or develop naturally over time. These can include things like artistic abilities, musical talent, or athletic prowess. Talents are usually things that come easily to you and that you enjoy doing.

Skills, on the other hand, are learned abilities that you acquire through education, training, and practice. These can include things like writing, public speaking, and computer programming. Skills are often things that you develop to be successful in your chosen career path.

Although talents are innate, skills are cultivated. They're the manifestations of your efforts to harness, hone, and heighten your natural talents. Through education, experience, and deliberate practice, you mold and refine your raw talents into formidable skills that serve you in diverse realms of life.

Recognizing and acknowledging your talents and skills fosters a profound sense of self-assurance. It becomes a wellspring of confidence, propelling you to take risks, embrace challenges, and navigate obstacles with resilience and resolve.

An awareness of your talents and skills offers clarity in your career and personal pursuits. It acts as a guiding light, illuminating paths and possibilities that align with your strengths, ensuring that your endeavors resonate with genuine passion and prowess.

You might start with a core set of talents and skills, but the canvas of human potential is vast and adaptable. With intention and effort, you can acquire new skills and nurture dormant talents, ensuring that you remain agile and relevant in an ever-evolving world.

Identifying your natural talents and cultivated skills is akin to discovering the unique melody that you bring to the world's orchestra. It's about recognizing your intrinsic worth, optimizing your potential, and shaping a life that not only celebrates your strengths but also consistently challenges you to evolve, expand, and excel.

Identifying your natural talents and skills allows you to focus on areas where you're naturally gifted and may have a higher likelihood of success. Here are some things you can do to identify your natural talents and skills:

>> **Reflect on your past experiences:** Think back to activities or tasks that you've enjoyed and excelled at in the past. What did you enjoy about them? What skills or talents did you use?

>> **Take an assessment:** You can take one of several assessments to help you identify your natural talents and skills. These can include personality tests, strengths assessments, and skills inventories. Some examples include the MBTI and the CliftonStrengths assessment.

>> **Ask for feedback:** Ask friends, family members, and colleagues to give you feedback on your strengths and areas where you excel. Sometimes others can see things in you that you don't see in yourself.

>> **Experiment:** Try new things and take on new challenges. This can help you identify new talents and skills that you may not know you have.

Once you've identified your natural talents and skills, you can use this knowledge to guide your career choices and pursue activities that bring you fulfillment and happiness.

REMEMBER

In terms of career development and personal fulfillment, it's important to recognize and develop both talents and skills. Whereas talents can provide a strong foundation for pursuing passions and developing expertise in related areas, skills can be developed and honed to increase competence and effectiveness in various roles and industries. By identifying and developing both talents and skills, you can increase your potential for success and fulfillment in both personal and professional pursuits. See Figure 2-6.

By completing Figure 2-6, you should have a better understanding of your natural talents and skills, as well as areas where you may need to focus on development. Use this information to guide your exploration of potential passions and career paths.

Identifying Your Natural Talents and Skills

This worksheet is designed to help you identify your natural talents and skills. For each question, think about your past experiences and abilities. Circle the answers that apply to you, and use the space provided to write down any additional thoughts or examples that come to mind.

1. What are some activities or tasks that come easily to you and that you enjoy doing?

2. What are some things you've always been interested in or curious about?

3. What are some skills you've developed through education, training, or practice?

4. What are some areas where you've received praise or recognition from others?

5. What are some things you've accomplished or achieved that you're proud of?

6. What are some things you've helped others with or been asked to assist with?

7. What are some things you've learned on your own or through self-study?

8. What are some areas where you've received feedback for improvement or areas where you feel you need more development?

9. What are some skills or abilities you admire in others and would like to develop in yourself?

10. What are some things you'd like to do or achieve in the future, and what skills or talents are required to accomplish them?

FIGURE 2-6: Recognizing your natural abilities.

To build on the identification of your natural talents and skills, you need to understand the role of practice and development in building skills. Although natural abilities can be a good starting point, skills require ongoing practice, refinement, and development.

For example, if you have a natural talent for playing the piano, you may still need to practice regularly to develop your skills and become a proficient pianist.

Similarly, if you have a talent for public speaking, you may still need to develop your skills through practice and training to become a confident and effective communicator.

Once you have a better understanding of your natural talents and skills and have begun to develop them, you can start to explore potential career paths that align with your abilities and interests. Look for industries, professions, or roles that require the skills you possess or are interested in developing.

For example, if you have strong analytical and problem-solving skills, you may consider a career in finance or data analysis. If you have excellent communication and interpersonal skills, you may be suited for a career in marketing or human resources.

Understanding your natural talents and skills is an important starting point in the journey toward finding a fulfilling and rewarding career, but identifying potential career paths based on your talents and skills is just one factor to consider when finding your passion. Also consider factors such as your values, interests, and personality.

The power of practice and development in building skills

The process of developing skills involves deliberate practice, which refers to a specific type of practice that involves breaking down a skill into smaller components and practicing each component repeatedly with focused attention and feedback. This process develops muscle memory and improves performance.

In addition to deliberate practice, you need to seek out opportunities for learning and development. This can include taking courses, attending workshops or conferences, or seeking out mentorship or coaching. These opportunities can broaden your skills and knowledge base and offer new perspectives and insights.

As you continue to practice and develop your skills, set goals and track your progress to keep you motivated and focused on your development. It's also important to be open to feedback and willing to make adjustments as you go.

Overall, the role of practice and development in building skills is crucial in the journey toward finding your passion. By identifying your natural talents and skills and actively working to develop them, you can increase your confidence, improve your performance, and ultimately find greater fulfillment in your personal and professional life.

Identifying potential career paths based on your talents and skills

The journey toward a fulfilling career is akin to navigating through a vast ocean. Your talents and skills serve as the compass guiding you toward the right shores. Instead of being swept away by external influences or fleeting trends, grounding your career choices in your inherent strengths ensures a voyage that's not just successful but also deeply gratifying.

In essence, the process of identifying potential career paths based on your talents and skills is a strategic endeavor to ensure that your professional life is a reflection of your true self. It's about choosing not just a job, but a journey — one that celebrates your unique contributions, challenges you in the right ways, and champions your growth both as a professional and as an individual.

Identifying potential career paths based on your talents and skills can be a helpful way to explore your passion and find a career that aligns with your strengths and interests. Here are some steps to take:

1. **Take an inventory of your talents and skills:** Make a list of all the things you're good at, whether it's something you learned in school or through a hobby or interest. Don't be afraid to include soft skills like communication or problem-solving. They're often just as important as technical skills.

2. **Identify your interests:** What are the things that excite and inspire you? What subjects or topics do you enjoy learning about or spending your free time on? Consider which potential career paths align with your interests.

3. **Research potential careers:** Look up job descriptions and requirements for careers that align with your skills and interests. You can use online resources like job boards or career exploration websites to get an idea of what's out there.

4. **Consider your values:** Think about what's important to you in a career, such as work-life balance, salary, job security, or making a difference in the world. Make sure the careers you're considering align with your values.

5. **Seek out opportunities to gain experience:** Once you've identified some potential career paths, seek out opportunities to gain experience in those fields. This can include internships, volunteering, or taking on projects or freelance work.

6. **Narrow down your options:** As you gain more experience and learn more about the careers you're interested in, you may find that some are a better fit than others. Take the time to reflect on your experiences and narrow down your options to the ones that align best with your talents, interests, and values.

Remember, finding your passion and identifying potential career paths takes time and exploration. Don't be afraid to try new things and step outside of your comfort zone. By taking an inventory of your talents and skills, identifying your interests, researching potential careers, and gaining experience, you're well on your way to finding a career that aligns with your passions and brings you fulfillment.

Mapping skills to opportunities

The world of work is diverse, with myriad roles and responsibilities. By understanding your unique set of skills and talents, you can draw parallels to professions where these attributes are highly valued, optimizing your chances for success and satisfaction.

Beyond the traditional roles

Today's dynamic work environment continually evolves, presenting new professions that might not have existed a decade ago. Being anchored in your strengths allows you to identify and adapt to these emerging opportunities, ensuring your relevance and resilience.

Intrinsic motivation

A career aligned with your innate talents and honed skills rewards you more than just monetarily; it offers intrinsic motivation. The sheer joy of doing what you're naturally good at, day in and day out, fuels your drive, enthusiasm, and commitment, leading to sustainable success.

Personal growth and professional development

When you choose a career that resonates with your strengths, the line between work and passion blurs. Such alignment creates opportunities for constant learning and growth, turning everyday tasks into avenues for personal development and professional progression.

Authenticity in the workplace

Embracing a profession that reflects your genuine talents and skills fosters authenticity. When you're true to yourself in your work, you engage more deeply, communicate more effectively, and inspire trust and credibility among colleagues and superiors.

Chapter **3**

Overcoming Obstacles to Finding Your Passion

ew pursuits are as exhilarating, profound, and transformative as the quest to find your passion. Like an ember waiting to ignite, passion resides within you, often masked by layers of doubt, fear, and societal expectations. It's the driving force that, once unearthed and embraced, can illuminate the darkest paths and propel you toward your most authentic self. Yet, the journey to its discovery is rarely straightforward. It's a winding road, riddled with obstacles that can deter, disillusion, and dishearten even the most ardent seeker.

Many of these challenges are external — societal pressures, familial expectations, and financial constraints. But equally potent are the internal barriers — the voice of self-doubt, the weight of past failures, and the paralysis of indecision. Navigating through these challenges requires more than just determination; it demands introspection, resilience, and, most importantly, a belief in your inherent potential.

But why is it so crucial to overcome these barriers? Because passion, once found, transcends mere interest or hobby. It becomes a North Star, guiding decisions, shaping goals, and imbuing every endeavor with a sense of purpose. It's the spark that turns the mundane into the meaningful and the routine into the remarkable.

This chapter explores the common obstacles that stand between you and your passions. It demystifies them so that you can understand their origins, and, most crucially, equip yourself with the strategies to surmount them. By the end, you'll have not only a clearer understanding of what might have held you back but also the tools and the mindset to push forward, unwaveringly, toward the passions that await your embrace.

It's time to embark on this transformative journey, breaking free from the chains of constraint and soaring toward the horizons of your true calling.

Overcoming Common Barriers to Finding Passion

Discovering your passion is much like uncovering a hidden treasure; it's immensely valuable, yet often buried beneath layers of challenges. These barriers, whether internal or external, can sometimes cloud your vision, making the quest seem daunting. However, understanding these common obstacles and adopting effective strategies to overcome them can pave the way to a more enriched and purpose-driven life.

>> **Societal expectations:** One of the foremost barriers is the weight of societal norms and expectations. Maybe you, like many, have been groomed to tread a predefined path at the expense of your true calling. Overcoming this requires a conscious shift in perspective, valuing self-awareness over conformity and realizing that true success lies in authentic living.

>> **Financial constraints:** Practical concerns, especially financial ones, can deter you from chasing your dreams. Although these concerns are valid, you can navigate them with planning. This might involve pursuing passion as a side endeavor initially or seeking out scholarships, grants, or mentorships in your chosen field.

>> **Overwhelm and indecision:** In an age of endless options, the sheer volume of potential paths can be daunting. Overcoming this involves breaking down the journey into smaller steps, setting short-term goals, and celebrating small victories along the way.

>> **Past experiences:** Past failures or discouragements can cast a shadow on future endeavors. Separate past experiences from future potential. Reflecting on past challenges, extracting lessons, and using them as steppingstones rather than as barriers can be transformative.

In essence, even though the path to discovering your passion is strewn with challenges, each obstacle offers an opportunity for growth, resilience, and clarity. By recognizing these common barriers and equipping yourself with the strategies to navigate them, the journey becomes not just feasible but deeply enriching.

Overcoming the barriers to finding your passion is crucial to achieving personal and professional fulfillment. Here are some common barriers that may hold you back from pursuing your passion and how to overcome them.

Fear of failure and self-doubt

Fear of failure and self-doubt are common barriers that might prevent you from finding your passion. The fear of failure can be paralyzing and may block you from taking the necessary risks to pursue your passion. Self-doubt can cause you to question your abilities and talents, leading to a lack of confidence and motivation.

To overcome the fear of failure and self-doubt, acknowledge and confront these negative emotions. Recognize that failure is a natural part of the learning process and can provide valuable lessons and experiences. Reframe the way you think about failure, seeing it as an opportunity for growth rather than a setback.

Develop a growth mindset, which involves believing in your ability to learn and improve over time. You can achieve this by setting small, achievable goals and focusing on progress rather than perfection. Celebrate your successes and learn from your failures, using them as opportunities to refine your skills and abilities.

Also, seek support from others — mentors, friends, or coaches — who can guide and encourage you. It's natural to experience self-doubt at some point in your life. Just be kind and compassionate to yourself throughout the process.

Lack of confidence and self-esteem

Lack of confidence and self-esteem can be major barriers to finding your passion. When you lack confidence, you may feel like you're incapable of achieving your goals or pursuing your passions. Low self-esteem can cause you to doubt your abilities and value, leading to a lack of motivation and self-belief.

For example, maybe you dream of becoming a musician, but you lack confidence in your singing abilities. You may feel like you're not good enough to pursue your passion even though you have a natural talent for music. This lack of confidence can prevent you from taking the necessary steps to pursue your passion, such as practicing and performing in public.

To overcome a lack of confidence and self-esteem, identify the root cause of these feelings. This may involve reflecting on past experiences or seeking professional support from a therapist or counselor.

Practicing self-care, such as exercising regularly and getting enough sleep, can also boost your confidence and self-esteem. Additionally, setting small, achievable goals and celebrating successes can build your confidence over time.

You can seek out supportive communities, such as clubs or groups, that share similar interests. Being around others who share your passion and can offer encouragement and feedback can boost your confidence and give you a sense of belonging.

Building confidence and self-esteem takes time and effort, but it's a crucial step in pursuing your passion and achieving your goals.

Negative self-talk and limiting beliefs

Negative self-talk and limiting beliefs can be major barriers to finding your passion. These internal factors can lead to self-doubt, fear, and a lack of confidence, which can kill your passion pursuit. Table 3-1 covers some common examples of negative self-talk and limiting beliefs.

Overall, negative self-talk and limiting beliefs can be powerful barriers to finding your passion. Recognize and challenge these beliefs, and focus on building confidence, self-esteem, and a growth mindset.

TABLE 3-1   **Negative Self-Talk Barriers**

Negative Belief	How It Limits You
"I'm not good enough."	This belief can stem from a fear of failure or a lack of confidence in your abilities. It can prevent you from taking risks and trying new things, including pursuing your passions.
"I don't have enough time/money/ resources."	This limiting belief can make you feel stuck and unable to pursue your passions. However, with proper planning and prioritization, you likely can find ways to prioritize and allocate resources toward your passions.
"I'm too old/young/ inexperienced."	This limiting belief can make you feel that you're too old or too young to start something new. However, age and experience shouldn't be barriers to pursuing your passions.
"What will others think of me?"	This limiting belief can be particularly challenging if you're worried about social expectations and what others may think of you. Just remember that pursuing your passions can often lead to greater happiness and fulfillment. Others' opinions shouldn't hold you back from pursuing what you truly love.
"I don't have any passions."	This limiting belief can be particularly frustrating if you're struggling to find your passions. But remember that you can often discover what makes you tick through exploration and trying new things. This experimentation and self-discovery to find your passions may take time and effort, so have patience.

External factors such as societal expectations and financial constraints

External factors such as societal expectations and financial constraints can also act as barriers in finding your passion. Maybe you grew up in a family that valued financial stability and security above all else, making it difficult to pursue a career that may not provide immediate financial rewards. Similarly, societal or cultural expectations may dictate certain career choices, making it challenging to pursue a passion that goes against those expectations. To overcome these external barriers, first identify and acknowledge them. Then you can begin to explore alternative options or find ways to overcome the obstacles.

Financial constraints can make you feel stuck. Pursuing a passion may require investing time and money into education, training, or equipment, which may not be feasible for you. You may have to seek out financial assistance, such as scholarships or grants, or find creative ways to pursue a passion while maintaining financial stability.

Perhaps you're passionate about photography, but you don't have the financial resources to invest in high-end camera equipment or attend photography workshops. Even with meager financial resources, you might be able to invest in a basic camera and use free online resources to improve your skills. You can also look for part-time or freelance photography opportunities to build your portfolio and gain experience while still maintaining a stable income.

Don't let external factors define or limit your passion. With determination and creativity, you can overcome these barriers and follow your dreams.

Persevering Despite Setbacks

The pursuit of your dreams and passions is rarely a linear path. It's often interspersed with challenges and unexpected detours. These setbacks, an intrinsic part of any meaningful journey, aren't mere obstacles. Think of them as pivotal moments that test and shape your resolve. Understanding them as inevitable components rather than hindrances can be empowering. Setbacks offer a chance to learn, adapt, and grow, turning what might seem like a stumbling block into an invaluable learning experience.

A resilient approach toward setbacks involves both a shift in perspective and actionable strategies. By viewing these challenges as feedback, you can extract lessons and refine your course of action. The power of resilience is amplified when it's combined with a robust support system and a clear, unwavering vision of the end goal. Furthermore, flexibility in approach, while remaining anchored to the core objective, can lead to innovative solutions and pathways. In essence, true perseverance lies not in the absence of setbacks but in the ability to navigate, adapt, and thrive amidst them.

Persevering through setbacks is a crucial aspect of finding and pursuing your passion. No matter how passionate you are about something, setbacks and challenges are inevitable. These setbacks might be in the form of rejection, failure, or simply slower progress than you want.

Setbacks aren't a sign of failure or an indication that you should give up. In fact, they can teach you valuable lessons and insights that can help you refine your approach and get you even closer to your passion.

Here are some strategies for persevering through setbacks:

>> **Reframe your perspective:** Instead of viewing setbacks as failures, try to see them as opportunities to learn and grow. Ask yourself what you can learn from the experience and how you can use it to improve your approach.

>> **Stay motivated:** It can be easy to lose motivation when you encounter setbacks, but try to stay focused on your end goal. Remind yourself why you started pursuing your passion in the first place and the positive impact it will have on your life.

>> **Get support:** Having a support system can be crucial when you're facing setbacks. Talk to friends, family, or a mentor about what you're going through, and seek their encouragement and advice.

>> **Break it down:** If you're feeling overwhelmed by a setback, try breaking down your goals into smaller, more manageable steps. This can help you feel more in control and make progress toward your passion.

Persistence is key. Don't let setbacks discourage you from continuing to pursue what you love. Keep trying, stay positive, and trust that your hard work will pay off in the end. Setbacks are a natural part of finding and pursuing your passion. By persevering through them, you become even more resilient and better equipped to achieve your goals.

Developing a growth mindset

In the realm of personal and professional development, the concept of a growth mindset stands out as a transformative principle. Coined by psychologist Carol Dweck after extensive research, a growth mindset is the belief that you can develop abilities and intelligence through dedication, hard work, and a love of learning.

Whereas in a fixed mindset you believe your talents and abilities are static, with a growth mindset you have a more dynamic and adaptive approach to challenges.

With a growth mindset, you view challenges as opportunities rather than threats. You perceive mistakes and failures as feedback — essential ingredients for learning and improvement. This perspective fosters a resilience against setbacks, ensuring that you remain undeterred in the face of difficulties. Furthermore, a growth mindset nurtures a perpetual love for learning. With an understanding that there's always room for enhancement, you remain curious, open to new experiences, and continually seek ways to better yourself.

Equally essential is the understanding that effort plays a crucial role in achievement. A growth mindset recognizes the value of persistence, ensuring that you stay committed even when tasks become challenging. This emphasis on effort and strategy, rather than innate talent, levels the playing field, giving you the potential to grow, evolve, and achieve.

In the broader context, adopting a growth mindset has profound implications not just for your own growth but for team dynamics, leadership, education, and organizational culture. It fosters environments where risks are embraced, innovation thrives, and continuous learning becomes the norm. In a rapidly evolving world, nurturing a growth mindset isn't just an advantage; it's a necessity if you're aspiring to lead, innovate, and make meaningful contributions.

Developing a growth mindset involves five elements:

>> **Embracing challenges:** Instead of avoiding challenges, you embrace them as opportunities to learn and grow.

>> **Embracing failure:** You see failure not as the end, but as an opportunity to learn from mistakes and improve.

>> **Persistence and effort:** Success requires effort and perseverance. You focus on the process of learning and improving rather than just the end result.

>> **Seeking feedback:** You welcome feedback because it can offer valuable insight into areas for improvement and help you grow.

>> **Learning from others:** You seek out role models and mentors who can provide guidance and inspiration in your pursuit of passion.

Developing a growth mindset can help you overcome the obstacles and setbacks that come with pursuing your passion. By focusing on the process of learning and improving and embracing challenges and failures as opportunities for growth, you can build the resilience and determination you need to achieve success.

Creating a support system

Creating a support system is critical to persevering through setbacks and challenges while pursuing your passion. The following steps help you create a support system:

1. **Identify who you can turn to:** Start by identifying people in your life who are supportive and positive. These can be family members, friends, colleagues, mentors, or even a therapist.

2. **Share your goals and challenges:** Once you've identified your support system, share your passion and goals with them. Be honest about your challenges, and ask for their support and encouragement.

3. **Seek accountability:** Ask your support system to hold you accountable for your goals and progress. Check in with them regularly to share updates on your progress.

4. **Participate in communities:** Consider joining groups or communities that share your passion. This can be a great way to connect with like-minded people and find additional support.

5. **Be supportive in return:** Remember that support is a two-way street. Be sure to offer support and encouragement to others in your support system when they need it.

By creating a strong support system, you can have a network of people who believe in you and can help you stay motivated and focused on your goals, even during challenging times.

Learning from mistakes and failures

Learning from mistakes and failures is a crucial part of the journey to finding your passion. Here are some tips for learning from mistakes and failures:

» **Reframe your mindset:** Instead of viewing mistakes and failures as negative experiences, reframe your mindset to see them as opportunities for growth and learning.

» **Analyze what went wrong:** Take a step back and analyze what went wrong. Try to identify the root cause of the mistake or failure and think about what you could have done differently.

- >> **Take responsibility:** Own up to your mistakes and take responsibility for your actions. Blaming others or making excuses will only hold you back from learning and growing.

- >> **Learn from others:** Seek out advice and guidance from others who have gone through similar experiences. Learn from their mistakes and successes.

- >> **Keep trying:** Don't let failures or setbacks discourage you. Keep trying and experimenting until you find what works for you.

- >> **Celebrate progress:** Even if you haven't achieved your ultimate goal, celebrate the progress you've made along the way. Every step forward is a step closer to finding your passion.

Remember, learning from mistakes and failures is an ongoing process. Embrace the journey, and use each experience as an opportunity to grow.

Practicing self-care and stress management

Self-care and stress management are essential for maintaining a healthy and balanced lifestyle while pursuing your passion. Consider these key strategies:

- >> **Prioritize self-care:** Make sure to take time for yourself every day, whether it's through exercise, meditation, reading, or simply relaxing.

- >> **Set boundaries:** Learn to say no to commitments that don't align with your values or that take away from your well-being.

- >> **Manage stress:** Identify sources of stress in your life and develop coping strategies, such as deep breathing exercises or mindfulness practices.

- >> **Practice good sleep hygiene:** Getting enough rest is crucial for maintaining physical and mental health. Establish a consistent sleep schedule and create a comfortable sleep environment.

- >> **Stay connected:** Maintain strong relationships with friends and family, and seek out support from like-minded individuals who share your passion.

- >> **Take breaks:** Take regular breaks from pursuing your passion to avoid burnout and maintain balance in your life.

Practicing self-care and stress management better equips you to handle the ups and downs of pursuing your passion so you can maintain a healthy, fulfilling lifestyle.

Turning Setbacks into Opportunities

Turning setbacks into opportunities for growth and learning is a crucial skill to develop when pursuing your passion. Failure and setbacks are inevitable, but it's important to reframe them as learning opportunities instead of letting them derail your progress.

One way to do this is by examining the situation and identifying what it can teach you. Ask yourself questions like, "What did I do well? What could I have done better? What did I learn from this experience?"

Another way is to embrace challenges as opportunities for growth and use them as motivation. When faced with a difficult situation, try to focus on the potential positive outcomes rather than the potential negative consequences. For example, instead of thinking, "I might fail," try thinking, "If I succeed, I'll learn so much and feel a great sense of accomplishment."

By reframing setbacks as opportunities, you can maintain a positive mindset and keep moving forward on your path toward finding your passion. Setbacks are just part of the journey.

Reframing failures and setbacks as learning opportunities

Reframing failures and setbacks as learning opportunities is a key aspect of perseverance and growth. Rather than viewing failures as negative, reframing them can help you see them as opportunities for improvement.

Take the inspiring journey of Marie Curie, a pioneering physicist and chemist. In her pursuit of scientific knowledge, Curie faced numerous challenges and setbacks. Her groundbreaking research on radioactivity led to the discovery of radium and polonium, but the path was fraught with obstacles. Despite societal biases against women in science and the immense personal sacrifices she made, Curie's resilience in the face of adversity showcases how passion can fuel the pursuit of knowledge.

Also, consider the life of Temple Grandin, an accomplished scientist and autism advocate. Grandin, who herself is on the autism spectrum, encountered numerous challenges in a world not yet fully understanding of neurodiversity. However, she turned her unique perspective into an advantage. Grandin's passion for animal science led her to design humane livestock handling facilities, revolutionizing the agricultural industry. Her story demonstrates how embracing one's differences and channeling passion can lead to innovative breakthroughs.

By reframing failures and setbacks as opportunities for learning, you can develop a growth mindset and become more resilient in the face of challenges. Instead of giving up when you encounter obstacles, you can use them as opportunities to learn and grow, ultimately becoming better equipped to pursue your passions and achieve your goals.

Embracing challenges and using them as motivation

Using challenges as motivation is an important aspect of turning setbacks into opportunities for growth and learning. Challenges and obstacles are often seen as roadblocks to success, but with the right mindset, they can become opportunities for personal and professional development.

Imagine that you're an aspiring writer who has been struggling to get published. You've received numerous rejections from publishers and are feeling discouraged. Instead of giving up on your dream, you can use this setback as motivation to improve your writing skills and try new approaches to getting published. You can take writing classes, join writing groups, and seek feedback from other writers to help you improve your craft. By embracing the challenge of getting published and using it as motivation to improve, you can turn a setback into an opportunity for growth and learning.

Similarly, in the business world, entrepreneurs often face challenges and obstacles in starting and growing their businesses. Instead of seeing these challenges as roadblocks to success, successful entrepreneurs use them as motivation to innovate, pivot, and improve. For example, the cofounder of Airbnb, Brian Chesky, faced numerous challenges in the early days of the company, including struggling to get investors and finding a sustainable business model. However, he used these challenges as motivation to improve the user experience and create a more innovative and unique platform. Today Airbnb is a thriving business that has disrupted the travel industry.

Overall, embracing challenges and using them as motivation can help individuals and businesses turn setbacks into opportunities for growth and learning. By reframing failures and obstacles as learning experiences and using them as motivation to improve, you can achieve your goals and reach new heights of success.

Chapter **4**

Exploring Different Areas of Interest

In the journey to finding your passion, it's crucial to explore different areas of interest. Life has endless possibilities. By broadening your horizons, you open yourself up to a world of exciting opportunities. This chapter is dedicated to encouraging you to step outside your comfort zone and embark on a journey of exploration.

Exploring different areas of interest allows you to discover new hobbies, activities, and even potential career paths that you may have never considered before. It's a chance to break free from the familiar and embrace the unknown so you can encounter new experiences and perspectives.

This chapter delves into the importance of exploration and curiosity, helps you seek out new and unfamiliar areas of interest, and shares the benefits that come from expanding your horizons. By the end of this chapter, you'll be equipped with the knowledge and tools to embark on a journey of self-discovery and adventure.

So get ready to step outside your comfort zone, embrace the thrill of the unknown, and explore the vast array of possibilities waiting to be uncovered. It's time to ignite your curiosity and embark on an exciting journey of exploring different areas of interest to find what truly sparks your passion.

Broadening Your Horizons and Trying New Things

Broadening your horizons and trying new things is an important mindset and practice when it comes to finding and exploring your passions. Sometimes people get caught up in routines. They keep doing the same things year in and year out, and that begins to define the scope of their passions and hobbies. To forge new paths, you need to break camp with routine. You have to step out of your usual patterns to try new things. Doing that brings several benefits:

>> **Expanding possibilities:** Trying new things allows you to discover new interests and passions you may not have been aware of before. It opens up a world of possibilities and introduces you to different perspectives, experiences, and activities.

>> **Overcoming fear and limitations:** Trying new things requires stepping out of your comfort zone and challenging yourself. The reward is overcoming fear, self-doubt, and limitations that may be holding you back from pursuing your passions. By pushing your boundaries, you expand your personal growth and development.

>> **Uncovering hidden talents:** When you try new things, you may discover hidden talents or skills you didn't know you had. Exploring diverse activities and experiences allows you to tap into unique aspects of your abilities and creativity.

>> **Building resilience:** Trying new things often involves facing obstacles and setbacks. When you push through, you develop resilience and adaptability as you navigate unfamiliar territories. This resilience can be valuable when pursuing your passions because it allows you to persevere in the face of challenges.

>> **Gaining new perspectives:** Trying new things exposes you to different cultures, ideas, and people. It broadens your perspective and understanding of the world around you, enhances your creativity, and fosters empathy.

Wondering what you can do to broaden your horizons and try new things? How about these:

>> **Step outside your comfort zone:** Challenge yourself to try activities or experiences that are unfamiliar or outside your usual preferences. This might be taking a dance class, learning a musical instrument, or trying a new cuisine.

>> **Embrace curiosity:** Cultivate a curious mindset and seek out new opportunities for exploration. Attend workshops, events, or conferences in areas that intrigue you. Read books or articles on diverse topics.

>> **Travel and explore:** Traveling allows you to immerse yourself in different cultures, traditions, and environments. It broadens your perspective and exposes you to extraordinary experiences and ideas.

>> **Network and connect:** Engage with diverse communities, join clubs or organizations, and connect with people who have interests and passions that you don't. Collaborating with others can lead to fresh insights and opportunities.

REMEMBER

The process of trying new things should be enjoyable and fulfilling. Embrace the journey of self-discovery, and keep an open mind. By broadening your horizons, you increase your chances of finding and nurturing your passions.

The importance of exploration and curiosity

Many people are too afraid to step outside their comfort zone and try new things. But doing so is essential to discovering what truly excites and motivates you. Embrace your curiosity, and don't hesitate to sidestep the usual.

Exploration and curiosity are essential when it comes to finding your passion. Being open to new experiences and ideas can broaden your perspective, challenge your assumptions, and spark interests you've never considered before.

For example, imagine that you've always been interested in technology and have pursued a career in programming. However, through exploration and curiosity, you discover a passion for photography. You may have never thought of trying photography before, but you find it fulfilling and rewarding.

Similarly, trying new things and exploring an assortment of interests can lead to unexpected discoveries about your talents. For instance, if you take an online Spanish or German class, you might find that you have a knack for a new language.

In essence, exploration and curiosity are crucial for finding your passion because they allow you to dip your toe into fresh waters that may expand your interests and passions.

Identifying new and unfamiliar areas of interest

Take some time to think about what you're naturally drawn to. What topics do you find yourself reading about or watching videos on? What hobbies or activities do you gravitate toward? Don't limit yourself to what you think you're "supposed" to be interested in. Instead, be open to exploring what's unfamiliar.

Identifying unknown areas of interest can be a great way to discover a new passion. This section looks at a few ways to identify new interests.

Attending events

Attending concerts, plays, art exhibitions, and festivals can expose you to new and exciting experiences. You might discover a love for a certain type of music or a passion for a particular form of art.

Traveling

Traveling can broaden your horizons and introduce you to thrilling cultures, foods, and activities. You might uncover a new hobby, such as surfing or hiking, that you never considered before.

Reading books and watching documentaries

Reading books and watching documentaries can spark your curiosity. You might become interested in history, science, or a particular culture.

Volunteering

Volunteering for worthwhile causes can introduce you to activities and interests. You might find a passion for environmental activism, animal welfare, or social justice.

Finding a new hobby

Trying new activities or hobbies can be a fun way to explore interests. Take a cooking class, see how you do at rock climbing, or join a community theater group.

By being open to these experiences and actively seeking out opportunities to explore, you might discover a passion.

Trying new activities and experiences

Once you've identified some potential areas of interest, start exploring them in more depth. Remember, the goal isn't to become an expert in everything you try. Rather, it's to expose yourself to alternative experiences and discover what resonates with you.

Trying new activities and experiences can be a great way to discover passions and interests. Here are some ways to do this.

Traveling

Book a trip overseas, across the country, or to an area you've never been in your own state. If you go to the mountains, rent skis and see how you like it. If you're a beachcomber, pick a different beach location, and instead of just tanning yourself and watching others, learn to surf. Or don a blindfold and blindly point to a spot on the map to be your next destination. Go and do what you haven't before.

Doing volunteer work

You don't have to save volunteer work for when you retire. Find a charity or organization that sounds interesting. Those running it will appreciate your time and effort, and you might find that you really look forward to the hours you're donating because you're passionate about the cause.

Joining a club or group

Looking to find new friends as you're exploring? Join a club or group focused around an interest you have. You'll meet like-minded people and perhaps discover new passions while you're at it. Do you have a yearning to hike the great outdoors? Bike across your state? Dress up in costumes and dance at public events? Get involved with your neighborhood board to make things better in your community? Your options are infinite.

Trying a new hobby

Have you always wanted to play the tuba but were too shy to sign up for band in high school? Maybe you have a flair for color and want to take up painting. Nothing's stopping you from trying a new hobby. You might discover an untapped talent.

Taking a class or workshop

Tired of eating the same frozen meals week in and week out? Consider signing up for a cooking class. You might find that you enjoy the culinary arts. Or sign up for a yoga class at the new place downtown and stretch your body in ways it hasn't before.

Attending events and festivals

Attending events and festivals centered around a particular interest, such as music or food, can be a great way to try new things and discover new passions. Maybe there's a music genre you're unfamiliar with but will really resonate with. Grab a friend and your blanket and go! Ever been to a pierogi festival? A beer or wine festival? What are you waiting for?

Exploring new foods

Don't limit yourself to eating what you grew up with. Make a reservation at a sushi restaurant. You might find that you love those particular tastes and textures, and starting with sushi can lead you down a path toward more Japanese cuisine.

If you have an international grocery store in your area, walk down the aisles. Grab some produce and other ingredients you've never had before but that sound interesting and invite someone over for a special dinner. Be open-minded about all that life has to offer.

Discovering Hobbies and Activities That Excite You

Hobbies and interests are a great way to explore your passions and discover new things about yourself. They offer an outlet for creativity and self-expression, relieve stress, and promote overall well-being. Hobbies and interests can make you feel happier, more relaxed, and fulfilled. They also supply an opportunity for you to learn new skills and make connections with others.

Table 4-1 offers some ways to discover hobbies and activities that excite you.

By following these tips, you can discover new hobbies and activities that excite you and bring more fulfillment to your life.

Identifying hobbies and activities that align with your values and interests

Identifying hobbies and activities that align with your values and interests is an important part of finding your passion. Table 4-2 offers some steps you can take to identify hobbies and activities that are a good fit for you.

TABLE 4-1   **Methods for Finding Passion in Your Hobbies and Activities**

Method	How to Carry It Out
Identify your values and interests	Think about what matters most to you and what you enjoy doing. Make a list of your values, interests, and what makes you happy.
Research new hobbies and activities	Use the internet to research new hobbies and activities that align with your values and interests. Explore different communities and forums to learn more about potential hobbies and how to get started.
Start small	Don't overwhelm yourself by trying to do too much at once. Start with one or two hobbies or activities that sound fun and see how you feel about them. You can always add more later.
Experiment	Try out some things to see what you enjoy most. You might surprise yourself with what you enjoy.
Find a community	Join a group or club that focuses on your hobby or activity. This way you can learn more and make new connections with people who share your interests.
Incorporate hobbies into your life	Make time for your hobbies and activities. Even if it's just a few minutes a day or a few hours a week, prioritize the things that make you happy and bring you joy.

BENEFITS OF HOBBIES AND OTHER INTERESTS BEYOND PASSION PURSUIT

Hobbies and interests are activities to enjoy in your leisure time. They're often pursued for personal enjoyment or satisfaction rather than for financial gain. Engaging in hobbies and interests has several benefits to your well-being. Some of these benefits include:

- **Stress relief:** Engaging in hobbies and interests can be a nice break from the stress and pressures of daily life. Participating in activities that you find enjoyable can reduce stress levels and improve your overall mood.

- **Improved mental health:** Hobbies and interests can promote positive mental health by giving you a sense of purpose and achievement. They can also increase your self-esteem and confidence.

- **Increased creativity:** Many hobbies and interests involve creative expression, which can help you tap into your imagination and develop your artistic abilities.

- **Improved physical health:** Some hobbies and interests, such as sports and dancing, can be sources of physical exercise and improve your overall fitness.

- **Social connections:** Engaging in hobbies and interests can help you meet new people and develop social connections with those who share similar interests.

(continued)

(continued)

For example, someone who enjoys painting may find that spending time creating artwork relieves their stress and improves their mood. Engaging in this hobby may also give them a sense of accomplishment and pride in their artistic abilities, leading to increased self-esteem and confidence. Additionally, attending art classes or joining a painting group can be a way to meet new people and make social connections.

Hobbies and interests can serve an important role in your overall well-being. Pursue them regularly as a form of self-care.

TABLE 4-2 **Steps for Identifying Which Hobbies and Activities Fit Your Needs**

Step	How to Accomplish It
Make a list of your values.	Consider what's important to you in life, such as helping others, finding ways to be creative, or developing yourself personally. This can help you identify hobbies and activities that align with your values.
Reflect on your interests.	Think about what you enjoy doing in your free time. This can include anything from reading to playing sports to cooking. Consider how you can incorporate these interests into your hobbies and activities.
Try new things.	Be open to trying new hobbies and activities. Attend events, join clubs, and experiment with hobbies until you find something that excites you.
Consider your skills.	Think about your strengths and areas where you excel. Consider how you can incorporate these skills into your hobbies and activities.
Evaluate your time and resources.	Consider the amount of time and money you have available for hobbies and activities. Look for hobbies and activities that fit within your schedule and budget.

Table 4-3 presents ideas for aligning your hobbies and activities with your values and interests.

By identifying hobbies and activities that align with your values and interests, you can discover new passions and find fulfillment in your leisure time.

Incorporating hobbies and interests into your life

Incorporating hobbies and interests into your life can bring a sense of fulfillment and balance. This section includes some ways to make it happen.

TABLE 4-3   Merging Your Values with Your Hobbies

Value	Possible Hobby or Activity
Helping others	Volunteering at a local charity or non-profit organization, mentoring or tutoring others, or participating in community service projects
Creativity	Painting, drawing, photography, writing, or playing a musical instrument
Personal growth	Practicing yoga or meditation, reading personal development books, attending workshops or seminars, or learning a new skill or language
Sports and fitness	Running, hiking, swimming, cycling, or joining a sports team
Cooking and baking	Trying new recipes, hosting dinner parties, or attending cooking classes

Schedule time for your hobbies

Make a weekly or monthly schedule that includes time for your hobbies and stick to it. If painting makes you happy, set aside a few hours every weekend to work on a new piece.

Find a community

Joining a club or group related to your hobby can be a source of community and support. Maybe you like to hike. You could join a local hiking group and meet others who share your passion for the outdoors.

Make it a priority

Prioritize your hobbies and make them a non-negotiable part of your routine. If you enjoy playing music, set aside time every day to practice, and make it a priority in your life.

Incorporate your hobby into your work

If possible, find a way to incorporate your hobby into your work. If you find joy in photography, offer to take photos for your company's website or social media accounts.

Explore new opportunities

Continuously explore new opportunities to learn and grow within your hobby. If cooking is your jam, attend a cooking class or try out new recipes to expand your knowledge and skills.

Understanding Different Career Paths and Industries

Researching careers and industries is an essential step in finding your passion. It involves understanding the roles and responsibilities of different job positions as well as the industry or field they belong to. You can start by researching online job boards, professional associations, and industry reports. You can also network with professionals in the field or attend career fairs to gain more insights.

Identifying careers that align with your values and interests is another crucial step. It's important to consider your core values, personality type, and natural talents when selecting a career path. For example, if you value helping others and have excellent communication skills, you might consider a career in counseling or social work. If you enjoy working with numbers and have a talent for problem-solving, you might consider a career in finance or data analysis.

Exploring different ways to pursue your passion within your career is important also. This involves identifying your specific area of interest within a particular field and finding ways to incorporate it into your job. For example, if you're passionate about writing and work in marketing, you might find opportunities to create content for the company's website or social media platforms. Alternatively, you might consider starting a blog or freelance writing on the side.

Finding your passion doesn't necessarily mean changing careers or industries. Sometimes it's possible to pursue your passion within your current job or by taking on side projects. The key is to be open to new opportunities and explore different ways to incorporate your interests into your life.

Researching the careers and industries

Researching numerous careers and industries is an essential step in finding your passion and pursuing a fulfilling career. It helps you gain knowledge and insight into various industries and job roles and allows you to make informed decisions about your future career path.

Keep in mind that researching these careers and industries is an ongoing process. Continue to explore new opportunities and learn more about different fields throughout your career journey.

When it comes to identifying and pursuing your passion, let your interests lead the way. You can conduct research on various fields and occupations to gain a better understanding of what's available.

For instance, if you have a passion for helping others, you might explore a career like social work, counseling, or healthcare. Or if you have an interest in technology, you might look into software development, cybersecurity, or data analytics.

Researching different careers and industries can involve conducting online research, attending job fairs and networking events, conducting informational interviews, reading articles and books, job shadowing, and seeking advice from career counselors. All these ways help you gain a better understanding of the skills and education required for different career paths, as well as the day-to-day responsibilities and opportunities for growth within each industry.

Conduct online research

Use online resources like LinkedIn, Glassdoor, and industry-specific websites to learn about job roles, industries, and companies. Read job descriptions, company reviews, and salary information to determine what each job entails.

Attend job fairs and networking events

Attend job fairs and networking events to meet professionals in different industries and learn about their experiences. This can help you gain valuable insights and connections that can aid in your job search.

Conduct informational interviews

Reach out to professionals in industries that interest you and request informational interviews. These conversations can lead to valuable insight into what the job entails, what skills are required, and what the day-to-day tasks involve.

Consider job shadowing

Job shadowing allows you to observe professionals in their daily work, gaining firsthand experience of what the job is really like. It's an excellent way to find out more about different careers and industries.

Seek advice from career counselors

Career counselors can give you guidance and support as you explore careers and industries. They can help you identify your strengths and interests and suggest potential career paths that align with them.

Identifying careers that align with your values and interests

When trying to identify a career that aligns with your values and interests, consider what you're passionate about, what your core values are, and what skills and talents you possess. For instance, if you're passionate about social justice and advocacy, you may be interested in pursuing a career in non-profit organizations, human rights organizations, or political campaigns. On the other hand, if you're passionate about science and technology, you may be interested in pursuing a career in engineering, research, or computer science.

Here are some examples of how identifying careers that align with values and interests can be beneficial:

TIP

» If you value creativity and artistic expression, pursuing a career in the arts or creative industries, such as graphic design or advertising, may light up your world.

» If you value helping others, a career in healthcare or social work may align with your values and interests.

» If you value environmental sustainability and preservation, a career in environmental science, renewable energy, or sustainability consulting may be just what recharges you.

» If you value innovation and problem-solving, a career in technology, engineering, or entrepreneurship may align with your values and interests.

By identifying careers that fit your values and interests, you can find greater fulfillment and meaning in your work, which can lead to greater job satisfaction and overall happiness.

Exploring ways to pursue your passion within your career

Once you've identified a career path that aligns with your values and interests, you can explore ways to pursue your passion within that field. Networking, volunteering, continuing education, side projects, and job shadowing can help you do that.

Networking

Attend industry conferences and events, and connect with professionals in your field who share similar interests. This can lead to new opportunities and insights on how to further pursue your passion within your career.

Volunteering

Find opportunities to volunteer within your field or related areas of interest. This can offer valuable experience and help you discover new aspects of your passion that you may not have considered before.

Continuing education

Look for courses, workshops, or certifications that enable you to develop new skills and knowledge related to your passion within your career. They can help you stay up-to-date with industry trends and advancements.

Side projects

Consider taking on side projects or freelance work that allows you to explore your passion further. This can also help you build a portfolio and gain experience that can lead to new opportunities within your career.

Job shadowing

Shadow professionals in your field who are already pursuing their passion. This can shine a light on how to successfully pursue your own passions within your career.

REMEMBER

By exploring different ways to pursue your passion within your career, you can continue to grow and develop professionally while staying true to your values and interests.

Improving Your Mental Health by Finding Your Passion

Finding your passion can have a significant positive impact on your mental health. It's common to feel lost, stuck, or unfulfilled when you're not doing what you truly love. Pursuing your passion can give you a sense of purpose, direction, and fulfillment that can greatly improve your overall mental health.

Research has shown that people who pursue their passion experience lower levels of stress, anxiety, and depression. When you're doing something you're passionate about, you're more likely to experience positive emotions like happiness, satisfaction, and joy. This can lead to a more positive outlook on life and greater resilience to stress.

For example, if someone's working in a career they don't enjoy, they come home feeling drained and unfulfilled every day. They may be more prone to negative thoughts and feelings of stress and anxiety, which affects their relationships with others. However, if they were to find their passion and pursue it, they may come home feeling energized and fulfilled, leading to a more positive outlook on life, improved mental health, and better relations with their family and friends.

Pursuing your passion can provide a sense of mastery and accomplishment. When you're doing something you love, you're more likely to put in the effort and time to become skilled and successful in that area. This sense of mastery and accomplishment can boost your self-esteem and confidence, which can have a positive impact on your mental health.

2

Going After What You Want

Chapter **5**

Setting Goals in Pursuit of Your Passion

Goals play a vital role both personally and professionally. They direct you, motivate you, and foster a sense of purpose. I dive into the art of setting meaningful and achievable goals in this chapter. Whether you're striving to excel in your career, pursue a personal passion, or make positive changes in your life, this chapter guides you through the process of effective goal setting.

Setting goals isn't just about having a vague idea of what you want to achieve. It involves thoughtful planning, clarity of purpose, and a systematic approach. This chapter offers you the tools and strategies to set goals that are meaningful, aligned with your values, and designed to propel you toward success.

These next few pages explore the importance of setting specific, measurable, achievable, relevant, and time-bound (SMART) goals. They also delve into the power of visualization and positive affirmation in goal setting, as well as the significance of breaking down larger goals into manageable steps.

The goal of this chapter is your clear understanding of how to define your goals, create actionable plans, and stay motivated along the way. Whether you're a beginner or have previous experience with goal setting, this chapter has valuable insights and practical strategies to set you up for success.

So get ready to unleash your potential, unlock your aspirations, and embark on a journey of intentional goal setting. It's time to define your path, control your destiny, and achieve the meaningful and achievable goals to bring fulfillment and joy to your life.

The Importance of Setting Goals in Finding Passion

I can't emphasize enough the importance of setting goals in the process. Goals serve as guideposts that lead you closer to your true passions and help you navigate the path of self-discovery.

Setting goals bestows a clear sense of direction and purpose. Without goals, you may find yourself wandering aimlessly, unsure of where you want to go or what you want to achieve. Goals give you a focal point, a target to aim for, and they help you channel your energy and efforts toward the things that truly matter.

When it comes to finding your passion, goals act as steppingstones toward self-discovery. They allow you to explore different areas, try new things, and gain valuable insights about yourself and what truly resonates with you. By setting goals, you create a roadmap that guides you toward activities, experiences, and opportunities that align with your passions and interests.

Moreover, setting goals helps you stay focused and motivated during the journey of finding your passion. It's easy to become overwhelmed or discouraged along the way, but having well-defined goals keeps you on track and reminds you of the bigger picture. Goals grant a sense of purpose and drive, pushing you forward even when faced with obstacles or setbacks.

In addition, goals bring structure and accountability to your pursuit of passion. They allow you to break down your aspirations into manageable steps, making them more attainable and less daunting. By setting measurable and time-bound goals, you create a framework that enables you to track your progress, celebrate your achievements, and adjust your approach as needed.

REMEMBER

Setting goals to find your passion isn't about imposing rigid expectations or putting unnecessary pressure on yourself. Instead, it's about setting intentions and creating a framework that supports your exploration, growth, and self-discovery. It's about embracing the journey, being open to new experiences, and allowing yourself the freedom to evolve and redefine your goals as you gain clarity on what truly excites you.

Different types of goals and their role in pursuing passion

Goals aren't one-size-fits-all; they come in various forms and serve distinct purposes in your journey of self-discovery. Goals come in different types and can contribute to your pursuit of passion, empowering you to create a fulfilling and purposeful life.

Setting the right types of goals is essential toward aligning your actions and aspirations with your passion. Each type of goal serves a specific purpose and offers unique benefits, creating a holistic approach to uncovering and pursuing your passion. By understanding these different categories of goals, you can tailor your goal-setting process to maximize its effectiveness in your personal journey.

The first category is *outcome goals*, which are the ultimate vision or destination you strive to achieve. These goals paint a vivid picture of what success looks like for you and offer a sense of direction. They act as a North Star, guiding your actions and decisions as you embark on your passion-fueled journey. For example, if your passion is photography, your outcome goal might be to become a renowned professional photographer or to publish a book featuring your breathtaking images.

Another category is *performance goals*, which focus on specific milestones and achievements that contribute to your overall outcome goal. These goals are measurable and help you track your progress and growth. They act as tangible targets that motivate and challenge you along the way. In the photography example, a performance goal might be to complete a photography course or to participate in a prestigious photography competition.

Process goals play a crucial role in the pursuit of passion by emphasizing the actions and behaviors you need to engage in consistently. These goals focus on the daily habits, routines, and practices that nurture and develop your passion. They're about the journey itself, the steps you take, and the skills you cultivate. Continuing with the photography passion, a process goal might be dedicating at least an hour every day to practice capturing different subjects or learning a new photography technique each week.

Personal development goals are another important goal type that contributes to your pursuit of passion. These goals revolve around self-improvement, expanding your knowledge, and honing your skills. They support your growth as an individual and enhance your abilities related to your passion. In the photography context, a personal development goal might be attending workshops or seminars to enhance your editing skills or studying the works of renowned photographers to gain inspiration and knowledge.

The final category is *lifestyle goals*, which encompass the broader aspects of your life that your passion influences. These goals focus on integrating your passion into various areas, such as your career, relationships, and overall well-being. They ensure that your passion becomes an integral part of your lifestyle, bringing fulfillment and purpose to every aspect of your life. For example, a lifestyle goal related to photography might involve establishing a photography business or creating a blog showcasing your photographic journey.

How different types of goals shape the pursuit of passion

Different goals play a pivotal role in shaping your pursuit of passion by building structure, direction, motivation, and a sense of purpose. Each type of goal contributes in its own way, creating a multifaceted approach to uncovering and nurturing your passions. Here's how these different goals shape your journey:

>> **Outcome goals:** These big-picture goals define your ultimate vision and serve as a guiding star. They offer a clear destination to strive for and create a sense of purpose and direction. Outcome goals help you visualize the desired outcome of your passion, fueling your motivation and determination to achieve it. They give you a sense of accomplishment when you reach significant milestones, reinforcing the belief in the pursuit of your passion.

>> **Performance goals:** These goals focus on specific achievements and milestones along the way. They serve as measurable targets that allow you to track your progress and celebrate your accomplishments. Performance goals break down the broader outcome goal into manageable steps, making the journey to your passion more tangible and attainable. By setting performance goals, you create a roadmap of smaller victories that build confidence and momentum, propelling you forward.

>> **Process goals:** These goals concentrate on the daily actions, habits, and behaviors that contribute to your growth and development in your passion. Process goals emphasize the journey rather than the end result. They help you cultivate consistency, discipline, and dedication in your pursuit of passion. By setting process goals, you establish a routine of deliberate practice, learning, and improvement, allowing you to refine your skills and deepen your connection to your passion.

>> **Personal development goals:** These goals focus on self-improvement and expanding your knowledge and skills related to your passion. They support your growth as an individual and enhance your ability in your chosen area. Personal development goals drive you to continuously learn, evolve, and stay abreast of new trends and advancements in your field of interest. They push

you outside your comfort zone, enabling you to unlock your full potential and excel in your pursuit of passion.

» **Lifestyle goals:** These goals integrate your passion into various aspects of your life. They ensure that your passion becomes part of who you are and how you live. Lifestyle goals help you align your career, relationships, and overall well-being with your passion. By setting lifestyle goals, you create a harmonious and fulfilling life that revolves around your passion, allowing you to experience joy, fulfillment, and purpose in all areas of your existence.

By incorporating these different types of goals into your pursuit of passion, you create a comprehensive framework that propels you forward. They contribute to your growth, resilience, and perseverance and help you stay focused, motivated, and committed, even when faced with challenges or setbacks. Additionally, these goals garner a sense of accomplishment, satisfaction, and fulfillment as you make progress and witness the tangible results of your efforts.

Ultimately, the interplay between these different goals shapes your pursuit of passion by providing structure, purpose, and continuous growth. They create a roadmap that supports your personal and professional development, ensuring that you stay aligned with your true passions and lead a purpose-driven life.

Identifying SMART goals

Identifying SMART goals is a crucial aspect of setting meaningful and achievable goals in the pursuit of passion. SMART goals supply a clear framework that helps you clarify your intentions, track your progress, and stay focused on the path to your passion. It's time to delve into each component of SMART goals so you can see how they contribute to your journey:

» **Specific:** A SMART goal should be well defined and specific. It should answer the questions of who, what, where, when, and why. By being specific, you create a clear target and direction for your efforts. For example, instead of setting a vague goal like "improve my skills," a specific goal might be "attend a photography workshop to enhance my composition techniques."

» **Measurable:** Measurability ensures that you can track your progress and determine whether you've achieved your goal. It involves quantifying or using tangible indicators to assess your success. Measurable goals enable you to stay accountable and motivated. For instance, a measurable goal might be "practice playing the guitar for 30 minutes every day" or "increase my monthly website traffic by 20%."

» **Achievable:** SMART goals should be realistic and achievable. They should stretch you outside your comfort zone but remain within the realm of possibility. Setting achievable goals allows you to build confidence, maintain momentum, and avoid setting yourself up for disappointment or burnout. For example, if you're starting a new fitness routine, an achievable goal might be "run a 5K race in six months" rather than aiming for a marathon right away.

>> **Relevant:** A SMART goal should align with your passion, values, and overall aspirations. It should be relevant to your personal and professional growth. By ensuring relevance, you maintain focus and invest your time and energy in pursuits that truly matter to you. For instance, if your passion lies in sustainable fashion, a relevant goal might be "launch an eco-friendly clothing line" rather than pursuing a completely unrelated business venture.

>> **Time-bound:** Setting a deadline or timeframe is crucial for SMART goals. It lends a sense of urgency, prioritizes your efforts, and prevents procrastination. Time-bound goals create a sense of structure and enable you to track your progress effectively. For example, a time-bound goal might be "complete the first draft of my novel within six months" or "achieve fluency in a foreign language within one year."

By incorporating the SMART criteria into your goal-setting process, you enhance your chances of success and maintain a sense of clarity and focus. SMART goals lay out a roadmap that guides your actions, keeps you accountable, and ensures that your efforts are aligned with your passion. They help you break down your larger aspirations into smaller, manageable steps, making the path to your passion more tangible and attainable.

REMEMBER

Setting SMART goals isn't a one-time activity but an ongoing process. As you progress and achieve your goals, it's essential to reassess, revise, and set new SMART goals that continue to challenge and inspire you on your journey of pursuing your passion.

Creating a Plan to Achieve Your Goals

Creating a plan to achieve your goals is a critical step in turning your passion into a reality. While having a vision and setting goals is essential, it's equally important to develop a roadmap that outlines the necessary steps, resources, and timelines to bring your aspirations to fruition. Without a well-thought-out plan, your goals may remain mere dreams, and the path to your passion can feel overwhelming and uncertain.

This section explores the process of creating a plan to achieve your goals. It dives into the key components and strategies that help you map out a clear and actionable plan, ensuring that you make progress toward your passion in a structured and organized manner.

TIP

Having a plan results in numerous benefits in your journey toward fulfilling your dreams. It brings focus, direction, and a sense of purpose to your actions. It allows you to break down complex goals into manageable steps, which in turn gives you a sense of progress and accomplishment along the way. A well-designed plan also serves as a guide, helping you navigate obstacles, make informed decisions, and stay motivated during challenging times.

REMEMBER

Creating a plan doesn't involve a rigid set of rules, but a flexible framework that allows for adjustments and iterations along the way. It's an iterative process that requires reflection, evaluation, and refinement as you gain new insights and experiences.

So embark on this journey of creating a plan to achieve your goals and bring your passion to life. This book explores the essential elements and practical techniques to guide you toward success and fulfillment. Get ready to take the next step and turn your aspirations into a well-crafted plan of action!

Breaking down larger goals into smaller, achievable steps

Breaking down larger goals into smaller, achievable steps is a fundamental strategy for effective goal setting and a key ingredient in the recipe for success. When you have ambitious and significant goals, it's easy to feel overwhelmed and uncertain about where to begin. However, by breaking them down into smaller, actionable steps, you can gain clarity, maintain focus, and make progress toward your ultimate objectives.

TIP

One of the primary advantages of breaking down larger goals is that it allows you to create a roadmap of smaller milestones along the way. These milestones serve as markers of progress and offer a sense of accomplishment as you achieve each one. Celebrating these smaller victories keeps you motivated and reinforces your belief in your ability to reach the larger goal.

Moreover, breaking down goals into smaller steps enhances your clarity and understanding of the necessary actions required. It offers a clear sense of direction and eliminates the ambiguity that often hinders progress. By identifying and organizing the specific tasks and actions needed, you can allocate your time, energy, and resources more effectively, resulting in increased productivity and efficiency.

Another significant benefit of breaking down goals is that it helps you overcome procrastination and overwhelm. When faced with a daunting and massive goal, it's easy to fall into the trap of procrastination or become discouraged by the enormity of the task. However, when you break a goal down into smaller, more manageable steps, it becomes less intimidating. You can approach each step with greater focus and confidence, knowing that you're making tangible progress.

Breaking down larger goals also allows for increased flexibility and adaptability. As you work through the smaller steps, you gain valuable insights and feedback that may necessitate adjustments to your approach. By having a more granular view of your goals, you can readily adapt and modify your plans to align with new circumstances or changing priorities. This flexibility enables you to stay nimble and responsive, ensuring that you remain on track toward your ultimate vision.

Breaking down larger goals into smaller, achievable steps is a powerful strategy for effective goal attainment. It's a roadmap for success, enhancing clarity and focus, boosting motivation, and allowing for flexibility and adaptability. By mastering the art of breaking down goals, you can navigate your path toward passion with purpose and confidence, consistently moving closer to your desired outcome.

REMEMBER

Progress is made one step at a time, and by breaking down your larger goals into smaller, actionable steps, you set yourself up for steady progress and a greater likelihood of achieving your dreams. So embrace the power of breaking down your goals, and watch as you transform your aspirations into reality.

Creating a timeline and schedule for achieving goals

Creating a timeline and schedule for achieving goals is a vital component of effective goal planning and execution. It produces structure, accountability, and a clear roadmap for turning your aspirations into reality. By setting specific deadlines and allocating time to each task and milestone, you increase your chances of success and stay on track toward accomplishing your goals.

One of the key advantages of creating a timeline and schedule is that it instills a sense of urgency and purpose. When you have a designated timeframe for completing your goals, you have a sense of time-bound pressure that motivates you to take action and make consistent progress. It helps you avoid the trap of procrastination and encourages you to stay focused and committed to your goals.

A well-defined timeline and schedule also supply a practical framework for managing your time and resources effectively. By breaking down your goals into smaller, actionable tasks and allocating specific time slots for each, you can prioritize your activities and ensure that you're dedicating adequate time to the most crucial aspects of goal attainment. This helps prevent overwhelm, improves productivity, and maximizes your efficiency in working toward your objectives.

Furthermore, creating a timeline and schedule enables you to set realistic expectations and milestones. It allows you to assess the feasibility of your goals and ensure that you're allocating sufficient time for each step. By breaking your goals into manageable chunks and assigning specific timeframes, you can gauge your progress, identify potential bottlenecks, and make necessary adjustments along the way. This iterative process keeps you on track and allows for continuous improvement.

TIP

In addition, a well-structured timeline and schedule facilitates effective time management and reduces the likelihood of burnout. It helps you strike a balance between pursuing your passion and maintaining a healthy lifestyle. By allocating time for self-care, rest, and rejuvenation, you prevent exhaustion and maintain your overall well-being, which is crucial for long-term success and sustainable goal achievement.

Moreover, a timeline and schedule are valuable tools for tracking and monitoring your progress. By regularly reviewing and updating your schedule, you can evaluate your performance, identify any deviations, and make adjustments to ensure you're on the right path. This self-assessment allows you to celebrate milestones, learn from setbacks, and make informed decisions so you can keep moving forward.

Creating a timeline and schedule for achieving goals is an indispensable practice for effective goal management. It provides structure, accountability, and a clear roadmap for success. By setting deadlines, allocating time, and managing your resources wisely, you increase your productivity, maintain focus, and enhance your chances of achieving your goals. So embrace the power of a well-crafted timeline and schedule, and witness how it propels you toward your passion with purpose and efficiency.

REMEMBER

Time is a valuable asset. By creating a timeline and schedule, you take control of your journey and maximize your potential for success. So set your goals, create your timeline, and embark on your path toward turning your dreams into reality.

Developing a timeline and schedule for achieving goals is an essential step in effective goal planning and execution. Here are some tips for creating a well-structured timeline and schedule:

>> **Start with a clear understanding of your goals:** Before you can create a timeline, it's crucial to have a clear understanding of your goals. Define what you want to achieve, break it down into specific objectives, and identify the tasks required to accomplish them.

>> **Set realistic deadlines:** Be realistic when setting deadlines for your goals and tasks. Consider the complexity of the task, your available resources, and any

external factors that may affect your timeline. Setting achievable deadlines helps you stay motivated and avoid unnecessary stress.

>> **Break down your goals into smaller tasks:** Break down your goals into smaller, manageable tasks. This makes them less overwhelming and easier to schedule. Identify the individual steps required to reach each goal, and assign them specific time slots on your schedule.

>> **Prioritize your tasks:** Determine the priority of each task based on its importance and urgency. Focus on high-priority tasks first to ensure progress toward your goals. Consider using techniques like the Eisenhower Matrix (categorizing tasks as urgent, important, not urgent, or not important) to prioritize effectively.

>> **Allocate sufficient time for each task:** Estimate a realistic time required to complete each task. Consider factors such as the complexity of the task, potential obstacles, and your own capabilities. Avoid overcommitting, and ensure you've allocated enough time for each task to maintain a realistic and achievable schedule.

>> **Use a visual calendar or scheduling tool:** Utilize a visual calendar or scheduling tool to create your timeline. Whether it's a physical planner, a digital calendar, or project management software, find a method that works best for you. Ensure your chosen tool allows you to easily view and update your schedule as needed.

>> **Consider dependencies and constraints:** Take into account any dependencies or constraints that may affect your timeline. If certain tasks rely on the completion of others or if external factors might influence your schedule, factor them in when allocating time to each task.

>> **Allow buffer time:** Include buffer time in your schedule to account for unexpected delays, revisions, or unforeseen circumstances. This helps you manage unexpected challenges without derailing your entire timeline.

>> **Regularly review and adjust your schedule:** Regularly review your timeline and make adjustments as needed. Assess your progress, identify any bottlenecks or deviations from the plan, and make necessary modifications to keep yourself on track. Flexibility and adaptability are key to maintaining a realistic and effective timeline.

>> **Stay committed and disciplined:** Creating a timeline is just the first step; you must also stay committed and disciplined in following it. Stick to your schedule as much as possible, avoid unnecessary distractions, and hold yourself accountable for completing tasks within the allocated timeframes.

Developing a timeline and schedule requires careful planning and ongoing monitoring. By following these tips, you can create a realistic and effective schedule to help you stay organized, focused, and motivated as you work toward achieving your goals.

Identifying potential obstacles and developing contingency plans

Identifying potential obstacles and developing contingency plans is a crucial aspect of goal planning and execution. Although it's important to stay optimistic and focused on your goals, it's equally important to anticipate and prepare for potential challenges along the way. Here's my expert opinion on the matter:

1. **Anticipate common obstacles:** Take some time to brainstorm and identify potential obstacles that may arise during your journey toward achieving your goals. These obstacles can include lack of resources, time constraints, unexpected events, or even internal factors like self-doubt or procrastination. By proactively identifying these obstacles, you can be better prepared to address them.

2. **Assess the impact and likelihood:** Once you've identified potential obstacles, assess their impact and likelihood of occurring. Determine how significant each obstacle might be in hindering your progress and the probability of it actually happening. This assessment helps you prioritize and allocate resources accordingly.

3. **Develop contingency plans:** Once you've identified potential obstacles and their impact, it's time to develop contingency plans. Contingency plans are alternative strategies or approaches that you can implement if an obstacle occurs. Consider different scenarios and outline specific actions you can take to mitigate or overcome the obstacle.

4. **Be flexible and adaptable:** Remember that your journey toward achieving your goals may not always go as planned. Being flexible and adaptable is key to navigating unexpected obstacles. Embrace the mindset that setbacks are temporary challenges you can overcome with the right mindset and approach. Remain open to adjusting your plans as needed while keeping your ultimate goal in sight.

5. **Seek support and resources:** Don't hesitate to seek support from others who can guide or assist you when you're facing obstacles. Reach out to mentors, friends, or colleagues who may have expertise or experience in dealing with similar challenges. Additionally, consider exploring resources such as books, online courses, or workshops that can offer valuable insights and strategies to tackle obstacles effectively.

6. **Maintain a positive mindset:** Your mindset plays a significant role in how you perceive and overcome obstacles. Cultivate a positive and resilient mindset that embraces challenges as opportunities for growth and learning. Believe in your ability to overcome obstacles, and view them as steppingstones toward your ultimate success.

7. **Regularly review and update contingency plans:** As you progress toward your goals, periodically review and update your contingency plans. As new obstacles arise or circumstances change, adjust your plans accordingly. Regularly evaluate the effectiveness of your contingency plans and make necessary modifications to ensure they remain relevant and effective.

By identifying potential obstacles and developing contingency plans, you're proactively equipping yourself to navigate challenges effectively. This level of preparedness not only helps you overcome obstacles but also enhances your confidence, resilience, and ability to stay on track toward achieving your goals. Remember: Obstacles aren't roadblocks but opportunities for growth and success.

Looking at common obstacles and contingency plans

Here are some common obstacles you will encounter and methods of overcoming them.

» **Lack of time:** If you find yourself struggling to find time to work on your goals, consider breaking down your tasks into smaller, manageable chunks. Allocate specific time slots in your schedule dedicated to working on your goals, and eliminate or delegate less important tasks to create more time.

» **Lack of resources:** If you face resource constraints, such as limited finances or access to certain tools, explore alternative options. Look for cost-effective alternatives, seek out free resources, or consider collaborating with others who may have the resources you need. Additionally, you can explore crowdfunding or grants to secure funding for your endeavors.

» **Procrastination and lack of motivation:** When faced with procrastination or a lack of motivation, figure out the underlying reasons. Break your goals into smaller, achievable tasks, and set deadlines to stay accountable. Find ways to stay motivated, such as rewarding yourself for completing milestones or seeking support from an accountability partner or mentor.

» **Fear of failure:** Fear of failure can be paralyzing and prevent you from taking necessary risks. Develop a growth mindset by reframing failure as a learning opportunity. Embrace the belief that mistakes are steppingstones to success. Seek support from mentors or peers who can guide and reassure you during challenging times.

» **External distractions:** External distractions, such as social media or excessive commitments, can hinder your progress. Create a conducive environment for focus by eliminating distractions and setting boundaries.

>> **Lack of support:** If you feel unsupported in pursuing your goals, seek out like-minded individuals or communities who share similar interests. Join relevant networking groups, online forums, or local meetups where you can find support, encouragement, and valuable insights. Surrounding yourself with a supportive network can significantly boost your motivation and resilience.

>> **Unexpected events or setbacks:** Life is unpredictable, and unexpected events can disrupt your progress. Maintain a flexible mindset, and be prepared to adapt your plans when unforeseen circumstances arise. Have backup options or alternative approaches ready, and be willing to adjust your timeline or expectations as needed.

REMEMBER

These are just some examples of common obstacles. The contingency plans may vary based on your specific goals and circumstances. The key is to anticipate potential challenges, develop a proactive mindset, and be resourceful in finding solutions.

Tracking Your Progress and Celebrating Milestones

Tracking your progress and celebrating milestones are essential aspects of achieving your goals and pursuing your passion. In the journey toward your desired outcome, make sure you have a clear understanding of how far you've come and acknowledge the significant milestones you've reached along the way.

TIP

Tracking your progress lends valuable insights, keeps you motivated, and allows for course corrections if needed. Additionally, celebrating milestones boosts your confidence, reinforces positive behavior, and commits you to your path.

This section explores the importance of tracking your progress and celebrating milestones and how these practices contribute to your overall success. It delves into practical strategies and techniques that can help you effectively monitor your progress, identify areas of improvement, and appreciate the significant milestones you achieve.

Whether you're embarking on a personal development journey, starting a new project, or pursuing a long-term goal, tracking your progress and celebrating milestones are powerful tools to keep you engaged, motivated, and accountable. Dive in and discover how you can track your progress and celebrate each step toward your passion and success.

The importance of tracking progress in achieving goals

I can't overstate the importance of tracking progress in achieving goals. Tracking progress is a fundamental practice that enables individuals to stay on course, maintain focus, and make necessary adjustments along the way. When you set goals, whether they're short-term or long-term, tracking your progress allows you to assess your performance, measure your achievements, and gain valuable insights into your journey.

Tracking your progress paints a clear picture of how far you've come and how much closer you are to your desired outcome. It helps you evaluate the effectiveness of your strategies and actions, allowing you to identify areas of improvement and make the necessary adjustments. Without tracking your progress, you may find yourself moving aimlessly, lacking direction, and unable to gauge whether you're making meaningful strides toward your goal.

Moreover, tracking progress provides a sense of accountability. By keeping a record of your progress, you hold yourself responsible for taking consistent action and making measurable progress. It eliminates the tendency to procrastinate or become complacent because you have a tangible measure of your efforts.

Another crucial benefit of tracking progress is the ability to stay motivated. When you see how far you've come and observe the milestones you've achieved, it fuels your motivation and determination to continue pushing forward. It serves as a reminder of your capabilities, the progress you've made, and the distance you've traveled on your path to success.

TIP

Tracking progress also allows for course corrections. It helps you identify any deviations from your intended path and make adjustments to ensure you stay aligned with your goals. By regularly monitoring your progress, you can identify potential obstacles, anticipate challenges, and develop strategies to overcome them effectively.

In summary, tracking progress is vital for goal achievement. It produces clarity, accountability, motivation, and the ability to make necessary adjustments. It empowers individuals to take control of their journey, stay focused, and ultimately achieve their desired outcomes. So embrace the practice of tracking progress, and witness the transformative impact it has on your goal pursuit and passion fulfillment.

TOOLS THAT CAN HELP YOU
TRACK YOUR PROGRESS

Several effective tools and methods are available to track your progress in achieving goals. Here are a few examples.

Goal-tracking apps: Goal-tracking apps are a convenient way to set and track your goals, allowing you to input tasks and deadlines and track your progress. Some popular goal-tracking apps include:

- Todoist (https://todoist.com/)

- Trello (https://trello.com/)

- Habitica (https://habitica.com/)

Spreadsheets: Using spreadsheet software like Microsoft Excel or Google Sheets, you can create a customized tracking sheet to monitor your progress. You can set up columns for tasks, deadlines, and progress updates, and you can create visual charts to visualize your progress over time.

Bullet journals: Bullet journaling is a popular method that combines planning, organization, and creative expression. With a bullet journal, you can create custom layouts to track your goals, tasks, and milestones. It offers flexibility and allows for personalized tracking methods.

Habit trackers: Habit trackers are useful for tracking daily or recurring activities that contribute to your overall goals. You can use physical habit tracker journals or digital habit-tracking apps such as these:

- Habitify (https://habitify.me/)

- Loop Habit Tracker (https://loophabit.com/)

Project management tools: If your goals involve complex projects or collaborations, project management tools can be valuable for tracking progress, assigning tasks, and managing deadlines. Some popular project management tools include:

- Asana (https://asana.com/)

- Monday.com (https://monday.com/)

- Basecamp (https://basecamp.com/)

The choice of tracking tool depends on your personal preferences and the nature of your goals. Experiment with different tools and methods to find the one that works best for you. Ultimately, the goal is to find a tracking system that is intuitive, easily accessible, and has the necessary features to monitor and celebrate your progress effectively.

Identifying metrics for measuring progress

When tracking progress toward your goals, you need to identify relevant metrics that can effectively measure your advancement. Metrics offer measurable and tangible indicators of progress, helping you assess how close you are to achieving your goals. Here are some steps to identify appropriate metrics for measuring progress:

1. **Clarify your goal:** Clearly define your goal and the specific outcome you want to achieve. The more specific and well defined your goal, the easier it is to identify relevant metrics.

2. **Break down your goal:** Break your overarching goal into smaller, manageable milestones or subgoals. Each milestone should contribute to the overall objective.

3. **Identify key indicators:** Determine the key indicators or performance factors that align with each milestone. These indicators should directly reflect progress toward your goal. For example, if your goal is to increase website traffic, relevant metrics might include the number of unique visitors, page views, or conversion rates.

4. **Consider leading and lagging indicators:** Leading indicators are proactive measures that can predict future progress, whereas lagging indicators reflect past performance. Both types are valuable for measuring progress. For example, a leading indicator for weight loss might be the number of gym sessions attended, whereas a lagging indicator might be the number of pounds lost.

5. **Determine measurement methods:** Once you've identified the key indicators, consider the methods you'll use to measure them. This might involve using software analytics tools, surveys, feedback forms, or manual tracking.

6. **Set targets and benchmarks:** Establish specific targets or benchmarks for each metric to provide a clear benchmark for success. These targets can be quantitative (e.g., reaching a specific sales target) or qualitative (e.g., achieving a high customer satisfaction rating).

7. **Track and review regularly:** Regularly monitor and track your metrics to evaluate progress. Set a schedule for reviewing and analyzing the data to identify trends, recognize areas for improvement, and celebrate milestones achieved.

REMEMBER

The metrics you choose should align with your goals and offer meaningful insights into your progress. Regularly reassess and refine your metrics as needed to ensure they remain relevant throughout your journey.

Examining common genetic metrics to track

When tracking progress toward your goals, the choice of metrics depends on the nature of your goal and what you aim to achieve. The following are some common examples of metrics that you can track in various areas.

Sales and revenue:

>> Total sales revenue

>> Conversion rates

>> Average order value

>> Customer lifetime value

>> Repeat purchase rate

Website and online presence:

>> Website traffic (unique visitors and page views)

>> Conversion rates, such as leads, sign-ups, and purchases

>> Bounce rate, including percentage of visitors who leave after viewing one page

>> Click-through rate (CTR) for online ads

>> Social media engagement, including likes, shares, and comments

Fitness and health:

>> Body weight and measurements

>> Body fat percentage

>> Strength and endurance benchmarks, such as weight lifted and running distance

>> Resting heart rate

>> Blood pressure levels

Learning and skill development:

>> Number of courses or workshops completed

>> Skill proficiency ratings

>> Test scores or grades

>> Time spent practicing or studying

>> Feedback from mentors or instructors

Project management:

>> Completion time for project milestones

>> Budget adherence and cost control

>> Stakeholder satisfaction ratings

>> Number of tasks completed

>> Quality assurance metrics, such as defect rate and customer complaints

The choice of metrics should align with your specific goals and produce meaningful insights into your progress. It's important to select metrics that are relevant, measurable, and reflect the desired outcomes. Additionally, consider using tools and software that can track and visualize these metrics effectively, such as project management software, analytics platforms, or fitness tracking apps.

Please note that the specific metrics to track might vary depending on your industry, goals, and individual circumstances.

Celebrating milestones and successes along the way

Celebrating milestones and successes along the way is an essential component of goal achievement. It not only provides a sense of accomplishment and motivation but reinforces positive behaviors and encourages continued progress. The following sections outline an expert perspective on the importance of celebrating milestones.

Acknowledgment of progress

Celebrating milestones allows you to recognize and appreciate the progress you've made toward your goals. It serves as a reminder of how far you've come and boosts your confidence in achieving future milestones.

Motivation and momentum

Celebrating successes is a motivational boost to keep moving forward. It serves as a reminder of the rewards and benefits of your efforts, reinforcing your commitment and determination to reach your ultimate goal. By celebrating milestones, you maintain a positive momentum that propels you toward further success.

Positive reinforcement

Celebration acts as a positive reinforcement for the behaviors and actions that have led to your accomplishments. It reinforces the belief that your efforts are worthwhile and that you're on the right track. This positive reinforcement strengthens your commitment to your goals and encourages you to continue taking the necessary steps toward achieving them.

Enhanced well-being and satisfaction

Celebrating milestones contributes to your overall well-being and satisfaction. It allows you to experience joy and fulfillment in the journey toward your goals, rather than solely focusing on the endpoint. By appreciating and celebrating the milestones, you cultivate a sense of happiness and contentment in the pursuit of your passion.

Resilience building

Celebrating milestones can also build resilience. These interim celebrations are a reminder that setbacks and challenges are part of the process, but they don't define your progress. By acknowledging and celebrating milestones, you develop the resilience to overcome obstacles and persevere through difficulties, ultimately leading to long-term success.

REMEMBER

Celebrating milestones doesn't always have to be grand or extravagant. It can be as simple as treating yourself to something you enjoy, sharing your achievements with loved ones, or taking a moment to reflect on your progress. The key is to recognize and appreciate the milestones along the way because they contribute significantly to your motivation, well-being, and ultimate success.

Chapter 6

Networking and Building Connections

N etworking plays a crucial role in finding your passion and pursuing a fulfilling career. In today's interconnected world, building and nurturing relationships with others can launch new opportunities, reveal valuable insights, and expand your professional horizons. Whether you're exploring different industries, seeking mentorship, or looking for collaboration opportunities, networking can be a game-changer in your journey to discovering and pursuing your passion. This chapter delves into the importance of networking and how it can significantly affect your ability to find and cultivate your true passion.

Networking goes beyond exchanging business cards and connecting on social media platforms. It's about building genuine relationships, fostering meaningful connections, and leveraging those connections to explore new possibilities. By actively engaging with a diverse network of individuals, you gain access to a wealth of knowledge, experiences, and perspectives that can shape your understanding of various fields and help you uncover potential passions.

The Importance of Networking

Networking exposes you to new ideas, industries, and career paths that you may not have considered before. Through conversations and interactions with professionals from diverse backgrounds, you can gain insights into other fields and discover potential areas of interest and passion.

REMEMBER

Networking isn't just a means to an end; it's an ongoing process that cultivates meaningful connections and expands your opportunities. By actively engaging in networking activities, you can tap into a wealth of resources, support systems, and opportunities that can propel you closer to finding and pursuing your passion. Embrace the power of networking, build authentic relationships, and unlock the doors to a world of possibilities in your quest for a fulfilling and passionate life and career.

Networking can help you gain insights and make strides toward finding your passion, as the following outlines:

>> **Learning from others' experiences:** Networking offers an opportunity to learn from the experiences of others who have already found their passion or are further along in their career journeys. Their stories, advice, and guidance can offer valuable insights and inspiration as you navigate your own path.

>> **Access to mentorship and guidance:** Building relationships with experienced professionals can lead to mentorship opportunities. Mentors can offer guidance, share their expertise, and support you as you explore and pursue your passion. Their mentorship can help you navigate challenges, set realistic goals, and stay motivated.

>> **Collaboration and synergy:** Networking creates opportunities for collaboration and synergy. By connecting with like-minded individuals or those with complementary skills, you can find potential collaborators, partners, or even cofounders for projects that align with your passion. Working together with others who share your enthusiasm can amplify your impact and bring new perspectives to your endeavors.

>> **Career advancement and job opportunities:** Networking is a key driver in discovering job opportunities and advancing your career. Many job openings are filled through personal connections and referrals. By actively networking, you increase your chances of being exposed to hidden job markets, receiving recommendations, and securing interviews in industries and roles that resonate with your passion.

» **Building confidence and self-promotion skills:** Networking enhances your interpersonal and communication skills, allowing you to confidently express your interests, goals, and aspirations. As you engage in conversations with professionals and share your own story, you develop the ability to articulate your passion effectively and make a lasting impression.

The benefits of networking in personal and professional growth are manifold. Networking brings about opportunities, delivers valuable insights, and fosters personal and career development.

Networking is an essential aspect of finding your passion and achieving personal and professional growth. By actively engaging in networking activities, you create an ecosystem that grants access to opportunities, knowledge, support, and guidance. Embrace networking as a powerful tool in your journey toward discovering and pursuing your true passion. Networking has several benefits:

» **Knowledge and information sharing:** Through networking, you gain access to a wealth of knowledge and information. Interacting with professionals from diverse backgrounds and industries allows you to tap into their expertise, learn about trends and best practices, and stay up-to-date with the latest developments in your field of interest. This knowledge exchange enhances your understanding and competence, enabling personal and professional growth.

» **Expansion of your professional circle:** Networking helps you expand your professional circle and connect with individuals who can become mentors, collaborators, and even friends. These connections offer support, guidance, and insights that can accelerate your growth and lend valuable perspectives on your journey to finding passion. Building relationships with like-minded individuals also cultivates a sense of community and fosters a positive environment for personal and professional development.

» **Foundation of a strong personal brand:** Networking allows you to showcase your skills, expertise, and unique qualities to others. By actively engaging in conversations, sharing your experiences, and demonstrating your passion, you can build a strong personal brand. A positive reputation and a network of supporters can bring about new opportunities and increase your visibility in your chosen field.

» **Enhanced communication and interpersonal skills:** Networking is an excellent platform to hone your communication and interpersonal skills. Engaging in conversations, expressing your ideas, and actively listening to others develops effective communication techniques. These skills are essential not only in networking settings but also in various professional and personal interactions.

» **Access to mentorship and guidance:** Networking creates opportunities to connect with experienced professionals who can serve as mentors or guide you. These mentors can offer valuable advice, share their experiences, and furnish insights that can help you shape your career path and discover your true passion. Their support and guidance can be instrumental in navigating challenges, making informed decisions, and reaching your goals.

» **Discovery of hidden opportunities:** Networking unleashes hidden opportunities that may not be advertised through traditional channels. Many job openings and business collaborations are shared within trusted networks. By expanding your network, you increase your chances of being exposed to such hidden opportunities, enabling personal and professional growth in unexpected ways.

» **Boosted confidence and self-esteem:** Networking allows you to showcase your expertise, share your ideas, and engage in meaningful conversations. Receiving positive feedback, validation, and support from others boosts your confidence and self-esteem. The validation you receive from peers and professionals can inspire you to take bolder steps, explore new avenues, and pursue your passion with greater conviction.

» **Access to opportunities:** Networking gives you access to a range of opportunities that may not be readily available through traditional means. By connecting with professionals in your field of interest, attending industry events, and engaging in networking platforms, you increase your visibility and become aware of potential opportunities such as job openings, collaborations, projects, and even mentorship programs. These opportunities can be instrumental in discovering and pursuing your passion.

» **Support and encouragement:** Networking provides a supportive environment where like-minded individuals come together to share their journeys, challenges, and successes. By connecting with professionals who are passionate about their own endeavors, you can find a network of support, encouragement, and inspiration. Being surrounded by individuals who understand and relate to your aspirations can be invaluable in maintaining motivation and resilience as you navigate the path toward your passion.

» **Collaborative opportunities:** Networking yields collaborative opportunities that can propel you toward your passion. By connecting with individuals who have complementary skills or shared interests, you can form collaborations or partnerships or even join existing projects that align with your goals.

Collaboration not only enhances your skills and knowledge but allows you to contribute to a collective effort in pursuing a shared passion.

>> **Development of a reputation and personal brand:** Networking is an opportunity to showcase your expertise, passion, and unique qualities. By actively participating in conversations, sharing your insights, and contributing meaningfully to discussions, you can build a positive reputation within your network. This positive reputation can forge new connections, collaborations, and opportunities that align with your passion.

Understanding the Different Types of Networking

Understanding the different types of networking is crucial to maximizing its ben-efits. Networking can take various forms, but each type offers unique opportuni-ties and advantages. Consider these key types of networking:

>> **Professional networking:** This type of networking focuses on building connections within your industry or profession. It involves attending industry-specific events, joining professional associations or organizations, and engaging with professionals in your field. Professional networking helps you stay up-to-date with industry trends, expand your knowledge, and create connections that can lead to career opportunities.

>> **Social networking:** Social networking involves building connections in social settings, both online and offline. It includes attending social events, participat-ing in social clubs or groups, and engaging in social media platforms. Although social networking may not directly relate to your profession, it's an opportu-nity to meet people from diverse backgrounds to exchange ideas and build relationships that can offer new perspectives and unexpected opportunities.

>> **Informational interviews:** Informational interviews involve reaching out to professionals in your field of interest to gather insights and information about their career paths, experiences, and industries. It allows you to learn from others' expertise, gain valuable advice, and potentially develop mentorship relationships. Informational interviews can produce clarity and direction in your pursuit of passion when you learn from those who have already achieved success in related areas.

>> **Online networking:** In the digital age, online networking has become increasingly important. It involves utilizing online platforms and social media channels to connect with professionals, join industry-related groups or

communities, and engage in online discussions. Online networking offers the convenience of connecting with individuals worldwide, expanding your reach, and accessing a vast pool of knowledge and resources.

>> **Peer networking:** Peer networking involves connecting with individuals who share similar interests, aspirations, or goals. These individuals may be in the same stage of their career as you are or may be pursuing similar passions. Peer networking encourages a supportive environment where you can exchange ideas, offer mutual support, and share experiences. Peer networks impart a sense of community and understanding, helping you stay motivated and inspired on your journey.

>> **Mentorship networking:** Mentorship networking involves seeking out mentors who can guide and support you in your pursuit of passion. Mentors are typically those with experience and expertise in your field of interest. They can dispense valuable advice, share their knowledge, and issue guidance based on their own experiences. Mentorship networking allows you to tap into the wisdom of someone who has already achieved success and can help you navigate challenges and make informed decisions.

>> **Alumni networking:** Alumni networking involves connecting with individuals who have graduated from the same educational institution as you. This type of networking can be beneficial for accessing a network of professionals who share a common background and educational experience. Alumni events, online platforms, and alumni associations are great resources for engaging in alumni networking.

>> **Industry-specific networking:** Industry-specific networking focuses on building connections within a particular industry or sector. This type of networking allows you to connect with professionals who work in the same industry, attend industry conferences and events, and join industry-specific online communities. Industry-specific networking furnishes opportunities to learn about industry trends, developments, and potential career paths.

>> **Volunteer networking:** Volunteering is a unique opportunity to network while making a positive impact. By volunteering for causes or organizations aligned with your interests, you can meet like-minded individuals, build relationships, and showcase your skills and dedication. Volunteer networking allows you to connect with individuals who share your passion for a particular cause or community.

>> **Cross-functional networking:** Cross-functional networking involves connecting with professionals from different departments or areas of expertise within your organization or industry. This type of networking allows you to broaden your knowledge, gain insights from different perspectives, and build collaborative relationships. Cross-functional networking can enhance your problem-solving abilities and launch new opportunities within your organization or industry.

REMEMBER

The key to successful networking is to approach it with genuine interest, professionalism, and reciprocity. Building meaningful connections takes time and effort, but the benefits can be substantial in terms of personal and professional growth, accessing new opportunities, and finding support and guidance on your journey toward passion.

Building and maintaining professional relationships

Building and maintaining professional relationships is a crucial aspect of personal and career development. The connections you form and nurture throughout your professional journey can open doors, provide support, and help you grow both personally and professionally. This section explores the importance of building strong professional relationships, discusses effective strategies for networking, and presents guidance on how to maintain and nurture these relationships for long-term success.

Whether you're just starting your career, seeking new opportunities, or aiming to advance in your current role, the ability to build and maintain professional relationships is essential. These relationships extend beyond mere acquaintanceships; they're based on trust, mutual respect, and shared interests. Building and maintaining professional relationships goes beyond networking events and LinkedIn connections; it requires genuine engagement, active communication, and a willingness to offer support and collaboration.

The benefits of building strong professional relationships are numerous. They can lead to job opportunities, partnerships, mentorship, knowledge sharing, and personal growth. By fostering meaningful connections, you create a network of individuals who can vouch for your abilities, guide you, and serve as a source of inspiration. Additionally, professional relationships can enhance your visibility in your industry or field and contribute to your overall professional reputation.

However, building and maintaining professional relationships isn't always easy. It requires effort, time, and effective communication skills. It's important to approach relationship-building with authenticity, professionalism, and a genuine interest in others. This section delves into practical strategies, tips, and techniques for building and maintaining professional relationships, both in-person and in the digital realm.

Whether you're a recent graduate, a mid-career professional, or a seasoned expert, the principles and strategies discussed in this section help you navigate the complex landscape of professional relationships and cultivate connections that can support your pursuit of passion and career success. By investing in these relationships, you're investing in your own growth, opportunities, and long-term fulfillment in your chosen field. It's time to dive in and explore the art of building and maintaining professional relationships!

Identifying potential networking opportunities

Networking is a powerful tool for personal and professional growth. It allows individuals to expand their professional circle, create meaningful connections, and find new opportunities. To harness the full potential of networking, you need to identify and seize relevant opportunities that align with your goals and interests:

» **Industry-specific events and conferences:** Keep an eye out for conferences, seminars, trade shows, and industry-specific events related to your field. These gatherings bring together professionals, experts, and thought leaders who share a common interest. Attending these events is an excellent opportunity to connect with like-minded individuals, gain insights from industry leaders, and expand your knowledge base.

» **Professional associations and organizations:** Joining professional associations and organizations relevant to your field is an excellent way to network with peers and industry professionals. These associations often organize networking events, workshops, and forums where you can engage in meaningful conversations, exchange ideas, and build relationships with individuals who share your professional interests.

» **Alumni networks:** Leverage your educational background by connecting with alumni networks from your alma mater. Many universities and colleges have alumni associations that host events, career fairs, and networking opportunities exclusively for alumni. Engaging with fellow alumni allows you to tap into a vast network of individuals who have shared educational experiences and may have similar career paths.

» **Online networking platforms:** In today's digital age, online networking platforms have become indispensable for connecting with professionals worldwide. Platforms like LinkedIn offer a virtual space to showcase your skills, engage in industry discussions, and reach out to individuals of interest. Actively participate in relevant groups and discussions, share valuable insights, and connect with professionals who align with your career aspirations.

» **Local business events and meetups:** Explore local business events, meetups, and networking groups in your area. These gatherings often bring together professionals from diverse industries in a casual and relaxed environment for building connections. Research local business chambers, entrepreneurial meetups, and industry-specific groups to find events that align with your interests.

>> **Volunteering and community involvement:** Engaging in volunteer work and community initiatives not only allows you to make a positive impact but also is a source of networking opportunities. Volunteering often brings together individuals from various backgrounds who are passionate about a common cause. By contributing your time and skills, you can connect with like-minded individuals, expand your network, and showcase your abilities in a meaningful way.

>> **Personal referrals and introductions:** Leverage your existing network by seeking referrals and introductions. Reach out to trusted colleagues, friends, or mentors who may have connections in your desired industry or field. Personal introductions often carry more weight and can facilitate the establishment of meaningful relationships.

REMEMBER

Networking isn't just about collecting business cards or accumulating a large number of connections. It's about building authentic relationships, fostering mutual support, and creating a valuable network of professionals. Be proactive, approach networking opportunities with an open mind, and maintain a genuine interest in others. By identifying and seizing potential networking opportunities, you pave the way for personal and professional growth, uncover new possibilities, and increase your chances of finding your passion.

Developing a strong elevator pitch

In today's fast-paced world, where first impressions matter, having a strong elevator pitch can make all the difference in networking and professional interactions. An elevator pitch is a concise and compelling introduction that effectively communicates who you are, what you do, and the value you bring in a short span of time, typically within 30 to 60 seconds. It's a powerful tool to grab attention, create interest, and leave a lasting impression.

Here is a step-by-step guide on how to go about developing a strong elevator pitch. If you follow through these steps, you should be able to draft your first elevator pitch and you can keep polishing it up as you go along.

>> **Clearly define your goal:** Before crafting your elevator pitch, you need a clear understanding of your objective. Ask yourself, "What do I want to achieve through this introduction?" Whether it's creating new business opportunities, seeking career advancement, or simply making connections, a well-defined goal shapes the content and tone of your pitch.

>> **Be concise and engaging:** The essence of an elevator pitch lies in its brevity. Focus on delivering a concise message that captures attention and sparks interest. Avoid jargon and complex technical terms that may confuse your listener. Instead, use simple language and compelling storytelling techniques to engage your audience from the start.

>> **Highlight your unique value proposition:** Your elevator pitch should clearly articulate the unique value you bring to the table. Identify your key strengths, skills, and experiences that differentiate you from others in your field. Highlight how your expertise can solve a specific problem or address a particular need. Make it clear why you're the best choice or why your work stands out.

>> **Adapt to your audience:** Tailor your elevator pitch to the specific audience or context. Different situations may require different angles or emphasize different aspects of your background and accomplishments. Research your audience beforehand to understand their needs, interests, and pain points. This allows you to customize your pitch and make it more relevant and compelling to the listener.

>> **Practice and refine:** Crafting an effective elevator pitch takes practice. Start by writing down your pitch, and then rehearse it until it flows naturally. Practice in front of a mirror or with friends or family, or even record yourself to assess your delivery and make necessary improvements. Refine your pitch over time based on feedback and your own observations to ensure it resonates with your audience.

>> **Use powerful and memorable language:** Choose your words carefully to make your pitch memorable. Incorporate impactful language, vivid imagery, or a captivating anecdote that showcases your passion and expertise. Make sure to communicate your message with enthusiasm and confidence because your delivery is just as important as your content.

>> **Be authentic and genuine:** Although it's important to craft a compelling pitch, authenticity is key. Be genuine, sincere, and true to yourself. Let your passion and enthusiasm shine through to create a lasting impression and make your pitch memorable. Avoid sounding rehearsed or overly scripted by allowing your personality to come through in your delivery.

REMEMBER

An elevator pitch isn't just a one-time introduction but a versatile tool that you can adapt to various networking situations. Continually refine and adapt your pitch based on feedback and experience. By developing a strong elevator pitch, you can effectively communicate your value, leave a lasting impression, and seize opportunities for meaningful connections and professional growth.

Developing a strong elevator pitch takes time and practice. Use the worksheet shown in Figure 6-1 as a guide to help you craft a compelling introduction that effectively communicates your value and leaves a lasting impression.

Define Your Objective:

What's your goal in creating this elevator pitch?

What do you want to achieve through this introduction?

Identify Your Unique Value Proposition:

List your key strengths, skills, and experiences that differentiate you from others.

How can your expertise solve a specific problem or address a particular need?

What sets you apart from others in your field?

Craft Your Message:

Write a concise and engaging introduction that captures attention.

Use simple language, and avoid jargon or technical terms.

Incorporate storytelling techniques to make it memorable.

Adapt to Your Audience:

Identify the specific audience or context for your elevator pitch.

Research their needs, interests, and pain points.

Customize your pitch to make it relevant and compelling to the listener.

Practice and Refine:

Rehearse your pitch until it flows naturally.

Practice in front of a mirror or with friends and family.

Record yourself to assess your delivery and make improvements.

FIGURE 6-1:
Developing a strong elevator pitch.

Use Powerful Language:

Choose impactful words to make your pitch memorable.

Incorporate vivid imagery or a captivating anecdote.

Communicate your message with enthusiasm and confidence.

Be Authentic and Genuine:

Stay true to yourself, and be genuine in your delivery.

Let your passion and enthusiasm shine through.

Avoid sounding rehearsed or overly scripted.

Seek Feedback:

Share your elevator pitch with others and ask for their input.

Consider their feedback and make necessary improvements.

Refine and Adapt:

Continuously refine your pitch based on feedback and experience.

Adapt your pitch to different networking situations as needed.

Practice Delivery:

Practice delivering your elevator pitch with confidence and poise.

Pay attention to your tone, body language, and overall presence.

FIGURE 6-1:
Continued

Practicing effective communication and active listening

Effective communication and active listening play a crucial role in building and maintaining both personal and professional relationships. As you navigate your journey to finding your passion, honing these skills enhances your ability to connect with others, learn from their experiences, and gain valuable insights. Here are some of the reasons it's important to practice effective communication and active listening:

>> **Building strong connections:** Effective communication is the foundation of any successful relationship. By articulating your thoughts clearly, expressing your ideas, and actively listening to others, you can establish strong connections with people who share similar interests or can offer valuable guidance. These connections can lead to new opportunities, collaborations, and insights into different fields.

>> **Sharing and gathering information:** Effective communication allows you to share your experiences, aspirations, and knowledge with others. By effectively conveying your thoughts and ideas, you can inspire and motivate others while gathering information from their experiences. This exchange of information can give you valuable insights, show you new perspectives, and help you make more informed decisions in your pursuit of passion.

>> **Active listening:** Active listening is a vital component of effective communication. It involves fully engaging with the speaker, paying attention to their words, and understanding their underlying emotions and perspectives. By actively listening, you demonstrate respect, empathy, and a genuine interest in the person speaking. This creates a positive and supportive environment that encourages open and honest conversations.

>> **Developing empathy and understanding:** Effective communication and active listening foster empathy and understanding. When you listen attentively and seek to understand others, you gain insights into their experiences, challenges, and passions. This empathy allows you to connect with them on a deeper level, build trust, and develop mutually beneficial relationships. It also expands your understanding of different perspectives and broadens your horizons.

>> **Resolving conflicts and navigating challenges:** Effective communication and active listening are essential in resolving conflicts and navigating challenges that may arise along your journey. By clearly expressing your thoughts and concerns while actively listening to the other person's perspective, you can find common ground, seek solutions, and maintain positive relationships even in the face of disagreements. These skills enable you to handle conflicts constructively and learn from diverse viewpoints.

>> **Practicing continuous improvement:** Practicing effective communication and active listening is an ongoing process of learning and growth. As you engage in conversations, reflect on your communication style, and seek feedback, you can refine your skills and become a more effective communicator. This continuous improvement not only enhances your ability to convey your passion but deepens your understanding of others, fostering meaningful connections and collaborations.

Effective communication and active listening are skills that you can develop through practice and intentional effort. By prioritizing these skills and integrating them into your interactions, you can build strong relationships, gain valuable insights, and create a supportive network that propels you closer to discovering and pursuing your passion.

Following up and staying in touch with contacts

In the realm of networking, following up and staying in touch with your contacts is a crucial aspect of building and nurturing professional relationships. It demonstrates your commitment, reliability, and genuine interest in maintaining connections. Following up and staying in touch with your contacts has the following benefits:

>> **Solidifying connections:** Following up after initial meetings or interactions solidifies the connections you've made. It shows that you value the relationship and are interested in continuing the conversation or collaboration. By promptly reaching out and expressing gratitude for the interaction, you leave a positive impression on your contacts, increasing the likelihood of future engagement.

>> **Building trust and reliability:** Consistently staying in touch with your contacts reinforces trust and reliability. Regular communication shows that you're committed to maintaining the relationship and that you value your contacts' input and support. It establishes you as someone dependable and professional, which can lead to opportunities for collaboration, mentorship, or referrals.

>> **Nurturing long-term relationships:** Following up and staying in touch is essential for nurturing long-term relationships. Relationships take time to develop, and regular communication allows you to deepen the connection over time. By sharing updates, exchanging insights, and showing genuine interest in your contacts' endeavors, you create a foundation for meaningful and mutually beneficial relationships.

>> **Leveraging opportunities:** Staying in touch with your contacts can lead to new opportunities for you. As you maintain regular communication, you remain on your contacts' radar, increasing the likelihood of being considered for relevant projects, collaborations, or career advancements. By staying top of mind, you position yourself as a valuable resource and increase your chances of receiving referrals or recommendations.

>> **Exchanging knowledge and resources:** Regular contact with your network allows for the exchange of knowledge, insights, and resources. By keeping the

lines of communication open, you can share industry trends, best practices, and valuable resources that can benefit both parties. This reciprocity strengthens the bond and fosters a supportive community where everyone can learn and grow together.

>> **Personal and professional growth:** Following up and staying in touch with your contacts contributes to your personal and professional growth. Engaging in conversations, seeking advice, and staying updated on industry developments can expand your knowledge, broaden your perspectives, and produce valuable learning opportunities. It also helps you stay informed about potential career advancements, collaborations, and new ventures.

TIP

Follow up and stay in touch in a thoughtful and genuine manner. Tailor your communication to each contact, acknowledging their interests and accomplishments. Use various communication channels, including email, phone calls, and social media platforms, to stay connected. By investing time and effort into nurturing your network, you can cultivate strong and lasting professional relationships that can support and guide you on your journey to finding and pursuing your passion.

Strategies for following up and staying in touch with contacts

You can employ several effective strategies to stay in touch with contacts and ensure you don't let the potential of the connection fade. You can follow up with and retain your connection when networking in several ways:

>> **Promptly send a follow-up message:** After meeting someone new or attending a networking event, send a personalized follow-up message within 24–48 hours. Express your appreciation for the interaction, reference specific points of discussion, and reiterate your interest in maintaining contact.

>> **Use a customer relationship management (CRM) system:** Consider using a CRM system to organize your contacts, set reminders for follow-ups, and track your interactions. This can help you stay organized and ensure you don't miss any important follow-up opportunities.

>> **Engage on social media:** Connect with your contacts on professional social media platforms such as LinkedIn and engage with their posts by commenting, liking, or sharing relevant content. This keeps you visible and allows for ongoing interaction.

>> **Offer value:** Be an asset to your contacts by sharing relevant articles, resources, or insights that align with their interests or professional goals. Show that you're genuinely interested in helping them succeed, and be a resourceful connection.

>> **Schedule regular check-ins:** Set a schedule to periodically reach out to your contacts. This can be a quarterly email, a monthly catch-up call, or a meeting for coffee. Consistency in communication maintains the relationship and shows your dedication.

>> **Attend industry events:** Stay involved in industry events, conferences, and networking functions where you're likely to encounter your contacts. Actively participate in discussions, exchange business cards, and follow up with a personalized message afterward.

>> **Collaborate on projects:** Seek opportunities to collaborate on projects or initiatives with your contacts. By working together, you build a deeper connection and create a shared experience that can strengthen the professional relationship.

>> **Be genuine and authentic:** Approach your follow-ups with sincerity and authenticity. Show a genuine interest in your contacts' endeavors, congratulate them on their achievements, and be open to providing support or guidance when needed.

>> **Personalize your interactions:** Tailor your communication to each contact. Acknowledge their specific interests, milestones, or challenges in your conversations. This personal touch demonstrates that you value the individual and their unique journey.

>> **Be proactive and responsive:** Be proactive in initiating communication, but also be responsive when your contacts reach out to you. Promptly respond to emails, calls, or messages to maintain a timely and professional interaction.

REMEMBER

The goal is to foster meaningful relationships built on trust, reciprocity, and shared interests. By implementing these strategies and maintaining consistent communication, you can effectively follow up and stay in touch with your contacts, enhancing your networking efforts and creating a strong professional network.

Finding Mentors and Role Models

Finding mentors and role models can be instrumental in your personal and professional growth. Mentors are individuals who share guidance, support, and valuable insights based on their own experiences, whereas role models are individuals who inspire and motivate you through their achievements and character. Both mentors and role models play a crucial role in helping you navigate your path, gain new perspectives, and achieve your goals.

This section explores the importance of finding mentors and role models and how they can positively affect your journey toward finding passion and success. It delves into the qualities to look for in mentors and role models, strategies to connect with them, and the benefits of fostering these relationships.

Mentors can be a source of valuable advice, encouragement, and constructive feedback. They can share their wisdom, knowledge, and lessons learned from their own experiences, helping you navigate challenges, make informed decisions, and avoid common pitfalls. Mentors can also bring inspiration and motivation, pushing you to reach your full potential.

Similarly, role models can inspire and influence your aspirations. By observing and learning from individuals who have achieved success in their chosen fields or have admirable qualities, you can gain insights into their mindset, work ethic, and strategies for success. Role models can inspire, guide you toward your own passions, and help you envision what's possible.

Throughout this chapter, I offer practical tips and strategies to help you identify potential mentors and role models, establish meaningful connections with them, and leverage their guidance and inspiration in your own journey. Whether you're seeking guidance in a specific industry or looking for mentors and role models who align with your values and interests, this chapter equips you with the tools to find and nurture these valuable relationships.

REMEMBER

Mentors and role models can have a profound impact on your personal and professional development. They can lend guidance, inspiration, and support as you explore your passions and work toward achieving your goals. By actively seeking out mentors and role models, you can accelerate your growth, gain valuable insights, and make meaningful connections that can propel you toward success.

How a mentor or role model helps in finding passion

Having a mentor or role model can be a game-changer when it comes to finding your passion. These individuals lend invaluable support, guidance, and inspiration that can significantly influence your journey of self-discovery and personal growth. Here are some key benefits of having a mentor or role model in your pursuit of passion:

>> **Gaining valuable insights and perspective:** A mentor or role model has likely walked a similar path to the one you aspire to take. They have firsthand

experience, knowledge, and insights that can help you navigate the challenges, pitfalls, and opportunities that lie ahead. By sharing their wisdom and perspective, they can shine a light on your own passions, strengths, and aspirations.

»» **Expanding your network and opportunities:** Mentors and role models often have extensive networks and connections in their respective fields. By fostering a relationship with them, you gain access to a broader professional network, unearthing new opportunities, collaborations, and mentorship from other industry experts. Their guidance and introductions can further your chances of finding meaningful opportunities related to your passion.

»» **Accelerating your learning curve:** One of the greatest advantages of having a mentor or role model is the chance to learn from their successes and failures. They can offer practical advice, share best practices, and impart valuable insights based on their own experiences. By leveraging their expertise, you can avoid common pitfalls, learn from their mistakes, and fast-track your own personal and professional growth.

»» **Building confidence and self-belief:** Having a mentor or role model who believes in your potential can boost your confidence and self-esteem. Their encouragement, validation, and support can help you overcome self-doubt and push your boundaries. They can be your inspiration when you need it most, reminding you that your dreams and passions are valid and achievable. Their belief in you can be a powerful catalyst in finding and pursuing your passion.

»» **Challenging your limits:** Mentors and role models often challenge you to step outside your comfort zone and push your limits. They encourage you to set ambitious goals, embrace new opportunities, and take calculated risks. By doing so, they help you unlock your full potential and discover passions and talents you may not have been aware of. Their guidance and belief in your abilities can motivate you to embrace challenges and pursue growth with enthusiasm.

»» **Providing emotional support:** Pursuing your passion can be a rollercoaster ride, with ups and downs along the way. During challenging times, mentors and role models can bring essential emotional support. They can offer a listening ear, empathize with your struggles, and guide you through overcoming obstacles. Their encouragement and reassurance can help you stay resilient, maintain focus, and navigate through setbacks.

Mentors and role models can be transformative in your passion journey. Their guidance, support, and inspiration can shape your mindset, expand your opportunities, and accelerate your personal and professional growth. By cultivating these relationships and leveraging the benefits they offer, you increase your chances of finding and pursuing your passion with clarity, confidence, and purpose.

Identifying potential mentors and role models

Identifying suitable mentors and role models is a critical step in your quest to find and pursue your passion. These individuals serve as guiding lights, offering valuable insights, knowledge, and inspiration to support your personal and professional growth. You can identify potential mentors and role models in several ways:

>> **Research within your field:** Start by researching professionals who have achieved success and recognition in your field of interest. Look for individuals who align with your values, have a track record of accomplishments, and possess the expertise you admire. Explore their backgrounds, achievements, and contributions to gain a deeper understanding of their impact in the industry.

>> **Seek recommendations:** Reach out to your network, whether it's colleagues, friends, or professors, and ask for recommendations of mentors or role models in your area of interest. They may be able to suggest individuals who have made a significant impact in your field or who possess valuable expertise that can benefit your personal and professional growth.

>> **Attend industry events and conferences:** Industry events and conferences are an excellent opportunity to connect with professionals who share your passion. Attend these events, engage in conversations, and network with like-minded individuals. Take note of those who exhibit qualities, skills, or achievements that resonate with your goals. These individuals may serve as potential mentors or role models.

>> **Utilize online platforms and communities:** Online platforms and communities focused on your field of interest can be valuable resources for finding mentors and role models. Participate in relevant forums, groups, and social media platforms where industry professionals gather. Engage in discussions, seek advice, and observe individuals who demonstrate expertise and passion in your area of interest.

>> **Reach out and connect:** Once you've identified potential mentors or role models, take the initiative to connect with them. Craft a thoughtful and personalized message expressing your admiration for their work and the impact they've made. Explain your goals, interests, and desire to learn from their experiences. Be respectful of their time, and consider proposing a meeting or a conversation to discuss your aspirations further.

>> **Consider diverse perspectives:** Although it's important to seek mentors and role models within your specific field, don't limit yourself to only one area. Look for individuals who have diverse experiences or who have successfully

pursued multiple passions. Their multidimensional insights can be a fresh perspective and inspire you to explore new avenues.

>> **Explore online mentorship platforms:** Online mentorship platforms, such as MentorCruise, Wisr, and MentorCity, connect mentees with mentors from various fields and industries. These platforms offer structured programs and resources to facilitate mentorship relationships. Research and explore reputable platforms that align with your goals and values to find potential mentors who can guide you on your path to discovering and pursuing your passion.

TIP

Please note that the availability and features of these platforms may change over time, so it's a good idea to visit their websites for the most up-to-date information and to determine which one best fits your mentoring needs.

Finding mentors and role models isn't just about their achievements and expertise; it's also about finding individuals who align with your values, share similar passions, and inspire you to reach your full potential. Cultivating these relationships requires mutual respect, open communication, and a genuine interest in learning from their experiences. By identifying suitable mentors and role models, you lay the foundation for meaningful connections that can shape your journey toward passion and success.

Use the checklist shown in Figure 6-2 to identify potential mentors and role models who can guide you in finding and pursuing your passion.

REMEMBER

The mentor or role model you choose should inspire and challenge you to grow, offering valuable insights and guidance on your journey to finding and pursuing your passion.

Approaching potential mentors and building a mentorship relationship

Building a mentorship relationship can be a transformative experience in your journey of finding and pursuing your passion. Use these tips to approach potential mentors and cultivate a meaningful mentorship relationship:

>> **Do your research:** Before approaching a potential mentor, invest time in researching their background, accomplishments, and expertise. Gain a thorough understanding of their work and contributions to your field of interest. This knowledge demonstrates your genuine interest and helps you make a compelling case for their mentorship.

Research within Your Field:

Identify professionals who have achieved success and recognition in your field of interest.

Consider their accomplishments, expertise, and impact in the industry.

Seek Recommendations:

Reach out to your network for recommendations of mentors or role models in your area of interest.

Ask colleagues, friends, professors, or industry contacts for their suggestions.

Attend Industry Events and Conferences:

Participate in industry events and conferences related to your field.

Observe and interact with professionals who exhibit qualities, skills, and achievements that resonate with your goals.

Utilize Online Platforms and Communities:

Engage in online platforms, forums, groups, and social media communities focused on your field of interest.

Seek advice, participate in discussions, and identify individuals who demonstrate expertise and passion.

Reach Out and Connect:

Craft personalized messages expressing admiration for their work and impact.

Explain your goals, interests, and desire to learn from their experiences.

Propose a meeting or conversation to discuss your aspirations further.

Consider Diverse Perspectives:

Explore mentors and role models with diverse experiences or who have successfully pursued multiple passions.

Look for individuals who can furnish a fresh perspective and inspire you to explore new avenues.

FIGURE 6-2:
Mentor and
role model
identification
checklist.

Research Online Mentorship Platforms:

Research reputable online mentorship platforms that align with your goals and values.

Explore structured programs and resources offered by these platforms to connect with potential mentors.

Evaluate Alignment:

Assess how well potential mentors or role models align with your values, goals, and areas of interest.

Consider their approach to personal and professional growth.

Mutual Compatibility:

Determine if there's potential for a mutually beneficial mentorship or role model relationship.

Look for individuals who are willing to guide, support, and share their experiences with you.

Nurture Relationships:

Once you've identified potential mentors or role models, foster the relationships by maintaining regular communication.

Show gratitude for their guidance, respect their time, and remain open to learning from their experiences.

FIGURE 6-2:
Continued

>> **Make a personal connection:** When reaching out to a potential mentor, strive to establish a personal connection. Share how their work has influenced and inspired you. Express your admiration for their achievements and articulate specific aspects that resonate with your own goals and aspirations. This personalized approach shows that you've done your homework and are genuinely interested in their guidance.

>> **Be clear and specific:** Clearly communicate your goals, challenges, and the areas in which you seek guidance. Outline what you hope to gain from the mentorship relationship. By being specific about your needs and expectations, you enable the potential mentor to assess whether they can give you the support you require.

>> **Demonstrate commitment and respect:** Approach potential mentors with professionalism, demonstrating your commitment to personal and professional growth. Respect their time and expertise by being concise in your communications and meeting commitments. Show a willingness to learn and implement their guidance.

>> **Be open to feedback and guidance:** A key aspect of mentorship is being open to receiving feedback and guidance. Embrace constructive criticism and use it as an opportunity for growth. Show your mentor that you're receptive to their insights and willing to make adjustments or explore new approaches.

>> **Take initiative:** In addition to seeking guidance, take the initiative to propose specific activities or projects where you can apply the mentor's advice. This demonstrates your proactive attitude and a desire to put their guidance into action. Show initiative in your personal and professional development.

>> **Maintain regular communication:** Once a mentorship relationship is established, maintain regular and open communication. Schedule regular check-ins or meetings to discuss progress, challenges, and new developments. Be proactive in sharing updates on your achievements and seeking further guidance as needed.

>> **Show gratitude and appreciation:** Express gratitude and appreciation for your mentor's time, expertise, and investment in your growth. Acknowledge the value they bring to your journey and how their guidance has influenced your personal and professional development. Show appreciation through thoughtful gestures, such as sending a thank-you note or recommending their work to others.

REMEMBER

Building a mentorship relationship is a two-way street. As you benefit from your mentor's guidance, offer your support and assistance whenever possible. Contribute to their work or projects, provide updates on your progress, and share relevant resources or insights that may be of interest to them. By nurturing the relationship and fostering a mutual exchange of knowledge and support, you can develop a strong and impactful mentorship bond.

Chapter 7

Finding Passion in Your Current Career

Many individuals find themselves searching for meaning and purpose in their professional lives. The desire to have a fulfilling and meaningful career is a natural aspiration because of the significant portion of your life you spend working. However, finding meaning and purpose doesn't always mean changing jobs or pursuing a new career path. You can often discover it right where you are, in your current job. The next dozen pages cover some strategies and insights for finding meaning and purpose in your current job, allowing you to experience greater fulfillment and satisfaction in your daily work life.

This chapter delves into the importance of finding meaning and purpose in your current job and how it can positively influence various aspects of your life. It explores practical steps and mindset shifts that can help you unlock the hidden potential within your current role and align it with your personal values and aspirations. By focusing on the tasks, relationships, and opportunities present in your current job, you can discover a sense of purpose and derive greater satisfaction from your work.

Finding meaning and purpose in your current job may require some self-reflection and intentional effort, but it's a worthwhile pursuit. It can bring a renewed sense of enthusiasm, motivation, and fulfillment to your daily work life.

Whether you're looking to make a long-term commitment to your current job or gain valuable experience and skills while working toward your future goals, this chapter presents practical strategies to cultivate meaning and purpose in your current job.

Finding meaning and purpose is a personal and individual journey. The insights and strategies shared in this chapter can serve as a guide to help you navigate your own path toward fulfillment in your current job. Embrace the opportunity to discover the hidden potential and purpose within your work, and let it propel you toward a more meaningful and satisfying professional life.

Finding Meaning and Purpose in Work

Finding meaning and purpose in your work isn't just a luxury or a nice-to-have; it's a fundamental aspect of leading a fulfilling and satisfying life. Your work takes up a significant portion of your time, energy, and mental capacity, and when you lack a sense of meaning and purpose in your professional endeavors, it can have profound negative effects on your overall well-being.

First and foremost, finding meaning and purpose in your work brings about a sense of fulfillment. It allows you to tap into your inherent human need for growth, contribution, and making a difference. When you feel that your work has a larger purpose and positively affects others, you experience a deep sense of satisfaction and fulfillment that goes beyond monetary rewards or external recognition.

Moreover, finding meaning and purpose in your work enhances your motivation and engagement. When you have a clear sense of why you do what you do and how it aligns with your values and personal aspirations, you're more likely to be motivated, committed, and enthusiastic about your work. You approach challenges with resilience and determination because you see them as opportunities for growth and progress toward your greater purpose.

Finding meaning and purpose in your work also affects your mental health and well-being. Engaging in work that aligns with your values and allows you to utilize your strengths and passions promotes a sense of authenticity and self-fulfillment. It reduces the likelihood of experiencing burnout, stress, and dissatisfaction that can arise from a disconnect between your true self and your work.

Additionally, when you find meaning and purpose in your work, it has a ripple effect on other areas of your life. It enhances your overall life satisfaction because work is an integral part of your identity and daily experience. It positively influences your relationships because you bring a sense of purpose and fulfillment home with you, fostering greater emotional well-being and connection with others.

From an organizational perspective, employees who find meaning and purpose in their work are more engaged, productive, and committed. They exhibit higher levels of creativity, innovation, and problem-solving because they're motivated by a deeper sense of purpose beyond external rewards. This benefits not only the individual but the organization as a whole, creating a positive work culture and driving sustainable success.

In conclusion, finding meaning and purpose in your work is essential for your personal and professional well-being. It brings fulfillment, enhances motivation, and positively shapes your mental health and overall satisfaction in life. It's a journey of self-discovery, aligning your values, passions, and strengths with the work you do. By actively seeking meaning and purpose in your work, you can create a more meaningful and satisfying professional life that enriches your overall human experience.

Identifying areas of your job that align with your values and interests

Finding areas of your job that align with your values and interests is crucial for creating a sense of fulfillment and satisfaction in your work. When your job aligns with what you value and enjoy, it becomes more meaningful, purposeful, and personally rewarding. It allows you to bring your authentic self to work and create a positive impact on yourself and the organization you're a part of.

First, identifying areas of your job that align with your values allows you to experience a greater sense of alignment and integrity. Values are the core principles and beliefs that guide your behavior and decision-making. When you can identify aspects of your job that resonate with your values, such as integrity, teamwork, or creativity, it creates a sense of coherence between your personal and your professional life. This alignment helps you feel more connected to your work and gives you a sense of purpose and meaning.

Similarly, identifying areas of your job that align with your interests taps into your intrinsic motivation and passion. When you're engaged in tasks or projects that align with your interests, you naturally feel more energized, enthusiastic, and eager to learn and grow. Your job becomes a platform for you to explore and utilize your skills and talents, which contributes to a sense of fulfillment and personal satisfaction.

Moreover, aligning your values and interests with your job enhances your overall job satisfaction and engagement. You feel a greater sense of ownership and commitment to your work when it resonates with what you value and enjoy. This positive attitude and engagement can lead to increased productivity, creativity, and a willingness to go above and beyond in your role. It also fosters a sense of pride and fulfillment in the contributions you make within your organization.

Identifying areas of your job that align with your values and interests also opens up opportunities for growth and development. When you actively seek out projects or tasks that align with your values and interests, you create a pathway for personal and professional growth. It allows you to expand your skills, acquire new knowledge, and develop expertise in areas that truly matter to you. This growth not only benefits you in your current role but can open doors to future career opportunities aligned with your passions and values.

In summary, identifying areas of your job that align with your values and interests is a key step toward finding meaning and fulfillment in your work. It allows you to experience a greater sense of alignment, authenticity, and personal satisfaction. By aligning your values and interests with your job, you create a solid foundation for long-term career satisfaction, growth, and a sense of purpose.

Practicing gratitude and mindfulness in your work

Practicing gratitude and mindfulness in your work can have a profound impact on your overall well-being, job satisfaction, and ability to find meaning and purpose in what you do. These practices allow you to cultivate a positive mindset, enhance your awareness of the present moment, and foster a deeper appreciation for the opportunities and experiences that your work provides.

First, practicing gratitude in your work involves recognizing and expressing appreciation for the aspects of your job that you may often take for granted. It's about acknowledging the people, resources, and opportunities that contribute to your professional growth and success. By regularly expressing gratitude, whether through verbal appreciation or written notes of thanks, you create a positive and supportive work environment. This can strengthen relationships, improve teamwork, and increase job satisfaction for you and your colleagues.

Additionally, mindfulness in your work involves being fully present and engaged in the tasks and interactions at hand. It means paying attention to the details, thoughts, and emotions that arise in the present moment without judgment. Mindfulness helps you become more attuned to your work environment, enabling you to make better decisions, manage stress more effectively, and enhance your overall well-being. By being mindful, you can cultivate a sense of clarity, focus, and purpose in your work.

Practicing gratitude and mindfulness in your work also allows you to find deeper meaning and purpose in the tasks you perform. When you approach your work with a grateful and mindful mindset, you start to notice the positive impact you can make, no matter how small. You become more aware of how your contributions align with your values and the greater mission of your organization. This awareness enhances your sense of purpose and fulfillment because you recognize the significance of your role and the value you bring to others.

Furthermore, gratitude and mindfulness practices help you navigate challenges and setbacks with resilience and a positive outlook. When you're faced with difficulties, expressing gratitude for the lessons you've learned or the support you've received can shift your perspective and open up new possibilities for growth. Mindfulness allows you to respond to challenges with clarity and composure rather than with impulse or overwhelm. These practices enable you to maintain a balanced and positive mindset, even during stressful or demanding times.

In summary, practicing gratitude and mindfulness in your work can transform your experience and bring greater meaning and purpose to your professional life. By cultivating a grateful mindset, expressing appreciation, and staying present in the moment, you can enhance your job satisfaction, improve relationships, and navigate challenges with resilience. These practices enable you to find fulfillment in the present moment and create a positive work environment where you can thrive.

Making Your Work More Fulfilling

In today's fast-paced and demanding work environments, it's crucial to find ways to make your work more fulfilling. Whether you're seeking greater satisfaction in your current job or striving to align your professional life with your passions and values, implementing strategies to enhance fulfillment can lead to increased motivation, engagement, and overall well-being. This section explores various approaches and techniques that can help you create a more meaningful and rewarding work experience.

Work takes up a significant portion of your life, and it's natural to desire a sense of fulfillment and purpose in the tasks you perform each day. However, many individuals find themselves feeling stuck or unfulfilled, lacking a sense of connection to their work. The good news is that you can employ practical strategies to transform your perspective and infuse your work with meaning.

This section delves into actionable strategies and approaches that go beyond the traditional notion of "just finding a new job." It acknowledges that, sometimes, the key to fulfillment lies in shifting your mindset, adjusting your behavior, and exploring new possibilities within your existing work environment.

The strategies presented here are designed to empower you to take proactive steps toward creating a more fulfilling work experience. They encompass both personal and professional aspects because finding fulfillment often requires a holistic approach that addresses various dimensions of your life.

Whether you're an employee, a manager, an entrepreneur, or someone in a transitional phase, you can adapt these strategies to suit your unique circumstances. By embracing them, you gain insights, tools, and techniques to enhance your job satisfaction, find purpose in your work, and create a more rewarding professional journey.

Finding fulfillment in your work is a personal and ongoing process. It requires self-reflection, experimentation, and a willingness to challenge the status quo. The strategies presented in this section serve as a starting point, providing you with guidance and inspiration to make positive changes in your work life.

It's time to dive in and explore a range of strategies that can help you make your work more fulfilling, empowering you to create a professional life that aligns with your passions, values, and aspirations.

Finding opportunities for growth and development in your job

Finding opportunities for growth and development in your job is an essential aspect of creating a fulfilling and meaningful professional experience. When you actively seek ways to learn, improve, and expand your skills and knowledge within your current role, you not only enhance your own capabilities but also invite new possibilities and advancement.

Continuous growth and development in your job has numerous benefits, both personally and professionally. It allows you to stay engaged and motivated, fosters a sense of progress and achievement, and increases your value as an employee. Additionally, embracing growth opportunities can help you adapt to changing work environments, seize new challenges, and position yourself for future career advancements.

Here are some key points to consider when seeking opportunities for growth and development in your job:

» **Embrace a growth mindset:** Cultivate a mindset that sees challenges and setbacks as opportunities for learning and improvement. Embrace the belief that you can develop your abilities through dedication and effort, and approach your job with a sense of curiosity and a willingness to take on new challenges.

» **Seek feedback and learn from others:** Actively seek feedback from your colleagues, supervisors, and mentors. This feedback can result in valuable insights into areas where you can improve and grow. Additionally, seek opportunities to learn from others' experiences and expertise, whether through mentorship programs, networking events, or professional development workshops.

» **Set learning goals:** Identify specific areas where you want to grow and develop within your job. Set clear and achievable learning goals that align with your interests, values, and the needs of your role. These goals can range from acquiring new technical skills to developing soft skills like leadership, communication, and problem-solving.

» **Take on new challenges:** Look for opportunities to stretch yourself and take on new challenges within your current job. Volunteer for projects that push you outside of your comfort zone, tackle complex tasks that require you to develop new skills, or seek out cross-functional collaborations that expose you to different areas of your organization.

» **Take advantage of training and development programs:** Many organizations offer training and development programs to support employees' growth. Take advantage of these resources, whether they're in-house workshops, online courses, or external conferences and seminars. Be proactive in identifying relevant opportunities, and communicate your interest in participating.

» **Build a professional network:** Networking is not only valuable for finding new job opportunities but also for professional growth. Engage with colleagues, attend industry events, join professional associations, and connect with individuals who inspire and challenge you. Building a strong professional network can provide access to mentorship, knowledge-sharing, and career guidance.

» **Reflect and iterate:** Regularly reflect on your experiences, achievements, and areas for improvement. Take time to evaluate your progress, celebrate milestones, and adjust your goals and strategies as needed. Use this reflection as a foundation for continuous growth and development.

REMEMBER

Finding opportunities for growth and development in your job doesn't depend solely on external factors. It requires proactive effort, self-motivation, and a commitment to lifelong learning — as well as opening yourself up to being more vulnerable and less fearful of making a mistake. By seeking out these opportunities and investing in your own professional development, you can create a fulfilling and dynamic career that aligns with your passions and goals.

Pursuing projects and initiatives that align with your interests and values

One of the key strategies to make your work more fulfilling is to actively pursue projects and initiatives that align with your interests and values. When you engage in work that resonates with who you are and what you believe in, you experience a greater sense of purpose, satisfaction, and motivation. Pursuing meaningful projects not only benefits your personal well-being but contributes to the overall success of your organization.

Here are some insights on the importance of pursuing projects and initiatives that align with your interests and values:

>> **Fulfillment and satisfaction:** When you work on projects that align with your interests and values, you're more likely to feel a sense of fulfillment and satisfaction. The work becomes personally meaningful, and you're motivated to give your best effort and make a positive impact. This fulfillment can enhance your overall job satisfaction and contribute to your long-term career happiness.

>> **Authenticity and alignment:** Engaging in work that aligns with your interests and values allows you to be authentic and true to yourself. It enables you to bring your unique strengths, perspectives, and passion to your work. When you're aligned with your core values, you're more likely to excel, be engaged, and make valuable contributions.

>> **Increased motivation and engagement:** Pursuing projects and initiatives that resonate with your interests and values naturally boosts your motivation and engagement. You're more likely to be energized and committed to the work, leading to higher levels of productivity, creativity, and innovation. This enthusiasm can have a ripple effect, inspiring and motivating those around you.

>> **Personal growth and development:** Working on projects aligned with your interests and values results in opportunities for personal growth and development. You're more likely to challenge yourself, acquire new skills, and expand your knowledge in areas that genuinely interest you. This continuous growth not only enhances your professional capabilities but ushers in new career opportunities.

>> **Positive impact and contribution:** When your work aligns with your interests and values, you have the opportunity to make a positive impact on others and the world around you. By pursuing projects that address social or environmental issues you care about, you can contribute to creating positive change and leave a lasting legacy through your work.

The following are strategies for pursuing projects and initiatives that align with your interests and values:

>> **Reflect on your passions and values:** Take time to identify your core passions and values. Consider the causes, subjects, or areas that truly resonate with you. This self-reflection can guide you in identifying projects that align with who you are and what you stand for.

>> **Seek alignment in your current role:** Evaluate your current job and responsibilities. Identify areas within your role where you can incorporate your interests and values. Look for projects or tasks that have a connection to what you care about, and explore ways to increase your involvement in those areas.

>> **Communicate and collaborate:** Express your interests and values to your supervisors and colleagues. Share your desire to work on projects that align with your passions. Collaborate with others who share similar interests, and find opportunities for joint initiatives. This collaboration can lead to more fulfilling projects and a supportive network.

>> **Explore new opportunities:** Keep an eye out for new projects, initiatives, or teams within your organization that align with your interests and values. Volunteer for cross-functional projects, or propose ideas that address the issues you care about. Be proactive in seeking out opportunities that allow you to make a meaningful impact.

>> **Expand your network:** Connect with individuals who are involved in projects or organizations related to your interests and values. Attend industry events, join professional groups, or participate in relevant online communities. Building a network of like-minded professionals can provide exposure to new projects and opportunities.

REMEMBER

Pursuing projects and initiatives that align with your interests and values requires proactive effort and ongoing exploration. It's important to stay open-minded and adaptable as you navigate your career path. Embrace opportunities for growth, and be willing to step outside of your comfort zone to pursue projects that truly resonate with you.

By aligning your work with your interests and values, you create a more fulfilling and meaningful professional journey. Not only will you experience greater satisfaction and personal growth, but you'll contribute your best work and make a positive impact in your organization and beyond.

Take the time to reflect on what truly matters to you, seek out opportunities that align with your passions, and be proactive in pursuing projects that ignite your enthusiasm. As you do so, you'll find that your work becomes more than just a job; it becomes a vehicle for personal fulfillment and professional success.

REMEMBER

Finding meaning and purpose in your work is a continuous journey. Stay committed to self-reflection, embrace new challenges, and never stop exploring opportunities to align your work with your interests and values. With each step forward, you move closer to a career that truly brings you joy and fulfillment.

Building positive relationships with colleagues and supervisors

Building positive relationships with colleagues and supervisors is a crucial aspect of making your work more fulfilling. When you have strong relationships in the workplace, you not only enjoy a more positive and supportive work environment but create opportunities for collaboration, growth, and career advancement.

Positive relationships with colleagues contribute to a sense of belonging and camaraderie. When you have a supportive network of coworkers, you're more likely to feel motivated, engaged, and satisfied in your job. These relationships can also be a source of valuable social and emotional support, making challenging situations easier to navigate.

Similarly, building positive relationships with supervisors can have a significant impact on your career. A good relationship with your supervisor can foster open communication, trust, and mutual respect. It creates an environment where you feel comfortable seeking feedback, discussing your goals, and receiving guidance. Your supervisor can become a valuable mentor and advocate, helping you develop professionally and providing opportunities for growth.

To build positive relationships with colleagues and supervisors, focus on effective communication, active listening, and empathy. Show genuine interest in others' perspectives and ideas, offer support and assistance when needed, and be proactive in fostering a collaborative and inclusive work environment.

Invest time and effort in getting to know your colleagues and supervisors on a personal level. Engage in team-building activities, participate in social events, and seek opportunities to collaborate on projects. Building these relationships takes time and consistent effort, but the rewards are worth it.

Remember that building positive relationships is a two-way street. Be willing to contribute positively to the workplace culture and support your colleagues and supervisors in their professional endeavors. By nurturing these relationships, you create a network of support and collaboration that enhances your work experience and contributes to your overall job satisfaction.

Building positive relationships with colleagues and supervisors is essential for making your work more fulfilling. These relationships provide support, collaboration, and growth opportunities, contributing to a positive work environment and your overall professional success. When you invest in fostering these connections, you experience greater satisfaction and enjoyment in your job.

Building positive relationships with colleagues and supervisors is crucial for a fulfilling work experience. Here are some practical tips to help you foster strong relationships:

>> **Practice active listening:** Pay attention to what others are saying, show genuine interest, and respond thoughtfully. Imagine that you're working on a team project with a colleague named Alex. During a meeting, Alex expresses concerns about meeting a tight deadline. Instead of dismissing those worries, actively listen and empathize with Alex's perspective. Offer support and suggest brainstorming solutions together.

>> **Show appreciation:** Recognize and acknowledge the contributions of your colleagues and supervisors. A simple thank-you or expression of gratitude for another's assistance can go a long way. If your supervisor, Sarah, provides valuable feedback on your presentation, take a moment to express your appreciation for her guidance and how it has improved your skills.

>> **Offer assistance:** Be proactive in supporting your colleagues and supervisors. Look for opportunities to lend a helping hand or share your expertise. If a colleague is struggling with a task, offer your assistance by suggesting resources or collaborating on finding a solution.

>> **Engage in social activities:** Participate in team-building activities or social events to connect with your colleagues on a personal level. Joining a work sports team or attending a virtual happy hour can build rapport and strengthen relationships outside of the formal work setting.

>> **Seek feedback and input:** Involve others in decision-making processes, and value their perspectives. When seeking input, consider a fictional scenario in which you're working on a project with a diverse team. Encourage each team member to share their ideas and opinions, fostering a collaborative environment where everyone's voice is heard.

>> **Maintain professionalism and respect:** Treat your colleagues and supervisors with respect, even in challenging situations. Avoid gossip or negative conversations, and focus on constructive communication. During a team meeting, if a disagreement arises between colleagues, maintain a respectful tone, and focus on finding a resolution.

Remember, building positive relationships takes time and effort. Be genuine, authentic, and consistent in your interactions. By investing in these relationships, you not only enhance your work experience but create a supportive network that contributes to your professional growth and success.

Knowing When and How to Transition to a New Career

Making a career transition can be a significant and life-changing decision. Whether you're seeking greater fulfillment, better work-life balance, or a change of industry, knowing when and how to transition to a new career is crucial. This chapter guides you through the process of recognizing the signs that it may be time for a career change and provides practical strategies for navigating the transition successfully.

Transitioning to a new career can bring a sense of excitement, growth, and renewed passion. It offers an opportunity to align your work with your values, interests, and goals. But approach this process with careful consideration and planning to ensure a smooth and successful transition.

Career transition involves self-reflection, skill assessment, and planning. Understanding how to evaluate your current situation, identify transferable skills, and explore new career possibilities is key. This section looks at practical steps to make a smooth transition, such as building a professional network, seeking additional education or training, and managing potential challenges along the way.

REMEMBER

A career transition requires courage, dedication, and a willingness to step outside of your comfort zone. It's a journey that can lead to new opportunities, personal growth, and a more fulfilling professional life. By understanding when it's time to make a change and equipping yourself with the right strategies, you can navigate the transition with confidence and set yourself up for success in your new career.

The following sections delve into the key considerations for knowing when it's time to transition and how to approach the process effectively. Whether you're looking for a complete career overhaul or a slight shift in your current field, this chapter provides you with valuable insights and practical advice to guide you toward a new and fulfilling career path.

Recognizing when it's time for a career change

Deciding when to make a career change is a deeply personal and introspective process. It requires careful reflection and self-awareness to recognize the signs that indicate it's time for a new direction in your professional life. Although the specific triggers may vary from person to person, some common indicators suggest it may be time for a career change. These are some of the ways to recognize these signs:

» **Dissatisfaction and lack of fulfillment:** If you consistently feel unfulfilled, unmotivated, or unhappy in your current job, your job may no longer align with your values, interests, or long-term goals. Pay attention to the persistent feelings of dissatisfaction and the sense that there's something more fulfilling waiting for you.

» **Lack of growth and development:** If you find yourself in a professional rut with limited opportunities for growth, learning, and advancement, perhaps you've outgrown your current role or industry. Stagnation in your career can be demotivating and hinder your long-term success and happiness.

» **Alignment with personal values:** If your current job conflicts with your core values and beliefs, it can create a sense of moral or ethical misalignment. Recognizing that your work isn't aligned with your values can be a powerful catalyst for considering a career change that allows you to contribute to something meaningful and in line with your principles.

» **Persistent stress and burnout:** Excessive stress, burnout, and a lack of work-life balance can have detrimental effects on your well-being and overall quality of life. If you find yourself consistently overwhelmed, exhausted, and unable to find joy in your work, your current career may not be sustainable in the long run.

» **Change in interests and passions:** Interests and passions can evolve over time. If you discover that your current career no longer aligns with your evolving interests and passions, you may need to explore new paths that ignite your enthusiasm and bring a sense of purpose to your work.

Recognizing these signs doesn't necessarily mean an immediate leap into a new career. It's a starting point for self-reflection and exploration. Take the time to evaluate your situation, consider your options, and weigh the potential risks and rewards of a career change. Engage in introspection, speak with trusted mentors or career counselors, and seek guidance to gain clarity about your aspirations and the feasibility of pursuing a new path.

Recognizing the need for a career change is the first step in a transformative journey. It's an opportunity to align your work with your passions, values, and goals, ultimately leading to greater fulfillment and satisfaction in your professional life.

Identifying potential career paths that align with your values and interests

Identifying potential career paths that align with your values and interests is an important step in finding professional fulfillment and meaning. It involves a deep exploration of your core values, passions, skills, and strengths to discover career options that resonate with who you are. Following are some of the steps that can enable you to identify potential career paths that align with your values and interests.

>> **Self-reflection:** Begin by engaging in self-reflection to gain a deeper understanding of your values, interests, and aspirations. Consider what matters most to you, what activities bring you joy and fulfillment, and what skills and strengths you possess. Reflect on your past experiences and moments when you felt energized and engaged. This introspection will illuminate the types of careers that align with your authentic self.

>> **Research and exploration:** Conduct thorough research on different industries, job roles, and career paths that match your identified values and interests. Explore online resources, career websites, industry publications, and professional networks to gather information about the opportunities available. Attend industry events, job fairs, and informational interviews to learn more about specific roles, and gain insights from professionals already working in those fields.

>> **Networking and mentorship:** Connect with professionals who are already working in your areas of interest. Reach out to them for informational interviews or mentorship opportunities to learn more about their career journeys and gain valuable advice. Networking can offer valuable insights into the day-to-day realities of various careers and help you assess whether they align with your values and interests.

>> **Transferable skills and training:** Evaluate your existing skills and identify the ones that are transferable across different industries or roles. Consider if any additional training or education might be required to bridge gaps in your skill set. This assessment assists in identifying career paths where you can leverage your existing strengths while developing new skills.

>> **Test and experiment:** It can be beneficial to test your interest in a potential career path before making a full commitment. Consider volunteering, freelancing, or taking on part-time work in the field of your interest to gain

hands-on experience and validate your assumptions about the career. This allows you to explore different options and gather firsthand insights to make informed decisions. It's also a way for a company to try you out and see how you will fit, which can lead to future opportunities such as tuition assistance or a better-paying job.

The journey of identifying potential career paths is an iterative process. It requires a combination of self-reflection, research, networking, and experimentation. Be open to new possibilities and willing to adapt as you gather new information. It's important to choose career paths that not only align with your values and interests but also offer growth opportunities, work-life balance, and long-term satisfaction.

By investing time and effort into this exploration process, you increase the likelihood of finding a career that brings purpose, fulfillment, and a sense of alignment with who you are as an individual.

Developing a plan for transitioning to a new career

Transitioning to a new career requires careful planning and strategic decision-making. It involves assessing your current situation, setting clear goals, acquiring new skills or qualifications, and creating a roadmap to navigate the transition successfully. What follows is a proposed approach on developing a plan for transitioning to a new career:

>> **Self-assessment:** Begin by conducting a comprehensive self-assessment to gain clarity on your motivations, strengths, and areas for improvement. Evaluate your skills, experiences, and interests to identify transferable assets and determine the type of career that aligns with your values and aspirations. Consider seeking the guidance of a career counselor or coach who can provide valuable insights and support during this process.

>> **Gap analysis:** Identify any gaps between your current qualifications and the requirements of your target career. Determine if you need to acquire additional education, training, or certifications to enhance your marketability. Consider enrolling in relevant courses, attending workshops, or pursuing online learning opportunities to bridge these gaps and acquire the necessary skills and knowledge.

>> **Building a professional network:** Cultivate a strong professional network in your desired industry or field. Attend industry events, join relevant professional associations, and engage with online communities to connect with

individuals who can provide guidance, mentorship, and potential job leads. Networking is crucial during a career transition because it fosters new opportunities and offers valuable insights into the industry.

>> **Career transition strategies:** Develop a step-by-step plan for transitioning to your new career. Set specific, measurable, achievable, relevant, and time-bound (SMART) goals to keep yourself focused and motivated. Break down the transition process into manageable tasks, such as updating your resume, building an online presence, and conducting informational interviews. Create a timeline for each task to ensure steady progress toward your ultimate career transition goal.

>> **Financial planning:** Assess the financial implications of your career transition. Consider any potential income changes, additional education or training costs, and the impact on your overall financial stability. Develop a financial plan to ensure you have the necessary resources to support yourself during the transition period.

>> **Execution and evaluation:** Execute your career transition plan while remaining adaptable to unforeseen circumstances or opportunities. Regularly evaluate your progress and adjust your plan as needed. Seek feedback from mentors, career advisors, and professionals in your network to fine-tune your approach and stay on track toward your new career goals.

REMEMBER

A successful career transition requires perseverance, patience, and a willingness to embrace new challenges. Accept the learning process, seek support from mentors and professionals, and stay committed to your vision. With a well-developed plan, determination, and proactive action, you can successfully navigate the transition to a new and fulfilling career.

Chapter 8

Leaping into Entrepreneurship

E ntrepreneurship is a dynamic and rewarding journey that offers a unique set of opportunities and challenges. As an entrepreneur, you have the freedom to shape your own destiny, pursue your passions, and create something meaningful. However, entrepreneurship also requires dedication, resilience, and a willingness to face uncertainties. This chapter explores the benefits and challenges of entrepreneurship, offering insights and perspectives to help you navigate this exciting path.

Starting a business or venturing into entrepreneurship comes with numerous advantages. First, it allows you to be your own boss, rewarding you with the autonomy to make decisions and chart your own course. This level of control over your professional life can be liberating and empowering. Second, entrepreneurship offers the potential for financial rewards and wealth creation. Successful ventures can generate substantial profits and a path to financial independence. Third, entrepreneurship often enables individuals to turn their passions and innovative ideas into reality. By pursuing projects and ventures that align with your interests, you can experience a deep sense of fulfillment and purpose in your work. Moreover, entrepreneurship fosters personal growth and learning because it pushes you to step out of your comfort zone, develop new skills, and overcome challenges.

However, entrepreneurship also comes with its share of challenges and risks. One of the primary challenges is the high level of uncertainty and the inherent risk of failure. Starting a business involves stepping into uncharted territory, where success isn't guaranteed. Managing finances, finding customers, and building a sustainable business model are complex tasks that require careful planning and execution. In addition, entrepreneurship often demands long hours, hard work, and a willingness to adapt and pivot in response to market dynamics. It requires a resilient mindset to navigate through setbacks and failures, learning from them and using them as steppingstones toward success. Finally, entrepreneurship can create a significant amount of stress and pressure because you're responsible for the success and growth of your business.

Despite these challenges, the rewards of entrepreneurship can far outweigh the difficulties. It offers the opportunity for personal and professional fulfillment, financial independence, and the ability to make a lasting impact. This chapter delves into the intricacies of entrepreneurship, exploring strategies, best practices, and insights to help you navigate the entrepreneurial journey with confidence and clarity.

Whether you're already an entrepreneur or considering embarking on this path, understanding the benefits and challenges of entrepreneurship is essential. By acknowledging the rewards and potential obstacles, you can better prepare yourself for the journey ahead, making informed decisions and leveraging the opportunities that entrepreneurship offers.

Pursuing Your Passion as an Entrepreneur

Entrepreneurship is a powerful vehicle for pursuing your passion and turning it into a thriving business venture. When you embark on the entrepreneurial path, you gain several distinct advantages that can significantly enhance your journey of following your passion.

First and foremost, entrepreneurship allows you the freedom and autonomy to build a business around your passion. Unlike traditional employment, where you may have limited control over the direction and scope of your work, as an entrepreneur, you have the opportunity to shape every aspect of your business. You can align your products or services with your true interests, values, and passions. This level of alignment lets you infuse your work with genuine enthusiasm, dedication, and authenticity, which can have a profound impact on your personal fulfillment and the overall success of your venture.

Moreover, entrepreneurship empowers you to create a meaningful impact in the world through your passion. When you pursue what truly drives you, you're more likely to develop innovative solutions, unique offerings, and compelling value propositions. By addressing a genuine need or problem with your products or services, you can make a difference in the lives of your customers or clients. This sense of purpose and impact can be deeply rewarding and motivate you to overcome challenges and persevere in the face of adversity.

Another advantage of entrepreneurship is the potential for financial rewards and long-term success. When you combine passion with a well-executed business model, you increase the chances of building a profitable and sustainable enterprise. As an entrepreneur, you have the opportunity to leverage your passion to differentiate yourself from competitors, attract loyal customers, and create a strong brand identity. This can translate into increased sales, customer loyalty, and ultimately, financial success. The ability to earn a living doing what you love is a tremendous advantage that entrepreneurship offers.

Additionally, entrepreneurship enables you to continually grow and evolve in your passion. As a business owner, you're constantly learning, adapting, and refining your skills and expertise. You have the freedom to explore new ideas, experiment with different strategies, and expand the boundaries of your passion. This ongoing growth and development not only enriches your professional journey but keeps your passion alive and thriving.

WARNING

Entrepreneurship isn't without its challenges. Building a business requires hard work, perseverance, and a willingness to navigate obstacles along the way. It requires a deep understanding of your passion, market dynamics, and business fundamentals. It also demands effective management of resources, strong leadership skills, and the ability to embrace failure as a steppingstone to success. It's crucial to approach entrepreneurship with a growth mindset and a willingness to continuously learn and adapt.

In sum, entrepreneurship affords a unique and advantageous platform for pursuing your passion. It empowers you to align your work with your true interests, make a meaningful impact, and potentially achieve financial success. By leveraging the benefits of entrepreneurship, you can turn your passion into a fulfilling and thriving business venture.

The challenges and risks of starting your own business

Starting your own business is an exciting and fulfilling endeavor, but it also comes with its fair share of challenges and risks. It's important to be aware of these potential obstacles and prepare yourself to navigate them effectively on your entrepreneurial journey.

One of the primary challenges of starting your own business is the inherent uncertainty and risk involved. Unlike traditional employment, marked by a stable income and a predefined set of responsibilities, entrepreneurship requires you to take calculated risks and make strategic decisions without the safety net of a regular paycheck. The financial stability and security that come with a job may be replaced with fluctuating income, unpredictable market conditions, and the need to invest your own resources into the business. You have to be financially prepared and have a contingency plan in place to mitigate these risks.

WARNING

Another significant challenge is the level of responsibility and workload that comes with running your own business. As an entrepreneur, you're responsible for all aspects of the business, from developing products or services to marketing, sales, operations, and financial management. This can be overwhelming and require a diverse skill set. Be prepared to wear multiple hats and continually learn and adapt to the demands of your business.

Building a customer base and establishing a brand presence can also be a daunting challenge for new entrepreneurs. In a competitive market, gaining visibility and attracting customers requires a well-defined target audience, effective marketing strategies, and exceptional customer experiences. It may take time and effort to build trust and credibility with your target market and establish your business as a reputable brand.

Additionally, managing the growth and scalability of your business can pose challenges. As your business expands, you may face the need to hire and manage employees, scale your operations, and maintain consistent quality and customer satisfaction. This growth phase requires strategic planning, effective systems and processes, and the ability to delegate and manage a team.

In the realm of entrepreneurship, failure is also a reality you need to acknowledge. Not all business ventures succeed, and setbacks and failures are part of the learning process. It's important to be resilient, learn from your mistakes, and be willing to adapt and pivot when necessary.

Despite these challenges, starting your own business can be immensely rewarding and provide a sense of fulfillment that's hard to find elsewhere. It offers the opportunity to be your own boss, pursue your passion, and create a legacy. With careful planning, strategic decision-making, and a willingness to persevere, you can overcome the challenges and mitigate the risks associated with starting your own business.

Although starting your own business comes with challenges and risks, it also offers the potential for personal and professional fulfillment. By understanding and preparing for these challenges and by approaching entrepreneurship with a growth mindset and a strong determination, you can navigate the journey of starting your own business with confidence and increase your chances of success.

Understanding the entrepreneurial mindset

The entrepreneurial mindset is a set of beliefs, attitudes, and behaviors that are essential for success in the world of entrepreneurship. It encompasses a unique way of thinking and approaching challenges, opportunities, and decision-making. Understanding and adopting an entrepreneurial mindset can significantly affect your ability to pursue your passion and thrive as an entrepreneur.

One key aspect of the entrepreneurial mindset is embracing a sense of purpose and vision. Successful entrepreneurs have a clear understanding of their goals, values, and the impact they want to make through their business ventures. They're driven by a strong sense of purpose that fuels their motivation and resilience in the face of obstacles.

Entrepreneurs also possess a high level of self-motivation and initiative. They're self-starters who are willing to take action and seize opportunities rather than waiting for things to happen. They have a proactive approach to problem-solving and are comfortable with taking risks and making decisions, even in the face of uncertainty.

Another critical element of the entrepreneurial mindset is a strong focus on innovation and creativity. Entrepreneurs constantly seek out new ideas, challenge the status quo, and find creative solutions to problems. They embrace change and are open to exploring unconventional approaches. This mindset enables them to identify opportunities that others may overlook and to develop unique value propositions for their businesses.

Resilience and a growth mindset are also integral to the entrepreneurial mindset. Entrepreneurs understand that setbacks and failures are part of the journey. They view these challenges as opportunities for learning and growth rather than as insurmountable obstacles. They bounce back from setbacks, adapt to change, and continually seek self-improvement.

Entrepreneurs are adept at building and leveraging networks and relationships. They understand the value of collaboration and surround themselves with a supportive community of mentors, advisors, and like-minded individuals. They actively seek feedback and guidance, and they're willing to learn from others' experiences.

Lastly, entrepreneurs exhibit a strong sense of ownership and responsibility for their businesses. They take accountability for their decisions and actions, and they're committed to delivering high-quality products or services to their customers. They're passionate about their work and willing to put in the necessary time and effort to make their ventures successful.

Understanding and cultivating the entrepreneurial mindset is crucial for aspiring entrepreneurs. It shapes attitudes, behaviors, and decision-making processes, and it sets the foundation for success in entrepreneurship. By adopting an entrepreneurial mindset, you can embrace challenges, think creatively, take calculated risks, and persist in the pursuit of your passion.

The entrepreneurial mindset encompasses purpose, self-motivation, innovation, resilience, networking, and a sense of ownership. It's a powerful framework that empowers individuals to pursue their passion and create successful ventures. By embracing the entrepreneurial mindset, you can unlock your full potential as an entrepreneur and increase your chances of building a thriving and fulfilling business. Read on for how to get started.

Getting Your Business off the Ground

Starting your own business can be an exciting and fulfilling journey. It allows you to turn your passion into a profession, be your own boss, and have the freedom to shape your own future. However, embarking on this path requires careful planning and strategic execution. This section explores the essential steps you need to take to start your own business successfully.

Whether you have a groundbreaking idea or a unique set of skills to offer, taking the leap into entrepreneurship requires a systematic approach. By following a structured process, you can navigate through the complexities of starting a business and increase your chances of long-term success.

This section delves into the key steps involved in starting your own business. It covers everything from conceptualizing your business idea to launching and growing your venture. Each step plays a crucial role in laying a solid foundation for your business and ensuring its viability in the marketplace.

Find out how to conduct market research to validate your business idea, develop a comprehensive business plan, secure funding, establish your legal structure, and build a strong brand identity. This section explores strategies for setting up your operations, hiring the right team, and marketing your products or services effectively.

Starting a business requires dedication, resilience, and a willingness to adapt to changing circumstances. It also demands careful attention to detail and a proactive mindset. By following the steps outlined in this section, you can navigate the path to entrepreneurship with confidence and increase your chances of building a successful business that aligns with your passion and goals.

Whether you aspire to launch a small-scale venture or aim to disrupt an entire industry, the steps outlined here serve as a roadmap to guide your entrepreneurial journey. Approach each step with thoroughness, creativity, and a willingness to learn from both successes and setbacks.

Starting your own business isn't without its challenges, but with the right mindset, knowledge, and a strong support system, you can overcome obstacles and transform your entrepreneurial dreams into reality. It's time to dive into the essential steps to start your own business and embark on a transformative entrepreneurial adventure.

Identifying a market need and developing a business idea

One of the crucial steps in starting your own business is identifying a market need and developing a business idea that addresses that need. This process lays the foundation for a successful and sustainable venture. By understanding the market demand and aligning it with your passion and skills, you can create a business that not only fulfills customer needs but brings you fulfillment and success.

To identify a market need, you need to conduct thorough market research. This involves studying the industry landscape, analyzing consumer trends, and identifying gaps or pain points that exist in the market. By observing customer behavior, listening to their feedback, and analyzing competitors, you can gain valuable insights into what customers are looking for and how you can supply a unique solution.

Once you've identified a market need, the next step is to develop a business idea that addresses that need effectively. This requires creativity, innovation, and a deep understanding of your own skills, strengths, and interests. Your business idea should be unique and differentiated, offering a solution that sets you apart from competitors.

Consider your own passion and expertise when developing your business idea. What are you truly passionate about? What are your skills and areas of expertise? By aligning your business idea with your own interests and capabilities, you increase the likelihood of long-term success and enjoyment in your entrepreneurial journey.

It's important to evaluate the feasibility and viability of your business idea. Conduct a thorough analysis of the market potential, competitive landscape, and potential barriers to entry. This way you can gauge whether your idea has a sustainable market opportunity and whether you have the resources and capabilities to execute it effectively.

Remember, the process of identifying a market need and developing a business idea is not a one-time task. It requires ongoing monitoring and adaptation to stay relevant in a dynamic business environment. Keep a pulse on market trends, customer feedback, and emerging technologies that may have an impact on your industry. Continuously refine and evolve your business idea to meet changing market needs and stay ahead of the competition.

In summary, identifying a market need and developing a business idea is the first step in starting your own business. It requires thorough market research, a deep understanding of customer needs, and aligning your passion and skills with a unique value proposition. By carefully assessing market potential and continuously refining your idea, you can lay a strong foundation for a successful and fulfilling entrepreneurial journey.

Conducting market research and developing a business plan

Conducting market research and developing a comprehensive business plan are essential steps in starting your own business. Market research provides valuable insights into your target market, competitors, and industry trends, and a well-crafted business plan guides your entrepreneurial journey. These activities help you make informed decisions, identify opportunities, and increase your chances of success.

Market research involves gathering and analyzing information about your target customers and their needs, preferences, and purchasing behavior. By understanding your target market, you can tailor your products or services to meet their specific demands. Market research also helps you identify potential competitors and assess their strengths, weaknesses, and market positioning. This knowledge allows you to differentiate yourself and identify unique selling propositions that give your business a competitive advantage.

You can conduct market research using several methods, including surveys, interviews, focus groups, and data analysis. These techniques lead to insights about customer preferences, market size, pricing strategies, distribution channels, and emerging trends. By leveraging both primary and secondary research, you can gather a comprehensive understanding of the market dynamics and make informed decisions.

Developing a business plan is equally important because it outlines the strategic direction and operational details of your business. A business plan directs you through various stages of your entrepreneurial journey. It typically includes an executive summary, market analysis, product or service description, marketing and sales strategies, operational plans, financial projections, and risk assessment.

A well-crafted business plan helps you clarify your business goals, define your target market, and outline your competitive advantage. It also allows you to assess the financial feasibility of your business, including startup costs, revenue projections, and potential funding sources. A business plan acts as a communication tool when seeking financing or partnerships, demonstrating your understanding of the market and your ability to execute your business concept.

Remember that market research and the business plan are not one-time activities. They require continuous monitoring and adjustments as market conditions and business environments evolve. Regularly update your market research to stay informed about changing customer needs, emerging trends, and industry shifts. Revise your business plan as you gain new insights and feedback, adapting your strategies to optimize business performance.

Conducting thorough market research and developing a comprehensive business plan are crucial steps in starting your own business. They yield valuable insights into your target market, competitors, and industry trends, enabling you to make informed decisions and develop effective strategies. By understanding customer needs, differentiating your business, and outlining a clear roadmap, you lay a solid foundation for a successful entrepreneurial venture.

Figure 8-1 is a worksheet you can use to formulate a market research approach and create your business plan.

REMEMBER

This worksheet is a guide to help you conduct market research and develop a business plan. Customize it according to your specific business idea and industry. Regularly revisit and update the worksheet as you gain new insights and progress in your entrepreneurial journey.

Market Research:

a. Define your target market: Describe the characteristics, demographics, and preferences of your ideal customers.

b. Competitor analysis: Identify your main competitors and analyze their strengths, weaknesses, and market positioning.

c. Customer surveys/interviews: Develop a questionnaire or interview guide to gather insights on customer needs, preferences, and purchasing behavior.

d. Industry trends: Research and document the current and future trends, innovations, and changes in your industry.

e. Market size and potential: Estimate the size of your target market and assess its growth potential.

Business Plan:

a. Executive summary: Summarize your business concept, mission, and key objectives.

b. Market analysis: Show a detailed overview of your target market, including customer segments, market trends, and competition.

c. Product/service description: Describe your offerings, highlighting their unique features, benefits, and value proposition.

d. Marketing and sales strategies: Outline your marketing and sales approach, including pricing, distribution channels, and promotional activities.

e. Operational plans: Define your operational processes, production/manufacturing requirements, and logistics.

f. Financial projections: Develop financial forecasts, including sales projections, expenses, and profitability analysis.

g. Risk assessment: Identify potential risks and challenges and propose strategies to mitigate them.

FIGURE 8-1:
Market research and business plan worksheet.

Ongoing Monitoring and Adjustments:

a. Continuous market research: Plan regular check-ins to stay updated on market trends, customer preferences, and competitor activities.

b. Business plan revisions: Schedule periodic reviews of your business plan to incorporate new insights, adjust strategies, and align with evolving market conditions.

Action Steps:

a. Set specific goals and timelines for completing each section of the worksheet.

b. Allocate time for market research activities, such as surveys, interviews, and data analysis.

c. Engage relevant stakeholders, such as industry experts or mentors, for feedback and guidance.

FIGURE 8-1:
Continued

d. Incorporate the findings from market research into your business plan.

TIP

Although this worksheet offers a structure for market research and business planning, consider seeking professional advice or utilizing specialized market research tools or business planning software for more in-depth analysis and guidance.

Financing your business and securing funding

Securing adequate financing is a crucial step in turning your business idea into a reality. As an entrepreneur, understanding the various options for financing your business and successfully securing funding can significantly contribute to your chances of success. Here's an expert perspective on financing your business and securing funding.

Entrepreneurs often face the challenge of finding the necessary capital to start or expand their businesses. Fortunately, multiple financing options are available, each with its own benefits and considerations. Here are some key insights on financing your business and securing funding:

>> **Self-funding:** Many entrepreneurs begin by using their personal savings, assets, or investments to fund their business. This method offers independence and control over your business but may limit the amount of capital available.

>> **Friends and family:** Borrowing from friends and family is a common source of initial funding. Just be sure to approach this option with professionalism and clear agreements to avoid straining personal relationships.

>> **Small business loans:** Traditional banks and financial institutions offer business loans specifically tailored for small businesses. These loans typically require a solid business plan, collateral, and a good credit history.

>> **Venture capital:** Venture capitalists invest in high-growth potential startups in exchange for equity. This option can provide substantial funding, industry expertise, and valuable connections. However, securing venture capital often involves relinquishing some control and providing a significant return on investment.

>> **Angel investors:** Angel investors are individuals or groups who provide capital to startups in exchange for ownership equity or convertible debt. They often bring industry experience, mentorship, and a network of contacts. Connecting with angel investors may require attending networking events or utilizing online platforms that facilitate investor-startup connections.

>> **Crowdfunding:** Crowdfunding platforms allow entrepreneurs to raise funds by presenting their business idea or project to a large pool of potential investors. This option can be effective at generating capital while also building a customer base and raising awareness.

>> **Grants and government programs:** Research grants and government-sponsored programs that support specific industries or initiatives are another option. These sources of funding often come with eligibility criteria and require detailed applications.

>> **Bootstrapping:** Bootstrapping refers to starting and growing a business with minimal external funding. This approach requires careful financial management, resourcefulness, and a focus on generating revenue from the early stages of the business.

TIP

When seeking funding, prepare a compelling business plan that demonstrates your market opportunity, competitive advantage, and potential for profitability. Investors and lenders want to see that you have thoroughly researched your target market, have a clear growth strategy, and understand the financial implications of your business.

Additionally, building relationships and networking within the entrepreneurial ecosystem can provide valuable insights, connections, and potential funding opportunities. Attending industry events, joining business associations, and seeking mentorship can open doors to potential investors or funding programs.

REMEMBER

Securing funding requires persistence, preparation, and effective communication. Develop a comprehensive financing strategy, understand the unique advantages and considerations of each funding option, and be prepared to present a compelling case for why your business is worthy of investment.

By understanding the financing landscape and pursuing the most suitable funding avenues, you can increase your chances of securing the necessary capital to fuel the growth and success of your business.

Turning Your Passion into a Successful Venture

Turning your passion into a successful venture is a dream for many aspiring entrepreneurs. It's an opportunity to pursue what you love while building a business that aligns with your values and interests. This section explores the essential steps and expert perspectives on turning your passion into a successful venture.

Whether you have a specific passion in mind or are still exploring different possibilities, this section guides you through the process of transforming your passion into a thriving business. From validating your ideas to developing a strong business model, it covers the essential elements to pave the way for a successful entrepreneurial journey.

REMEMBER

Turning your passion into a successful venture requires a combination of passion and practicality. It's important to balance your enthusiasm with a realistic understanding of the market, customer needs, and business fundamentals. Through careful planning, diligent execution, and continuous learning, you can transform your passion into a fulfilling and profitable venture.

The following sections delve into the crucial steps, strategies, and expert advice to empower you to turn your passion into a successful and sustainable business. Read on to discover how you can make your entrepreneurial dreams a reality.

Aligning your passion with your business idea

Aligning your passion with your business idea is a key factor in creating a successful and fulfilling venture. When your passion and business idea are in harmony, it brings a level of authenticity and enthusiasm that can drive your success and differentiate you in the market.

One of the first steps in aligning your passion with your business idea is to identify the core elements of your passion that you want to incorporate into your business. Consider the aspects of your passion that truly inspire you and that you want to share with others. These can be specific skills, values, or causes that resonate with you deeply.

Next, evaluate how these elements can be translated into a viable business idea. Think about the needs and desires of your target audience and how your passion can deliver a unique solution or value proposition. Look for areas where your passion intersects with market demand because this is where you can find the greatest potential for success.

Conduct market research and validate your business idea to ensure there's a viable market for your passion-driven product or service. This helps you understand your target customers, their preferences, and how your passion can meet their needs. By aligning your passion with a market need, you increase the chances of creating a sustainable and profitable business.

In addition, consider how your business idea aligns with your long-term goals and aspirations. Reflect on how it complements your values, lifestyle, and personal growth objectives. Building a business around your passion allows you to create a meaningful and fulfilling career that aligns with who you are and what you value most.

You need to strike a balance between passion and practicality. Although following your passion is crucial, it's equally important to assess the market potential, competitive landscape, and financial feasibility of your business idea. Conduct a thorough analysis of the market, evaluate the scalability of your idea, and develop a strong business plan that outlines how your passion will translate into sustainable revenue and growth.

Remember, aligning your passion with your business idea is an ongoing process. As you gain experience and feedback from customers, you may need to refine and adapt your business model. Stay open to learning, embrace feedback, and be willing to make adjustments along the way.

In conclusion, aligning your passion with your business idea is a powerful combination that can lead to both personal fulfillment and entrepreneurial success. By infusing your passion into every aspect of your business, you create a unique offering that resonates with customers and sets you apart from competitors. When you stay true to your passion, validate your idea, and adapt as needed, you're well on your way to building a business that brings you joy and drives your success.

Consider someone deeply passionate about sustainable living and eco-conscious practices. They identify their core elements: promoting sustainability, reducing carbon footprints, and spreading eco-awareness.

To turn their passion into a business, they tap into the growing market demand for eco-friendly products. Recognizing the need for sustainable solutions, they launch a business offering environmentally friendly household products. Extensive market research confirms a rising trend of eco-conscious consumers, aligning their passion with market demand.

Their business idea harmonizes with long-term goals: living in line with their values, promoting a sustainable lifestyle, and contributing to environmental well-being. This alignment brings personal fulfillment.

Balancing passion and practicality, they analyze the competitive landscape, consider scalability, and develop a comprehensive business plan. As they gain experience and customer feedback, they remain adaptable, refining their strategies to cater to evolving market needs.

Developing a strong brand and marketing strategy

Developing a strong brand and marketing strategy is essential for turning your passion into a successful venture. A well-defined brand and effective marketing approach helps you communicate your passion, connect with your target audience, and differentiate your business in the market.

Building a strong brand starts with clearly defining your business's unique value proposition and identifying the key attributes that set you apart from competitors. Consider how your passion, expertise, and offerings align with the needs and desires of your target audience. Develop a compelling brand story that captures the essence of your passion and communicates it in a way that resonates with your customers.

A strong brand identity encompasses visual elements such as a memorable logo, color scheme, and design elements that reflect the personality of your business and appeal to your target audience. Consistency in branding across all touchpoints, including your website, social media profiles, packaging, and marketing materials, establishes a recognizable and cohesive brand presence.

In addition to visual branding, a robust marketing strategy is crucial for reaching and engaging your target audience. Start by identifying the most effective marketing channels to reach your specific customer base. This can include digital platforms like social media, search engine marketing, content marketing, and traditional channels such as print media or events.

Craft compelling messaging that showcases your passion, addresses customer pain points, and highlights the unique benefits of your offerings. Tailor your marketing messages to resonate with your target audience and convey the value they can expect from engaging with your business.

Consistency is key in marketing. Create a consistent brand voice and messaging across all your marketing channels to reinforce your brand identity and build brand recognition. Develop a content strategy that showcases your passion, expertise, and offerings through various forms of content such as blog posts, videos, podcasts, or social media updates.

Don't forget the power of storytelling in your marketing efforts. Share the story behind your passion, the journey that led you to start your business, and the positive impact you aim to make. Authenticity and transparency in your storytelling can forge strong connections with your audience and foster trust and loyalty.

Regularly evaluate the effectiveness of your marketing efforts through metrics and analytics to identify which strategies are working well and which may require adjustments. Stay agile and adapt your marketing approach based on customer feedback, market trends, and industry insights.

Developing a strong brand and marketing strategy is essential for turning your passion into a successful venture. Figure 8-2 is a worksheet for helping you do so. By building a unique and compelling brand and implementing a targeted and consistent marketing approach, you can effectively communicate your passion, connect with your target audience, and drive the growth and success of your business. Remember to stay true to your passion, be consistent in your messaging, and continuously evaluate and adjust your marketing efforts for optimal results.

Building a strong brand and effective marketing strategy takes time and continuous refinement. Regularly review and update your strategies based on market trends, customer feedback, and business insights.

This worksheet is a guide to help you develop your brand and marketing strategy. Customize and adapt it to fit the specific needs of your business.

Define Your Brand Identity:

Describe your business's unique value proposition.

Identify key attributes that set you apart from competitors.

Consider how your passion aligns with the needs of your target audience.

Craft Your Brand Story:

Write a compelling narrative that captures the essence of your passion.

Highlight the journey that led you to start your business.

Emphasize the positive impact you aim to make.

Visual Branding:

Design a memorable logo and select a color scheme that reflects your brand's personality.

Choose consistent design elements for your website, social media profiles, packaging, and marketing materials.

Marketing Channels:

Identify the most effective marketing channels to reach your target audience.

List digital platforms (e.g., social media, search engine marketing) and traditional channels (e.g., print media, events) you plan to use.

Messaging Strategy:

Develop key messages that showcase your passion, address customer pain points, and highlight your unique offerings.

Tailor your messaging to resonate with your target audience.

FIGURE 8-2:
Developing a
strong brand
and marketing
strategy.

Content Strategy:

Determine the types of content that align with your brand and engage your audience (e.g., blog posts, videos, podcasts).

Create a content calendar outlining topics, formats, and publishing schedules.

Brand Voice and Consistency:

Define your brand voice and tone.

Ensure consistent messaging and branding across all marketing channels.

Storytelling:

Identify key stories that you can share to connect with your audience.

Determine how and where you will incorporate storytelling into your marketing efforts.

Metrics and Evaluation:

Determine key performance indicators (KPIs) to track the effectiveness of your marketing efforts.

Establish a system for regularly monitoring and evaluating your marketing performance.

Action Plan:

Set specific goals and deadlines for implementing your brand and marketing strategies.

Break down tasks into actionable steps and assign responsibilities.

FIGURE 8-2:
Continued

Building a team and establishing partnerships

As an entrepreneur pursuing your passion, you can't do it all alone. Building a strong team and establishing strategic partnerships can accelerate the growth of your business and bring valuable expertise to the table. Here's why it's important and how you can go about it:

>> **Leverage diverse skills and expertise:** Building a team allows you to tap into a diverse range of skills and expertise that complement your own. Look for individuals who possess the necessary skills and share your passion for the industry or field. This diversity brings fresh perspectives, creative solutions, and increased efficiency to your business.

- **Divide responsibilities and delegate:** As your business grows, you need to delegate tasks and responsibilities to your team members. Identify their strengths, and assign roles that align with their expertise. Effective delegation not only lightens your workload but allows team members to develop their skills and take ownership of their areas of responsibility.

- **Foster a positive and collaborative culture:** A strong team is built on a foundation of trust, open communication, and mutual respect. Create a positive work environment that encourages collaboration, creativity, and innovation. Foster a culture where team members feel valued, heard, and motivated to contribute their best.

- **Establish clear roles and responsibilities:** Clearly define the roles and responsibilities of each team member to avoid confusion and overlapping tasks. Establish clear communication channels, reporting structures, and decision-making processes to ensure smooth operations within the team.

- **Seek strategic partnerships:** Establishing partnerships with other businesses or individuals who share your values and complement your offerings can lead to new opportunities. Look for partners who can lend resources, expertise, or access to new markets. Collaborate on joint projects, co-marketing efforts, or cross-promotions to expand your reach and customer base.

- **Nurture relationships:** Building strong relationships with team members and partners requires ongoing effort. Regularly communicate and provide feedback to ensure everyone is aligned with the business goals. Offer opportunities for growth and development to retain top talent. Similarly, invest time and effort in maintaining and nurturing partnerships by seeking mutual benefits and maintaining open lines of communication.

- **Embrace collaboration and innovation:** Encourage a culture of collaboration and innovation within your team and partnerships. Foster an environment where ideas are freely shared and everyone feels empowered to contribute their unique perspectives. This collaboration can lead to breakthroughs, new opportunities, and continuous improvement.

Remember, building a team and establishing partnerships is a dynamic and ongoing process. As your business evolves, regularly assess your team's needs, evaluate existing partnerships, and seek new collaborations that align with your growth objectives.

By building a strong team and establishing strategic partnerships, you can leverage the collective knowledge, skills, and resources to fuel the success of your business and bring your passion to new heights.

Chapter **9**

Pursuing Education and Training

E ducation and training has the remarkable power to light the way toward your deepest passions. These twin forces are not just stepping stones to professional success; they are the gateways to discovering your true purpose, nurturing your talents, and unleashing your creativity.

Imagine education and training as keys that unlock the treasure chest of your potential. These are not mundane tools; they are the magical wands that can transform your aspirations into reality. They offer more than just knowledge and skills: They can lead to the self-assurance to take on the world, the adaptability to shape your dreams, and the tenacity to overcome any challenge that stands in your way.

In this chapter, we look at education and training, where learning becomes a journey of self-discovery, a quest for personal enlightenment, and a pathway to uncovering your passions. From structured learning programs to the untamed wilderness of self-directed exploration, the chapter will help you discover the right educational choices for you.

Keeping Yourself Current and Connected

In today's rapidly evolving world, where industries and technologies are constantly advancing, the value of continuous learning and professional development is immeasurable. Further education and training offer individuals a multitude of benefits that can enhance their personal growth, career prospects, and overall success. This chapter explores the various advantages of pursuing further education and training to expand your knowledge and skills:

>> **Stay current and relevant:** Further education and training allow individuals to stay up-to-date with the latest trends, advancements, and best practices in their field. They ensure that you remain relevant and competitive in an ever-changing job market. By acquiring new knowledge and skills, you can adapt to emerging industry demands and stay ahead of the curve.

>> **Expand your knowledge base:** Continuing education provides opportunities to delve deeper into a subject, broaden your knowledge base, and gain a comprehensive understanding of your field. It exposes you to new theories, research, and perspectives, enabling you to develop a well-rounded expertise and a deeper level of understanding.

>> **Enhance career opportunities:** Acquiring additional education and training opens doors to a wider range of career opportunities. It equips you with the necessary qualifications and credentials that can distinguish you from other candidates in the job market. Employers often prioritize candidates with advanced degrees or specialized certifications because they demonstrate a commitment to continuous learning and professional growth.

>> **Develop specialized skills:** Further education and training offer the opportunity to develop specialized skills that can set you apart in your field. Whether it's mastering a specific software, acquiring technical expertise, or gaining proficiency in a niche area, specialized skills can make you highly sought after by employers and clients.

>> **Increase earning potential:** Studies consistently show that individuals with higher levels of education tend to earn higher salaries and enjoy better job prospects. By investing in further education and training, you increase your earning potential and usher in more lucrative career opportunities.

>> **Enjoy personal growth and fulfillment:** Pursuing further education and training can be an enriching and fulfilling experience. It allows you to explore your passions, deepen your understanding of a subject, and challenge yourself intellectually. In turn, you're rewarded with a sense of personal growth, accomplishment, and fulfillment that goes beyond career advancement.

>> **Promote networking and collaboration:** Further education and training often involve interacting with professionals and peers from diverse backgrounds. This creates networking opportunities, facilitates knowledge sharing, and fosters collaborative relationships. These connections can be valuable for career advancement, mentorship, and future collaborations.

REMEMBER

Education and training are lifelong journeys. They enable you to continuously expand your horizons, adapt to new challenges, and unlock new possibilities. Whether it's pursuing a higher degree, attending workshops and seminars, or acquiring professional certifications, investing in further education and training is an investment in your personal and professional growth.

The following sections explore specific avenues for further education and training, such as degree programs, certifications, online courses, and professional development opportunities, to help you chart your path toward continued learning and success.

The advantages of formal education in pursuing passion

Formal education, such as earning a degree or attending a structured educational program, offers numerous advantages when it comes to pursuing your passion. Although you can take various paths to learning and acquiring knowledge, formal education provides a solid foundation and a range of benefits that can significantly support your journey toward following your passion. Here are some key advantages of formal education in pursuing your passions:

>> **In-depth knowledge and expertise:** Formal education offers a structured curriculum designed to provide comprehensive knowledge and expertise in a particular field or subject area. By pursuing a degree or completing a formal educational program, you gain a deep understanding of the foundational principles, theories, and practical applications related to your passion. This extensive knowledge can serve as a strong base for further exploration and specialization within your chosen field.

>> **Credibility and validation:** Obtaining a formal education in your passion area adds credibility and validation to your skills and knowledge. A recognized degree or certification from an accredited institution demonstrates to employers, clients, and peers that you've undergone rigorous training and met certain academic standards. It enhances your professional reputation and can give you a competitive edge in the job market.

>> **Access to expert faculty and resources:** One of the significant advantages of formal education is the access to experienced faculty members and

resources. Professors and instructors with expertise in your field can share valuable insights, mentorship, and guidance. They can challenge and inspire you to deepen your understanding, explore new perspectives, and refine your skills. Additionally, educational institutions often provide access to libraries, research databases, laboratories, and other resources that can further enrich your learning experience.

» **Skill development:** Formal education focuses not only on theoretical knowledge but on practical skills. Through assignments, projects, internships, and hands-on training, you have opportunities to apply what you've learned and develop relevant skills in your passion area. These skills can range from critical thinking and problem-solving to communication and collaboration, all of which are crucial for success in any field.

» **Networking and collaboration:** Engaging in formal education paves the way to a network of like-minded individuals, including fellow students, alumni, faculty, and industry professionals. These connections can lead to valuable collaborations, mentorship opportunities, and a supportive community that shares your passion. Networking within your educational institution can help you build relationships that may extend beyond the classroom and into your future professional endeavors.

» **Personal growth and self-discovery:** Pursuing formal education in your passion provides a platform for personal growth and self-discovery. It encourages you to delve deeper into your interests, explore new areas within your field, and challenge yourself intellectually. Through coursework, discussions, and exposure to diverse perspectives, you gain a broader understanding of your passion and its various facets, which can contribute to your personal and intellectual development.

» **Career opportunities:** Formal education often opens doors to a range of career opportunities related to your passion. Many professions and industries have specific educational requirements, and having the necessary qualifications can significantly expand your career prospects. A formal education also equips you with transferable skills, such as critical thinking, research abilities, and problem-solving, that are valuable in multiple fields and can make you adaptable to changing career landscapes.

REMEMBER

Formal education is just one pathway to pursuing your passion, and it may not be necessary or suitable for everyone. However, it offers unique advantages that can lay a strong foundation for your journey and support your long-term goals. Whether you choose to pursue a degree, enroll in a specialized program, or combine formal education with other learning experiences, consider how it aligns with your aspirations and contributes to your growth and fulfillment in following your passion.

The role of training and professional development in finding passion

Training and professional development play a vital role in finding and nurturing your passion. Although formal education makes for a solid foundation, ongoing training and professional development opportunities are crucial for staying current, expanding your skill set, and deepening your expertise in your chosen field. Training and professional development contribute to your journey of finding and pursuing passion in several ways:

» **Skill enhancement and specialization:** Training programs and professional development opportunities offer a focused approach to enhancing your skills and knowledge in specific areas of interest. These programs provide specialized training, workshops, seminars, and certifications that help you develop new competencies, refine existing skills, and stay up-to-date with emerging trends and technologies. By honing your expertise, you become better equipped to pursue your passion with confidence and competence.

» **Exploration and discovery:** Training and professional development initiatives often expose you to a range of topics and disciplines within your field. They bestow opportunities to explore different areas, techniques, and methodologies that may align with your passion. Through workshops, conferences, and networking events, you can engage with industry professionals, thought leaders, and peers, gaining valuable insights and discovering new possibilities that can fuel your passion.

» **Formation of a professional network:** Training and professional development activities offer excellent networking opportunities. Engaging with professionals in your field, connecting with like-minded individuals, and building relationships with mentors and role models can foster new opportunities and collaborations. Your professional network can supply support, guidance, and mentorship as you navigate your journey of finding and pursuing your passion.

» **Career advancement and adaptability:** Investing in training and professional development demonstrates your commitment to growth and continuous improvement. By acquiring new skills, knowledge, and certifications, you enhance your marketability and increase your chances of career advancement. Training and development also equip you with the flexibility and adaptability you need to thrive in a dynamic job market, allowing you to explore different career paths and adapt to evolving industry demands.

» **Confidence and self-efficacy:** Engaging in training and professional development programs boosts your confidence and self-efficacy. As you acquire new skills, broaden your knowledge, and gain practical experience, you develop a sense of mastery and competence. This newfound confidence empowers you to take risks, pursue challenging opportunities, and embrace new ventures aligned with your passion.

>> **Continuous learning and growth mindset:** Training and professional development foster a mindset of continuous learning and growth. They encourage you to remain curious, open-minded, and receptive to new ideas and perspectives. By embracing a growth mindset, you can navigate changes and setbacks with resilience, viewing them as opportunities for learning and personal development.

>> **Recognition and professional validation:** Participating in training and professional development activities brings external validation and recognition of your skills and expertise. Earning certifications, attending industry conferences, and acquiring new qualifications demonstrate your commitment to professional growth and can enhance your credibility and reputation within your field. This recognition can help you find new opportunities and collaborations, further fueling your passion.

REMEMBER

Training and professional development are ongoing processes that you should tailor to your individual needs and aspirations. Explore a variety of options, including workshops, online courses, industry certifications, mentorship programs, and conferences, to find the right opportunities that align with your goals and passions. By investing in your growth and development, you pave the way for a fulfilling and successful journey in pursuing your passion.

Identifying the Best Educational Opportunities for Your Passion

To pursue your passion and turn it into a fulfilling career, you need to acquire the necessary education and knowledge. Education grants you the skills, expertise, and foundation you need to excel in your chosen field. However, with the array of educational opportunities available today, it can be overwhelming to determine which ones are best suited for your specific passion. This chapter aims to guide you through the process of identifying the best educational opportunities for aligning with your interests, goals, and learning preferences.

Finding the right educational opportunities for your passion involves a thoughtful and strategic approach. It requires assessing your specific needs, researching available options, and considering factors such as credibility, relevance, and flexibility. By investing time and effort into this process, you ensure that you receive the education and training to pursue your passion with confidence and competence.

This section explores various strategies, tips, and resources to help you navigate the journey of identifying the best educational opportunities for your passion. From formal education programs to online courses, certifications, workshops, and more, it shares how to evaluate each option, align it with your unique requirements, and make informed decisions to propel you forward on your path to success.

Education is a lifelong pursuit. As you grow and evolve in your passion, you may discover the need for continuous learning and upskilling. Embrace the mindset of being a lifelong learner, and remain open to exploring new educational opportunities that can sharpen your knowledge and expertise. A clear understanding of your passion and a strategic approach to education can pave the way for a fulfilling and successful journey in your chosen field.

Researching educational options such as degrees, certifications, and workshops

When it comes to pursuing your passion, researching and exploring educational options is a crucial step in setting yourself up for success. The world of education offers a diverse range of opportunities, from traditional degrees to specialized certifications and workshops. Conducting thorough research allows you to make informed decisions and select the educational path that aligns best with your passion, goals, and learning style.

>> **Degrees:** Pursuing a degree in a field related to your passion can result in a comprehensive and structured education. Universities and colleges offer undergraduate and graduate degree programs that delve deep into specific subjects, offering theoretical knowledge, practical skills, and academic credentials. Research different institutions and their course offerings, curriculum, faculty expertise, and alumni success stories. Consider factors such as program duration, tuition fees, location, and potential networking opportunities.

>> **Certifications:** Certifications offer a focused and specialized approach to education. They're designed to impart targeted knowledge and skill development in specific areas, often recognized by industry standards. Research professional certifications that are relevant to your passion and desired career path. Look for reputable certification programs that align with your goals and yield practical skills that employers value. Consider the credibility of the certifying body, the curriculum, exam requirements, and any ongoing maintenance or renewal requirements.

>> **Workshops and short-term courses:** Workshops and short-term courses offer the opportunity to acquire specific skills and knowledge in a condensed and focused format. These options are often more flexible, allowing you to choose specific topics or areas of interest related to your passion. Research workshops and courses offered by reputable training organizations, industry associations, or online learning platforms. Look for content that aligns with your passion, course duration, instructor expertise, participant reviews, and any available certifications or recognition.

WARNING

Not every degree, certificate, or workshop will be worth its return when it comes to bringing you closer to finding and fulfilling your passion, so be sure to consider carefully whether the time and financial investment will be of true value.

Researching educational options requires dedication and thoroughness. Take the time to gather information, compare different options, and seek advice from professionals or mentors in your field of interest. By making well-informed decisions, you can embark on an educational journey that equips you with the knowledge and skills necessary to pursue your passion with confidence and excellence.

When researching educational options, consider several factors:

>> **Relevance:** Ensure that the educational option aligns closely with your passion and desired career path. Look for programs or courses that cover topics directly related to your interests, skills, and industry requirements.

>> **Credibility:** Verify the reputation and credibility of the educational institution, certifying body, or training organization. Review their accreditations, affiliations, faculty qualifications, and student testimonials to gauge the quality of education they provide.

>> **Flexibility:** Consider the flexibility of the educational option in terms of scheduling, format (online or in-person), and the ability to balance it with other commitments. Flexibility is particularly important if you're currently working or have other responsibilities.

>> **Cost:** Evaluate the cost of the educational option, including tuition fees, course materials, and any additional expenses. Consider the potential return on investment and the long-term value the education will bring to your passion and career.

Considering online learning and self-paced courses

In today's digital age, online learning and self-paced courses have revolutionized the acquisition of knowledge and skills. These flexible and accessible educational options offer numerous advantages for individuals seeking to pursue their passion. Online learning and self-paced courses can open up a world of opportunities, allowing you to study at your own pace, customize your learning experience, and access a wide range of subjects and resources.

>> **Flexibility:** Online learning and self-paced courses afford you the flexibility to study anytime and anywhere. Whether you have a busy schedule, work commitments, or other responsibilities, these options allow you to learn at

your own convenience. You can set your own pace, allocating time for learning that fits your lifestyle. This flexibility is particularly beneficial for individuals who want to pursue their passion while juggling other obligations.

>> **Variety of courses:** Online platforms and websites offer an array of courses covering diverse subjects and industries. Whether your passion lies in arts, business, technology, or any other field, you can find online courses that align with your interests. Take the time to research reputable online learning platforms, read course descriptions, check reviews, and consider the qualifications of instructors. Look for courses that provide comprehensive content, interactive learning materials, and practical exercises to ensure a valuable learning experience.

>> **Self-paced learning:** Self-paced courses allow you to learn at your own speed without strict deadlines or fixed schedules. This approach enables you to delve deep into topics that fascinate you, spend more time on challenging concepts, and progress faster through familiar subjects. Self-paced learning empowers you to take control of your education and adapt it to your individual learning style and preferences.

>> **Networking opportunities:** Online learning platforms often have forums, discussion boards, and communities where learners can connect and engage with fellow students, instructors, and industry professionals. These virtual networking opportunities can help you expand your professional network, share ideas, gain insights, and seek advice from like-minded individuals who share your passion. Engaging in online discussions and networking can be a resource for valuable connections and potential collaborations.

>> **Cost-effectiveness:** Online learning and self-paced courses are often more affordable than traditional educational options. They eliminate expenses such as commuting, accommodation, and material costs. Furthermore, many online platforms offer free or low-cost courses, making education more accessible to a wider audience. However, it's important to carefully assess the quality and credibility of the course provider to ensure you receive value for your investment.

Online learning and self-paced courses have revolutionized education by offering accessible and flexible opportunities for individuals to pursue their passion. By considering these options, you can embark on a learning journey that fits your lifestyle, caters to your interests, and equips you with the knowledge and skills necessary to excel in your chosen field.

When considering online learning and self-paced courses, keep the following in mind:

>> **Accreditation:** Verify the accreditation and credibility of the online learning platform or course provider. Ensure that the courses you choose are recognized and respected within your industry or field of interest.

>> **Course structure and support:** Assess the course structure, curriculum, and learning materials. Look for courses that offer engaging content, interactive elements, assessments, and support resources such as forums or instructor feedback. This ensures a comprehensive and enriching learning experience.

>> **Technical requirements:** Check the technical requirements for online courses, such as internet speed, software, and hardware compatibility. Ensure that you have the necessary resources to access the course materials and participate effectively.

Choosing the educational path that best aligns with your goals and interests

When it comes to pursuing your passion, choosing the right educational path is crucial. The educational path you embark on should align with your goals, interests, and aspirations, setting you up for success in your desired field. Here are some key considerations to help you make an informed decision when choosing the educational path that best suits your needs.

>> **Clarify your goals:** Begin by clearly defining your goals and what you hope to achieve through education. Are you looking to gain specific knowledge and skills to advance in your current career? Do you aim to transition into a completely new field? Understanding your objectives will help you narrow down your options and identify the most relevant educational paths.

>> **Research different educational paths:** Explore the various educational paths available to you, such as degree programs, certifications, vocational training, apprenticeships, and specialized workshops. Each option offers unique benefits and opportunities for growth. Take the time to research different programs, their curriculum, prerequisites, and potential career outcomes. Consider factors such as duration, cost, flexibility, and the reputation of the educational institution or program.

>> **Evaluate your learning style:** Consider your preferred learning style and how it aligns with the educational path you're considering. Some individuals thrive in a structured and traditional classroom setting, whereas others prefer self-directed learning or online formats. Reflect on your learning preferences, such as hands-on experience, collaborative projects, or individual study, and choose an educational path that accommodates your preferred style.

>> **Seek guidance and advice:** Reach out to professionals, career counselors, mentors, or individuals working in your desired field to seek guidance and advice. They can share insights into the educational paths that are most relevant and valued within the industry. Their experiences and perspectives

can help you make an informed decision and gain a realistic understanding of the educational requirements for your chosen field.

» **Consider industry requirements:** Some professions or industries have specific educational requirements or preferences. Research the industry standards and job postings to identify the educational qualifications that employers often seek. Although some fields may have flexibility, having the right educational credentials can enhance your credibility and competitiveness.

» **Evaluate practical considerations:** Take into account practical factors such as time commitment, financial investment, and your personal circumstances. Consider whether you can commit to full-time education or if part-time or online learning better suits your lifestyle. Assess the financial implications of pursuing a particular educational path, and explore scholarship or financial aid options if needed.

» **Follow your passion:** Ultimately, choose an educational path that ignites your passion and curiosity. The journey toward achieving your goals should be fulfilling and enjoyable. Look for programs or courses that align with your interests and include opportunities for hands-on learning, internships, or practical experiences. By following your passion, you're more likely to stay motivated, excel in your studies, and find long-term satisfaction in your chosen field.

REMEMBER

Choosing the right educational path is a personal decision that requires careful consideration. By clarifying your goals, conducting thorough research, seeking guidance, and aligning with your passion, you can make an informed choice that sets you on a path of growth, learning, and success.

Financing Your Education and Training

Embarking on an educational journey to pursue your passion requires careful consideration of the financial aspects involved. The cost of education and training can be a significant factor that affects your decision-making process. However, with proper planning and exploring various financing options, you can make your educational aspirations a reality. This section explores the strategies and resources available to help you finance your education and training, ensuring that financial constraints don't hinder your pursuit of passion.

Education and training can come in different forms, such as degree programs, certifications, workshops, and vocational training. Each has its own associated costs, including tuition fees, materials, books, and living expenses. You need to have a clear understanding of the financial commitment required for your chosen educational path. By addressing the financial aspect early on, you can better plan and make informed decisions about your education.

Investing in your education and training is an investment in your future. The financial aspect may seem daunting, but it shouldn't deter you from pursuing your passion and acquiring the necessary skills and knowledge. By understanding the options and resources available, you can make well-informed financial decisions and create a solid plan to finance your educational endeavors.

This section covers various financing options available to support your educational journey. It equips you with knowledge about scholarships, grants, loans, employer assistance programs, and other funding sources. It also explores practical tips on budgeting, financial planning, and maximizing resources to minimize the burden of educational expenses.

REMEMBER

The benefits of investing in your education and training extend beyond monetary value. It also opens doors to new opportunities, enhances your skills and expertise, and empowers you to pursue a career that aligns with your passion and aspirations. By exploring the strategies and resources outlined in this section, you can make your educational dreams a reality.

Identifying potential sources of funding, such as scholarships and grants

When considering financing options for your education and training, don't forget to explore potential sources of funding beyond personal savings or traditional loans. Scholarships and grants are valuable resources that can lend financial assistance and alleviate the burden of educational expenses. These funding opportunities are often awarded based on merit, financial need, or specific criteria related to your field of study or personal background.

Scholarships and grants offer numerous benefits to students pursuing their passion. They can significantly reduce or even eliminate the cost of tuition, books, and other educational expenses. Additionally, unlike loans, scholarships and grants don't require repayment, which means you can focus on your education without accumulating debt.

To identify potential sources of funding, such as scholarships and grants, conduct thorough research. Start by exploring scholarship databases — both general and specialized ones related to your field of interest. These databases have comprehensive listings of available scholarships, including criteria, application deadlines, and award amounts.

Scholarship and grant applications usually have specific requirements and deadlines. Take the time to carefully review the eligibility criteria and application instructions for each opportunity you consider. Pay attention to deadlines, and ensure that you submit all required documents accurately and on time.

When searching for scholarships and grants, consider the following:

» **Local, national, and international organizations:** Many organizations, including non-profit organizations, corporations, and foundations, offer scholarships and grants to support students pursuing their education. Research these organizations and their scholarship programs to find opportunities that align with your goals and interests.

» **Educational institutions:** Colleges, universities, and vocational schools often have their own scholarship and grant programs for enrolled students. Research the financial aid options available at the institutions you're considering, and be mindful of their application requirements and deadlines.

» **Professional associations and societies:** Many professional associations and societies offer scholarships and grants to support students within their respective fields. These opportunities often require applicants to demonstrate a commitment to the industry and show potential for future contributions.

» **Government and public-funded programs:** Governments at both the national and the local levels often provide scholarships and grants to support education and career development. Explore government websites, educational departments, and funding agencies to discover available options.

The competition for scholarships and grants can be intense, so make sure you present a strong application. Showcase your achievements, academic performance, extracurricular activities, community involvement, and any unique qualities or experiences that make you stand out. Craft well-written essays and personal statements that clearly communicate your passion and goals and why you deserve the funding.

By actively seeking out scholarships and grants and submitting strong applications, you increase your chances of securing financial assistance for your education and training. These funding opportunities can provide not only financial support but also recognition and validation of your dedication and potential. Start early, be proactive, and persevere in your search for scholarships and grants to make your educational journey more accessible and affordable.

Understanding the costs associated with different educational paths

Before embarking on an educational journey to pursue your passion, it's crucial to have a comprehensive understanding of the costs associated with different educational paths. By evaluating the financial aspects of your chosen path, you can make informed decisions and plan effectively for the investment required.

The costs of education can vary significantly depending on factors such as the type of institution, program duration, location, and specific requirements of your chosen field. Consider the following elements when breaking down the costs associated with different educational paths:

» **Tuition and fees:** Tuition and fees are major components of the overall cost of education. Research and compare the tuition and fees of different educational institutions and programs. Keep in mind that tuition costs may differ based on whether you choose a public or a private institution, in-state or out-of-state options, or online learning.

» **Books and learning materials:** Textbooks, reference materials, and other learning resources are often additional expenses. Consider the cost of books and materials required for your program, and explore options for purchasing used books or utilizing online resources to reduce expenses.

» **Housing and living expenses:** If you plan to attend a college or university away from home, factor in the costs of housing, meals, transportation, and other living expenses. Compare the cost of living in different locations, and explore options such as on-campus housing, shared accommodations, and commuting from home to find the most cost-effective solution.

» **Additional fees:** Be aware of additional fees that may be associated with your educational path, such as application fees, technology fees, laboratory fees, or membership fees for specific programs or associations. These costs can add up, so don't forget to consider them in your budget planning.

» **Scholarships and financial aid:** Investigate the availability of scholarships, grants, and other forms of financial aid that can offset the costs of education. Research eligibility requirements, application processes, and deadlines for various scholarship programs, and explore opportunities for work-study programs or part-time jobs on campus.

» **Opportunity costs:** Consider the potential income you may forgo while pursuing your education, especially if you plan to leave your current job or reduce your working hours. Factor in the loss of income and any associated expenses such as health insurance and retirement contributions.

Understanding the costs associated with different educational paths allows you to make realistic financial plans and consider your options. Evaluate the return on investment (ROI) of your chosen educational path, and weigh it against your long-term career goals and earning potential. Keep in mind that although some paths may have higher upfront costs, they may lead to greater opportunities and higher income in the future.

WARNING

Additionally, be mindful of the potential for unforeseen expenses or changes in financial circumstances. Create a financial contingency plan to handle unexpected costs or financial challenges that may arise during your educational journey.

By carefully assessing the costs associated with different educational paths, you can make informed decisions about the most viable and financially sustainable option for pursuing your passion. Remember to explore financial aid options, consider cost-saving strategies, and plan your budget effectively to ensure a successful and financially manageable educational experience.

Developing a budget and financial plan for pursuing education and training

When embarking on an educational journey to pursue your passion, you need to develop a comprehensive budget and financial plan to manage the costs associated with education and training, ensure financial stability throughout your learning experience, and make the most of your investment. Consider these key steps when developing a budget and financial plan:

>> **Assess your current financial situation:** Begin by evaluating your current income, savings, and any existing financial obligations. Take into account your regular expenses, such as rent, utilities, groceries, transportation, and debt payments. Understanding your financial standing is a good starting point for creating a realistic budget.

>> **Determine your educational expenses:** Identify and estimate the costs associated with your chosen educational path. Consider tuition fees, books and learning materials, housing and living expenses, transportation, and any additional fees specific to your program or institution. Research the average costs for these items, and use them as a basis for your budget.

>> **Create a budget:** Based on your financial assessment and estimated educational expenses, create a detailed budget that outlines your income and expenses. Allocate funds for education-related costs, and consider other necessary expenses. Be realistic, and ensure that your budget aligns with your financial capabilities.

» **Explore funding options:** Research and explore potential sources of funding, such as scholarships, grants, student loans, and employer-sponsored education programs. Consider the eligibility criteria, application processes, and deadlines for these funding opportunities. Incorporate any awarded funds into your budget.

» **Track your expenses:** Once you've established a budget, track your expenses diligently. Keep a record of all your spending, and compare it with your planned budget. This helps you identify areas where you may need to adjust your spending or find cost-saving measures.

» **Seek cost-saving strategies:** Look for ways to reduce your educational expenses without compromising the quality of your learning experience. Consider buying used textbooks, utilizing online resources, exploring open educational resources (OER), or sharing resources with fellow students. Look for student discounts on software, memberships, and transportation.

» **Plan for income and employment:** If possible, explore part-time job opportunities or work-study programs to supplement your income while studying. Research internships or co-op programs that offer practical experience and potential income. Factor in any potential income from employment when developing your budget.

» **Set financial goals:** Establish financial goals to stay motivated and focused on your financial plan. These goals may include saving a certain amount each month, paying off existing debt, or achieving specific financial milestones. Regularly review your progress and make adjustments as needed.

» **Seek financial advice if necessary:** If you're unsure about managing your finances or need assistance in creating a financial plan, consider seeking guidance from a financial advisor or counselor. This person can provide personalized advice based on your unique circumstances and help you optimize your financial situation.

» **Regularly review and update your financial plan:** As your educational journey progresses, regularly review and update your financial plan. Monitor any changes in expenses, income, or funding sources, and make necessary adjustments to ensure your financial plan remains relevant and effective.

Developing a budget and financial plan for pursuing education and training helps you manage your expenses, maximize available resources, and stay financially stable throughout your learning journey. By carefully planning and monitoring your finances, you can focus on your education and pursue your passion with confidence.

Chapter **10**

Developing Your Skills and Expertise

P icture your skills as the sails of your passion, catching the winds that propel you toward mastery. Mastery, we discover, is not a static destination but a dynamic expedition, and in this chapter, we unravel the art and science of honing the tools that will fuel your passion's growth.

At the heart of skill development lies deliberate practice, a concept explored in-depth. Delving into deliberate practice unveils the power of intentional, focused efforts to improve specific aspects of your craft.

This chapter probes deeper into the benefits of continuous learning and development, exploring various strategies, resources, and approaches to help you harness the power of lifelong learning in your quest to find and nurture your passion. Through ongoing personal and professional development, you can unlock your potential, embrace growth, and embark on a fulfilling journey of self-discovery and pursuit of your passion.

The following pages cover the strategies and principles that can guide you on your path to mastery. Explore the mindset, habits, and practices necessary to unlock your potential and become an expert in your chosen domain. Whether you're an artist, athlete, scientist, entrepreneur, or any other professional, the principles of mastery are universally applicable.

Through deliberate practice, focused learning, and a deep understanding of your craft, you can elevate your skills to exceptional levels. Discover how to cultivate expertise, harness your unique strengths, and navigate the challenges that come with the pursuit of mastery.

The Benefits of Continuous Learning and Development in Finding Passion

In today's rapidly evolving world, the pursuit of passion and personal fulfillment goes hand in hand with continuous learning and development. Whether you're looking to explore new interests, enhance your skills, or make a career transition, the journey of lifelong learning offers a multitude of benefits. This chapter covers the advantages of continuous learning and development in finding and nurturing your passion.

>> **Staying relevant in a dynamic world:** Continuous learning allows you to stay abreast of the latest advancements, trends, and technologies in your field of interest. By acquiring new knowledge and skills, you remain relevant in an ever-changing landscape, positioning yourself for greater opportunities and growth.

>> **Unlocking your potential:** Continuous learning empowers you to unlock your full potential. It's an avenue for self-discovery, enabling you to explore different areas of interest, uncover hidden talents, and tap into your unique abilities. Through ongoing development, you can push beyond your limits and discover new dimensions of passion and purpose.

>> **Expanding your perspectives:** Learning is a transformative process that broadens your horizons and expands your perspectives. By exposing yourself to diverse ideas, cultures, and experiences, you gain a deeper understanding of the world around you. This expanded worldview fuels creativity, innovation, and the ability to think critically, all of which are crucial elements in finding and pursuing your passion.

>> **Boosting confidence and self-efficacy:** Continuous learning builds confidence and self-efficacy. As you acquire new knowledge and skills, tackle challenges, and achieve personal milestones, you develop a sense of competence and belief in your abilities. This newfound confidence propels you forward, enabling you to take on new ventures and pursue your passion with conviction.

>> **Enhancing adaptability and resilience:** Learning isn't just about acquiring specific skills; it's also about cultivating adaptability and resilience. Continuous

learning equips you with the mindset and tools to navigate change, overcome obstacles, and bounce back from setbacks. These qualities are essential in the pursuit of passion because they enable you to embrace challenges, learn from failures, and keep pushing forward.

>> **Creating new opportunities:** The process of continuous learning ushers in new experiences. By expanding your knowledge base and skill set, you increase your value in the job market and open yourself up to a wider range of possibilities. Whether it's exploring different career paths, starting your own business, or pursuing creative endeavors, continuous learning creates a pathway for new and exciting opportunities aligned with your passions.

>> **Fostering personal growth and fulfillment:** Ultimately, continuous learning and development contribute to your personal growth and fulfillment. The pursuit of knowledge, skills, and self-improvement leads to a sense of purpose, meaning, and personal satisfaction. It ignites a lifelong journey of exploration, self-discovery, and the pursuit of your authentic passions.

The value of feedback and self-reflection in continuous improvement

Feedback and self-reflection play a crucial role in continuous improvement. They serve as powerful tools for personal and professional growth, enabling you to gain insights, identify areas for improvement, and make meaningful progress in your journey of continuous improvement. Feedback and self-reflection contribute to continuous improvement in several ways:

>> **Gaining objective insights:** Feedback, whether from others or yourself, bestows valuable and objective insights into your performance, actions, and behaviors. It offers a different perspective and helps you see yourself more accurately, highlighting strengths to leverage and areas that need development. By seeking and receiving feedback, you gain a clearer understanding of your strengths, weaknesses, and areas for growth.

>> **Identifying blind spots:** Feedback and self-reflection shed light on blind spots that may hinder personal and professional development. Blind spots are areas where you may be unaware of your shortcomings or areas where you could improve. Through feedback and self-reflection, you can uncover these blind spots, allowing for targeted efforts and improvement in those specific areas.

>> **Facilitating growth-oriented mindset:** Feedback and self-reflection foster a growth-oriented mindset. Instead of viewing feedback as criticism, you see it as an opportunity for growth and improvement. It encourages you to embrace challenges, learn from mistakes, and continuously seek ways to enhance your skills, knowledge, and capabilities.

- >> **Promoting accountability and ownership:** Feedback and self-reflection promote accountability and ownership over your growth and development. By actively seeking feedback and reflecting on your own performance, you take responsibility for your actions and strive for continuous improvement. This accountability fosters a proactive approach to growth and ensures you're actively engaged in your own development.

- >> **Enhancing self-awareness:** Feedback and self-reflection enhance self-awareness, a critical aspect of personal and professional growth. They help you gain a deeper understanding of your values, motivations, strengths, and areas that require development. This self-awareness enables you to align your actions with your aspirations, make better decisions, and maximize your potential.

- >> **Encouraging course correction:** Feedback and self-reflection afford opportunities for course correction. They enable you to identify areas where you need adjustments and make necessary changes to improve performance and outcomes. By actively seeking feedback and engaging in self-reflection, you can make informed decisions, refine your strategies, and adapt your approach for continuous improvement.

- >> **Supporting goal achievement:** Feedback and self-reflection are essential for goal achievement. They help you assess progress, identify areas of success, and pinpoint areas that require further attention. By regularly evaluating your performance and reflecting on your actions, you can refine your goals, adjust your strategies, and make the necessary improvements to stay on track toward your objectives.

The benefits of staying up-to-date with industry trends and changes

TIP

Staying up-to-date with industry trends and changes is vital for professionals across various fields. In today's fast-paced and ever-evolving business landscape, remaining current and informed about industry developments has become more important than ever. Staying up-to-date with industry trends and changes has its benefits:

- >> **Competitive advantage:** Being aware of industry trends and changes gives you a competitive edge. It allows you to anticipate market shifts, emerging technologies, and evolving customer preferences. By staying ahead of the curve, you can adapt your strategies, products, and services to meet changing demands, thus outperforming competitors.

Continuous learning plays a crucial role in building expertise and achieving mastery in any field. It goes beyond acquiring initial knowledge or skills and emphasizes the ongoing pursuit of knowledge, growth, and improvement.

Strategies for Continuous Learning and Development

Embracing a mindset of continuous improvement and actively seeking opportunities for growth are essential for personal and professional success. This section explores various strategies that you can employ to engage in continuous learning and development. By implementing these strategies, you can stay ahead of the curve, adapt to change, and unlock your full potential.

Whether you're a student, professional, entrepreneur, or lifelong learner, the strategies discussed in this section are practical approaches to cultivate a habit of continuous learning. Through intentional and consistent effort, you can expand your knowledge, sharpen your skills, and enhance your overall capabilities.

The strategies covered in this section encompass a range of learning methods, enabling you to choose the approach that best aligns with your learning preferences, lifestyle, and goals. These strategies include formal education, online courses, reading, workshops and conferences, professional associations, networking, mentorship, and use of technology for self-paced learning.

By exploring these strategies and incorporating them into your learning journey, you can:

>> **Stay relevant:** Continuous learning ensures that your knowledge and skills remain relevant in a rapidly changing world. It helps you stay up-to-date with the latest trends, advancements, and best practices in your field, enabling you to adapt and thrive in dynamic environments.

>> **Cultivate a growth mindset:** Continuous learning nurtures a growth mindset, a belief that you can develop your abilities through effort and perseverance. It encourages you to embrace challenges, view failures as opportunities for learning, and seek feedback for continuous improvement.

>> **Expand your skill set:** Engaging in continuous learning allows you to expand your skill set, acquire new competencies, and develop a diverse range of capabilities. It enables you to take on new challenges, pursue different career paths, and explore new areas of interest.

>> **Enhance problem-solving abilities:** Continuous learning sharpens your critical thinking and problem-solving skills. It equips you with the knowledge, tools, and frameworks to analyze complex problems, generate innovative solutions, and make informed decisions.

>> **Fuel personal and professional growth:** By consistently investing in your learning and development, you foster personal and professional growth.

Continuous learning opens doors to new opportunities, increases your marketability, and positions you for career advancement.

» **Foster adaptability and resilience:** The ability to adapt to change is crucial in today's fast-paced world. Continuous learning enhances your adaptability and resilience by equipping you with the knowledge and skills needed to navigate through uncertain and challenging circumstances.

» **Ignite creativity and innovation:** Continuous learning stimulates your creativity and fuels innovation. It exposes you to diverse perspectives, new ideas, and different ways of thinking, inspiring you to approach problems from fresh angles and develop innovative solutions.

Developing a growth mindset and embracing new challenges

In the pursuit of personal and professional growth, developing a growth mindset and embracing new challenges are essential. A growth mindset is the belief that you can develop your abilities and intelligence through dedication, effort, and a willingness to learn. It's a mindset that fosters resilience, curiosity, and a passion for continuous improvement.

When you adopt a growth mindset, you understand that your talents and skills aren't fixed but can be developed with practice and perseverance. You view challenges as opportunities for learning and growth rather than as obstacles to avoid. This mindset allows you to approach new challenges with enthusiasm and a willingness to step outside of your comfort zone.

REMEMBER

Embracing new challenges is crucial because it pushes you to expand your skills, knowledge, and capabilities. It enables you to overcome limitations, break through barriers, and discover your true potential. When you actively seek out and embrace new challenges, you develop a sense of confidence, adaptability, and a capacity for innovation.

Developing a growth mindset and embracing new challenges go hand in hand. Here's how they work together:

» **Resilience:** A growth mindset helps you bounce back from setbacks and view failures as opportunities for learning and growth. It enables you to persevere through challenges, maintain a positive attitude, and keep moving forward.

» **Curiosity and learning:** A growth mindset fosters a natural curiosity and a love for learning. This mindset makes you eager to explore new ideas, acquire new skills, and broaden your knowledge. You approach challenges as opportunities to gain new insights and expand your expertise.

>> **Creativity and innovation:** Embracing new challenges encourages you to think creatively and find innovative solutions. It pushes you to explore alternative approaches, think outside the box, and challenge conventional thinking. This mindset fosters a culture of innovation and continuous improvement.

>> **Personal growth and development:** By embracing new challenges, you push yourself to develop new skills, expand your capabilities, and broaden your perspectives. You continuously strive to improve and reach your full potential. This personal growth enhances your self-confidence and motivation.

>> **Adaptability:** A growth mindset enables you to adapt and thrive in a rapidly changing environment. It allows you to embrace uncertainty, navigate through challenges, and seize new opportunities. You're not afraid of change but embrace it as a chance to learn and grow.

Developing a growth mindset and embracing new challenges requires self-awareness, effort, and a commitment to continuous learning. It involves recognizing and challenging limiting beliefs, cultivating a positive attitude, and seeking out opportunities to stretch oneself. It also requires perseverance because facing new challenges can be uncomfortable and demanding.

By developing a growth mindset and actively seeking new challenges, you can unlock your potential, cultivate resilience, and achieve higher levels of personal and professional success. Embracing the unknown and stepping outside of your comfort zones, you can discover new passions, overcome obstacles, and make significant contributions in your chosen endeavors.

Identifying sources of learning and development opportunities

In the quest for continuous learning and development, it's crucial to identify diverse sources of opportunities that can enhance knowledge, skills, and expertise. By seeking out these sources, you can tap into a wealth of resources and experiences that contribute to your personal and professional growth. Here are some key sources to consider:

>> **Formal education:** Formal education institutions, such as universities, colleges, and vocational schools, offer a range of programs and courses that present structured learning experiences. These educational institutions lend access to specialized knowledge, certifications, and degrees that can deepen understanding and launch new opportunities.

>> **Professional training programs:** Many industries and organizations offer specialized training programs designed to enhance specific skills and knowledge relevant to a particular field. These programs may include workshops, seminars, conferences, and online courses. They supply targeted learning opportunities and the chance to network with industry professionals.

>> **Professional associations and industry events:** Professional associations and industry events can offer valuable learning and networking opportunities. These associations often organize conferences, webinars, and workshops where you can gain insights from industry leaders, participate in discussions, and stay updated on the latest trends and practices.

>> **Mentoring and coaching:** Engaging with mentors and coaches who have expertise in your field can be an invaluable source of learning and development. They can guide you, offer feedback, and share their experiences to help you navigate challenges and accelerate your growth. You can find mentoring programs and coaching services through professional organizations, networking connections, and specialized mentorship platforms.

>> **Online learning platforms:** The internet has revolutionized the availability of learning resources. Online platforms like Coursera, Udemy, LinkedIn Learning, and Khan Academy offer an array of courses and tutorials across various subjects. These platforms bring flexibility, allowing you to learn at your own pace and explore topics of interest conveniently.

>> **Books, blogs, and podcasts:** The written word and audio platforms offer a wealth of knowledge and inspiration. Books, blogs, and podcasts cover a wide range of topics, including personal development, industry insights, leadership, and specialized skills. By actively seeking out recommended readings and subscribing to relevant blogs and podcasts, you can access valuable information and gain fresh perspectives.

>> **Job rotations and cross-functional projects:** Within the workplace, opportunities for learning and development can arise through job rotations, cross-functional projects, and stretch assignments. These experiences provide exposure to different areas of the organization, broaden skill sets, and foster a deeper understanding of the business as a whole.

>> **Self-directed learning:** Taking initiative for self-directed learning involves proactively seeking out information and resources to expand your knowledge and skills. It includes conducting research, exploring online communities and forums, and engaging in self-study. By setting learning goals and leveraging available resources, you can pursue learning opportunities tailored to your interests and needs.

Setting learning goals and developing a learning plan

Setting learning goals and developing a learning plan are essential for focused and effective continuous learning. They help you identify areas of improvement, prioritize your learning objectives, and chart a clear path toward acquiring new knowledge and skills. Here are some key considerations when setting learning goals and developing a learning plan:

» **Assess your current skills and knowledge:** Begin by assessing your current skills and knowledge in your field of interest. Reflect on your strengths and weaknesses, and identify areas where you would like to expand your expertise. This self-assessment serves as a starting point for setting meaningful and achievable learning goals.

» **Employ SMART learning goals:** Set SMART (specific, measurable, achievable, relevant, and time-bound) learning goals. Specific goals help you pinpoint what you want to achieve, measurable goals allow you to track your progress, achievable goals ensure they're within reach, relevant goals align with your overall objectives, and time-bound goals establish a timeline for completion.

» **Prioritize learning objectives:** Determine the most important learning objectives based on their relevance to your current situation and long-term aspirations. Prioritizing your goals helps you focus your efforts and allocate resources effectively. Consider both the immediate needs of your field and your personal growth ambitions.

» **Break goals into actionable steps:** Break down your learning goals into smaller, actionable steps. This approach makes them more manageable and allows you to track progress more effectively. Each step should have a clear outcome and contribute to the overall achievement of your learning goals.

» **Create a learning plan:** Develop a structured learning plan that outlines the resources, activities, and timeline for achieving your learning goals. Consider various learning modalities such as online courses, workshops, books, mentorship, or hands-on experiences. Incorporate a mix of theoretical knowledge and practical application to deepen your understanding.

» **Allocate time and resources:** Dedicate specific time slots for your learning activities into your schedule. Treat your learning plan as a priority and allocate the necessary resources, such as budget for courses or materials, access to relevant tools or software, and a supportive learning environment.

» **Track progress and adjust as needed:** Regularly assess your progress toward your learning goals. Keep track of milestones, reflect on your achievements, and identify areas where you may need to adjust your approach. Flexibility and adaptability are key as you navigate the learning journey.

>> **Seek feedback and evaluation:** Seek feedback from mentors, peers, or instructors to gain insights into your learning progress. Engage in self-evaluation to assess your own growth and identify areas for improvement. Adjust your learning plan based on the feedback received to maximize your learning outcomes.

>> **Celebrate milestones:** Celebrate your achievements and milestones along the way. Recognize the progress you've made and the effort you've put into your learning journey. This motivates you and reinforces the value of continuous learning.

By setting learning goals and developing a well-structured learning plan, you can direct your efforts and make the most of your continuous learning journey. You can focus on acquiring the specific knowledge and skills that align with your interests, aspirations, and professional growth. Remember to regularly review and update your learning plan as you evolve in your field and embrace new opportunities for growth. See Figure 10-1.

Perform a Self-Assessment:

Reflect on your current skills and knowledge in your field of interest.

Identify your strengths and weaknesses.

Consider areas where you want to expand your expertise.

Set SMART Learning Goals:

Set specific, measurable, achievable, relevant, and time-bound learning goals.

Write down your learning goals based on your self-assessment.

Prioritize Learning Objectives:

Determine the most important learning objectives that align with your goals and aspirations.

Rank them in order of priority.

Break Goals into Actionable Steps:

Break down each learning goal into smaller, actionable steps.

Write down the steps required to achieve each learning goal.

FIGURE 10-1:
Setting learning goals.

Create a Learning Plan:

Develop a structured learning plan that includes resources, activities, and a timeline.

Specify the learning modalities you want to utilize, such as online courses, workshops, books, or a mentorship.

Allocate time slots in your schedule for learning activities.

Allocate Time and Resources:

Determine the necessary time and resources to achieve your learning goals.

Allocate a budget for courses or materials, if needed.

Identify any tools or software required for your learning.

Track Progress and Adjust:

Regularly assess your progress toward each learning goal.

Track milestones and accomplishments.

Reflect on your achievements and areas where you may need adjustments.

Seek Feedback and Evaluation:

Seek feedback from mentors, peers, or instructors on your learning progress.

Engage in self-evaluation and reflect on your growth.

Consider feedback received to refine your learning plan.

Celebrate Milestones:

Acknowledge and celebrate your achievements and milestones.

Take a moment to appreciate your progress and efforts.

FIGURE 10-1:
Continued

Building habits and routines that support continuous learning and development

Continuous learning and development require more than just sporadic efforts. They require the establishment of habits and routines that foster a lifelong commitment to growth. By intentionally building habits and incorporating them into your daily life, you can create a supportive environment for continuous learning and development. Here are some key insights on building such habits:

>> **Acknowledge that consistency is key:** Consistency is vital in forming habits. Set aside dedicated time each day or week for learning activities. Treat it as a non-negotiable commitment to yourself and prioritize it in your schedule.

>> **Create a conducive learning environment:** Designate a space where you can focus and immerse yourself in learning. Keep it organized, free from distractions, and filled with the necessary resources. This environment should inspire and motivate you to engage in continuous learning.

>> **Start small and build momentum:** Begin with manageable learning goals and gradually increase the complexity or intensity over time. Starting small helps to build confidence and ensures a higher chance of success. As you achieve smaller milestones, you gain momentum and are more motivated to tackle more significant challenges.

>> **Incorporate learning into daily routines:** Integrate learning into your daily routines and activities. For example, listen to educational podcasts or audio-books during your commute, read industry articles during breaks, or dedicate a portion of your evenings to online courses. By making learning a part of your everyday life, you'll maximize your exposure to new knowledge and skills.

>> **Use technology to your advantage:** Leverage technology tools and platforms that facilitate continuous learning. Online courses, webinars, podcasts, and educational apps offer convenient and accessible ways to expand your knowledge. Utilize tools for note-taking, organizing resources, and tracking your progress.

>> **Seek accountability and support:** Share your learning goals with others who can hold you accountable and support you. This can be a mentor, colleague, or a learning community. Engage in discussions, ask questions, and share your insights with others to enhance the learning experience.

>> **Reflect and review:** Regularly reflect on your learning journey. Take time to review your progress, evaluate the effectiveness of your learning strategies, and make adjustments as needed. Reflection enables you to identify areas for improvement, celebrate your achievements, and refine your approach to continuous learning.

>> **Embrace a growth mindset:** Adopt a growth mindset that embraces challenges, sees failures as learning opportunities, and believes in the potential for growth and development. Embracing a growth mindset fuels your motivation and resilience in the face of obstacles.

Building habits takes time and effort. Be patient with yourself and stay committed to your learning goals. With consistent practice, these habits become ingrained, and continuous learning and development become a natural part of your life.

Mastering Your Craft and Becoming an Expert

Mastering your craft is a lifelong endeavor that requires dedication, passion, and a thirst for continuous learning. It's the conscious choice to push beyond the boundaries of familiarity and comfort and to embrace challenges and setbacks as opportunities for growth. By committing to this pursuit, you not only elevate your own abilities but contribute to the advancement of your field and inspire others along the way.

Identifying your niche and developing specialized knowledge and skills

Identifying your niche requires introspection, research, and a deep understanding of your passions and interests. It involves recognizing the unique combination of skills, experiences, and perspectives that set you apart. By homing in on a specific area, you position yourself as a go-to authority, creating a unique value proposition that attracts opportunities and builds your reputation.

Once you've identified your niche, the journey toward expertise begins. It involves a commitment to continuous learning and development, constantly seeking new knowledge, and refining your skills. Specialized knowledge is a powerful asset that allows you to provide unique insights, solve complex problems, and innovate within your niche.

Developing specialized knowledge and skills requires a multifaceted approach. It involves staying updated with the latest trends, research, and advancements in your field. This can include reading scholarly articles, attending conferences and workshops, engaging in industry-specific forums, and participating in online courses. Mentors, experts, and thought leaders in your niche can guide you in ways that accelerate your learning.

Hands-on experience is another critical component of developing specialized expertise. Actively applying your knowledge and skills in real-world scenarios allows you to refine your abilities and gain a deeper understanding of the nuances within your niche. This can involve taking on challenging projects, volunteering for relevant opportunities, or even starting your own initiatives within your specialized area.

Networking within your niche is crucial. Connecting with like-minded individuals, professionals, and experts in your field opens doors to collaboration, mentorship, and opportunities for growth. Engage in industry events, join professional associations or groups, and actively participate in conversations and knowledge-sharing platforms to expand your network and exchange insights with others.

Lastly, don't underestimate the power of perseverance and dedication. Becoming an expert in your niche takes time and effort. Embrace the inevitable challenges and setbacks as opportunities for growth and learning. Stay committed to continuous improvement, remain curious, and be open to feedback and constructive criticism. The journey toward expertise is a lifelong pursuit, and by continually pushing the boundaries of your knowledge and skills, you can reach new heights of mastery within your chosen niche.

Practicing deliberately

Practicing deliberately and setting high standards for yourself are key elements in the pursuit of mastery and becoming an expert in your chosen field. Although talent and natural abilities play a role, deliberate practice and a commitment to excellence truly separate outstanding performers from the rest.

Deliberate practice involves a focused and intentional approach to improving your skills. It goes beyond simply repeating tasks or going through the motions. Instead, it requires structured and purposeful practice that targets specific areas for improvement. Deliberate practice involves breaking down complex skills into manageable components, identifying weaknesses, and working systematically to address them.

One crucial aspect of deliberate practice is setting high standards for yourself. By establishing ambitious benchmarks, you challenge yourself to continually strive for improvement and excellence. Setting high standards pushes you beyond your comfort zone and stretches your capabilities. It fuels a mindset of continuous growth and a relentless pursuit of mastery.

To practice deliberately and set high standards, it's essential to define clear goals and objectives. These goals should be specific, measurable, and aligned with your vision of expertise. By setting specific targets, you create a roadmap for your development and provide a framework for evaluating your progress.

Building a portfolio to showcase your expertise

Building a portfolio to showcase your expertise is a crucial step in establishing yourself as an expert in your field. In today's competitive landscape, having tangible evidence of your skills, accomplishments, and expertise can significantly enhance your professional credibility and lead to new opportunities.

A portfolio serves as a comprehensive collection of your best work, demonstrating your capabilities and showcasing your accomplishments. It's tangible evidence of your expertise, allowing others to assess the quality and depth of your skills. Whether you're a designer, writer, programmer, or any other professional, a well-crafted portfolio can leave a lasting impression on potential clients, employers, and collaborators.

To build an effective portfolio, start by carefully curating your work. Select projects, assignments, or examples that best represent your capabilities and demonstrate your expertise in action. Choose a diverse range of work that highlights different aspects of your skill set and your versatility.

When organizing your portfolio, consider presenting your work in a visually appealing and accessible manner. Use a consistent format and structure that allows viewers to navigate through your portfolio easily. Provide clear and concise descriptions for each project, outlining the objectives, your role, and the outcomes achieved. Including testimonials or feedback from clients or collaborators can further strengthen your portfolio's credibility.

In addition to showcasing completed projects, consider including works in progress or personal passion projects that demonstrate your commitment to continuous learning and improvement. This shows that you're actively engaged in honing your craft and staying at the forefront of industry trends.

Leverage digital platforms and technology to create an online portfolio that can be easily shared and accessed. Build a professional website or utilize portfolio platforms that allow you to showcase your work in a visually appealing and interactive manner. Optimize your online presence by utilizing search engine optimization (SEO) techniques to increase visibility and attract potential opportunities.

Networking is also a powerful tool for showcasing your expertise. Attend industry conferences, events, or meetups to connect with professionals in your field. Be proactive in sharing your portfolio with relevant individuals or organizations. Actively engage in online communities, forums, or social media groups to establish your presence and share your work with a wider audience.

Continuous updating and refinement of your portfolio is essential to keep it relevant and reflective of your current skills and achievements. As you complete new projects or acquire new skills, ensure that your portfolio accurately represents your latest capabilities. Regularly review and update the content, removing outdated work and adding new and more impactful examples.

REMEMBER

Building a portfolio is an ongoing process. It requires a commitment to continuous learning, professional growth, and showcasing your best work. Regularly seek feedback and evaluate the effectiveness of your portfolio. Strive for a balance between showcasing your expertise and demonstrating your potential for future growth and development.

Chapter 11

Harnessing the Power of Personal Branding

I n today's interconnected and competitive world, establishing a personal brand has become a pivotal aspect of finding success and fulfillment in both personal and professional endeavors. Your personal brand is the unique combination of your skills, experiences, values, and passions that sets you apart from others and shapes how you're perceived by the world. Just as companies carefully craft their brand identities, individuals can strategically shape their personal brands to create a lasting and positive impression on others.

This chapter explores the art of developing a compelling personal brand that aligns with your passions, values, and goals. It delves into the significance of authenticity and self-awareness in crafting a brand that genuinely reflects who you are and what you stand for. Moreover, it explores the ways in which a well-defined personal brand can elevate your visibility, credibility, and influence in the areas that matter most to you.

Why Personal Branding Is Important

Your personal brand reflects who you are, what you stand for, and what unique value you bring to the table. It's the impression that others have of you based on your actions, expertise, and manner of presenting yourself to the world. Developing a strong and authentic personal brand isn't just about self-promotion; rather, it's a powerful tool that can help you align your passions with your personal and professional goals.

Personal branding is a powerful tool that can play a transformative role in finding and pursuing your passion. By understanding the importance of aligning your brand with your true self, purpose, and values, you can create a path that leads you to a more fulfilling and purpose-driven life. Embrace the process of building your personal brand, and let it serve as a guiding light on your journey toward passion and fulfillment.

Establishing your personal brand

Personal branding starts with deep self-awareness. Understanding your passions, values, and strengths is essential in shaping a brand that's genuine and aligned with your true self. When you know what drives you and what truly matters to you, you can create a brand that resonates with your core identity.

A well-defined personal brand offers clarity in your purpose and direction. It helps you articulate your vision and goals, making it easier to identify the areas and opportunities that align with your passions. By understanding your purpose, you can focus your efforts on activities that bring fulfillment and avoid distractions that lead you away from your passions.

By showcasing your unique skills, experiences, and perspectives, you differentiate yourself and create a memorable impression on others. This differentiation becomes particularly important when pursuing opportunities that align with your passion.

A strong personal brand can enhance your credibility and build trust with others. When your brand reflects your expertise and values, people are more likely to trust your abilities and recommendations. This credibility is essential when seeking support, collaborations, or partnerships in your passion-driven endeavors.

Personal branding gives you the platform and freedom to express yourself authentically. It allows you to share your passion and enthusiasm with the world, inspiring others and creating a positive impact. Embracing your personal brand empowers you to be unapologetically yourself and pursue your passions with conviction.

Your personal brand isn't static; it evolves as you grow and develop. Through the process of building and refining your brand, you gain insights about yourself, your passions, and your goals. This continuous self-improvement journey contributes to your personal and professional growth.

Defining your values, strengths, and unique selling point

To successfully find and pursue your passion, you need a clear understanding of your values, strengths, and unique selling point (USP). These aspects form the foundation of your personal brand and play a pivotal role in shaping your journey toward fulfillment and success.

Values are the fundamental principles that guide your decisions and actions. They represent what's truly important to you and serve as a compass in both your personal and your professional life. Defining your core values requires introspection and self-awareness. Consider the qualities and beliefs that most resonate with you. These values will become the pillars of your personal brand and should align with the activities and causes that ignite your passion.

Your strengths are the unique talents, skills, and qualities that set you apart from others. Identifying your strengths involves acknowledging your natural abilities and areas where you excel. Reflect on the tasks or activities that energize you and bring out the best in you. Embracing your strengths boosts your confidence and enables you to contribute in ways that align with your passion.

Your USP is what makes you stand out in a crowded marketplace. It's your perspective, values, strengths, and experiences that makes you uniquely valuable to others. Your USP distinguishes you from others who may have similar skills or qualifications. Consider the specific qualities or aspects that make you different and how you can leverage them to make a significant impact in areas related to your passion.

The alignment of your values, strengths, and USP is crucial to finding your true calling. When these elements are in sync, you create a cohesive and authentic personal brand. Your brand should reflect the essence of who you are and what you bring to the table. The alignment provides a clear direction for your passion-driven endeavors and helps you make decisions that are in harmony with your core identity.

Defining your values, strengths, and USP isn't about conforming to external expectations or trying to fit into a predefined mold. It's about embracing your authenticity and expressing yourself genuinely. Your unique blend of qualities makes you compelling and relatable to others. Embrace your individuality, and let it shine through in your personal and professional pursuits.

Personal branding is an ongoing process. As you gain more clarity about your passions and goals, you may need to refine and evolve your brand to better align with your aspirations. Be open to self-discovery, and adapt your brand as you grow and learn.

Defining your values

Defining your values, strengths, and USP is essential in finding and pursuing your passion. It provides you with a solid foundation for building an authentic personal brand that reflects your true self and resonates with others. Embrace the process of self-discovery, and use it as a compass to navigate your journey toward passion, purpose, and fulfillment.

This is a crucial step in understanding yourself and aligning your actions with what truly matters to you. Values are the guiding principles that influence your decisions, behaviors, and interactions with others. They act as a moral compass, helping you make choices that are in line with your core beliefs and contribute to a fulfilling life.

Defining your values is an ongoing process of self-discovery and self-awareness. Embrace the journey with openness and curiosity, and let your values shape a purpose-driven life that brings you joy, fulfillment, and meaningful connections with others.

Start by reflecting on significant moments and experiences in your life. Consider times when you felt most fulfilled, proud, or satisfied. Identify the underlying factors that contributed to those positive feelings. For example, if you felt a sense of fulfillment when helping others, empathy and compassion might be important values for you.

Take a close look at how you allocate your time and energy. What activities and relationships are most important to you? Your priorities often reveal what you value most. If spending quality time with family is a top priority, it indicates the value you place on connection and relationships.

Consider the beliefs that guide your thoughts and actions. Your beliefs shape your worldview and influence your decision-making process. For instance, if you believe in the importance of environmental sustainability, you have a value for environmental consciousness.

Pay attention to your emotional responses to different situations and events. Emotions are powerful indicators of what matters to you deeply. If you feel a strong emotional reaction to social justice issues, you likely value fairness and equality.

Think about people you admire and respect, as well as those you don't. Identify the qualities and behaviors that attract or repel you. The positive traits you admire in others often align with your values, while the negative ones may conflict with your values.

Reflect on the impact you want to have on the world and the people around you. What kind of legacy do you want to leave behind? Values often revolve around making a positive difference in the lives of others.

Defining your strengths

Defining your strengths is a crucial step in understanding your abilities and potential for success in various areas of life. Your strengths are the natural talents and skills that come easily to you and energize you when you use them. Identifying your strengths allows you to leverage them to your advantage and pursue opportunities that align with your innate abilities.

This is an ongoing process, and it's okay to revisit this worksheet periodically as you gain more self-awareness and insight into your unique abilities. Celebrate your strengths, and use them as a guiding force on your journey to finding and pursuing your passion.

REMEMBER

Defining your strengths isn't about comparing yourself to others; it's about understanding your unique qualities and using them to lead a fulfilling life. Embrace your strengths, using them as a foundation to pursue your passions and achieve your goals.

Take time to reflect on your experiences, both past and present. Consider moments when you felt most confident, accomplished, and fulfilled. What were the activities or tasks involved in these experiences? What specific skills or qualities did you use to excel in those situations?

Sometimes you're not fully aware of our own strengths, and feedback from others can be insightful. Ask your friends, family, colleagues, or mentors about the strengths they see in you. This external perspective can give you valuable insights that you might not have recognized on your own.

Several online assessments and questionnaires can help you identify your strengths. These assessments are designed to measure your preferences, skills, and natural inclinations. Examples of such assessments include the Clifton-Strengths assessment, VIA Character Strengths, and StrengthsFinder.

Review past achievements and successes in various areas of your life. What skills or attributes contributed to your accomplishments? What actions did you take to achieve those goals? Analyzing your achievements can reveal patterns that indicate your strengths.

Defining your USP

USP is a marketing concept used to differentiate a product, service, or brand from its competitors in the marketplace. It's the distinctive feature or benefit that sets a business apart and makes it stand out in the eyes of consumers.

The USP answers the question, "Why should customers choose your product or service over others?" It highlights what makes the offering special, unique, or superior, creating a compelling reason for customers to choose it.

A well-crafted USP should be clear, concise, and easy for customers to understand. It should focus on addressing a specific customer need or pain point and emphasize the value that the product or service provides. The USP is often used in advertising and marketing materials to attract and engage potential customers.

Here's an example of a USP for a smartphone brand: "Our smartphones feature cutting-edge technology and long-lasting battery life, ensuring you stay connected and productive on the go."

In this example, the USP highlights the brand's focus on technology and battery life, which addresses a common consumer concern with smartphones.

Defining your USP involves identifying and articulating the key attributes that differentiate your product, service, or personal brand from others in the market. It's a critical step in creating a compelling and memorable message that sets you apart and resonates with your target audience. Here's a step-by-step guide to defining your USP:

1. **Identify your target audience:** Understand who your ideal customers or audience are. What are their needs, pain points, and preferences? Knowing your target audience is crucial for tailoring your USP to appeal directly to them.

2. **Research your competitors:** Analyze your competition to see how they position themselves in the market. What are their strengths and weaknesses? This research will help you identify opportunities for differentiation.

3. **List your unique features and benefits:** Make a list of the unique features, qualities, or benefits that your product, service, or personal brand offers. These could be specific features, superior quality, outstanding customer service, or a special approach to solving a problem.

4. **Identify the most compelling benefit:** From your list, identify the benefit that's most relevant and appealing to your target audience. This benefit should address a specific need or desire of your customers and set you apart from the competition.

5. **Make your USP clear and concise:** Craft a clear and concise statement that communicates your USP. Your USP should be easily understandable and memorable. Avoid jargon or technical language that might confuse your audience.

6. **Emphasize value:** Explain how your unique feature or benefit adds value to your customers' lives or addresses their pain points. Demonstrating the value of your USP will help customers see why they should choose your offering.

7. **Test and refine:** Once you've defined your USP, test it with your target audience to gather feedback. Use this feedback to refine and fine-tune your message until it resonates with your customers.

Be authentic and honest when crafting your USP and ensure that it aligns with your values and the promises you can deliver to your customers or audience.

Crafting a Personal Brand Statement and Elevator Pitch

A personal brand statement is a concise and compelling statement that communicates your unique value, strengths, and passions to your target audience. It's a strategic tool that helps you differentiate yourself from others and build a strong personal brand. Your personal brand statement is essentially a summary of who you are, what you stand for, and what you bring to the table.

This statement is often used in professional settings, such as networking events, job interviews, and social media profiles, to introduce yourself and leave a lasting impression on others. Your brand statement should be clear, authentic, and memorable, allowing people to understand your strengths and what you can offer in a matter of seconds.

Crafting your personal brand statement

A well-crafted personal brand statement is essential in today's competitive job market and business landscape. It helps you stand out, make a positive impact, and attract opportunities that align with your passions and career aspirations. By defining and refining your personal brand statement, you can confidently showcase your unique value point and build meaningful connections with your target audience.

Crafting a powerful personal brand statement takes time and self-reflection, but it's a valuable tool for presenting yourself with confidence and clarity. Use it in networking events, interviews, and when introducing yourself to others to leave a lasting impression that aligns with your passion and career goals.

Here are the steps for crafting your own personal brand statement.

1. **Define your unique selling point:** Start by identifying your key strengths, skills, experiences, and attributes that make you stand out from others. Consider what sets you apart and what you bring to the table in your personal and professional life. Your unique selling point is the foundation of your personal brand statement.

   Example: "I'm a creative problem solver with a passion for innovation. My ability to think outside the box and my keen eye for detail enable me to deliver unique and effective solutions that drive results for my clients."

2. **Understand your target audience:** Consider who you want to communicate with through your personal brand statement. Are you targeting potential employers, clients, or collaborators? Tailor your messaging to address their needs and interests.

   Example: "As a marketing professional, I'm dedicated to helping businesses reach their full potential. My expertise in digital marketing and my strategic approach resonate with businesses seeking to expand their online presence and customer base."

3. **Craft a clear and concise statement:** Your personal brand statement should be concise, straightforward, and easy to understand. Avoid using jargon or complex language that might confuse your audience. Aim to communicate your value in a few sentences.

   Example: "I'm a results-driven marketing specialist with a proven track record in driving brand awareness and engagement through strategic digital campaigns."

4. **Showcase your achievements:** Highlight key accomplishments and experiences that demonstrate your unique selling point. Share specific examples of how your skills and strengths have contributed to successful projects or outcomes.

Example: "During my tenure at Company XYZ, I led a team in developing and executing a social media campaign that generated a 40% increase in brand engagement and a 15% rise in website traffic."

5. **Emphasize your passion and core values:** Incorporate your passion and core values into your personal brand statement. Doing so helps others understand what drives you and what you care deeply about.

   Example: "I'm deeply passionate about creating meaningful connections between brands and their audiences. I believe in the power of storytelling and empathy to foster genuine relationships."

6. **Be authentic and memorable:** Make sure your personal brand statement reflects your authentic self. Avoid using generic statements that could apply to anyone. Make your statement memorable and uniquely yours.

   Example: "As an environmental advocate and sustainability enthusiast, I'm committed to using my expertise in finance to support businesses in making environmentally responsible decisions that drive both profit and positive impact."

7. **Practice and revise:** Practice delivering your personal brand statement until it flows naturally and feels authentic. Seek feedback from colleagues or mentors to refine your messaging and ensure it makes a strong impression.

Coming up with your elevator pitch

An elevator pitch is a brief and compelling introduction that succinctly conveys who you are, what you do, and what value you bring to the listener. It's called an *elevator pitch* because it should be concise enough to deliver within the time it takes to ride an elevator, which is typically between 30 seconds and 1 minute.

The purpose of an elevator pitch is to capture the attention of the listener and leave a memorable impression. It's commonly used in networking events, job interviews, business meetings, and any situation where you have a short amount of time to introduce yourself and make a positive impact.

A well-crafted elevator pitch should be tailored to your audience and highlight your USP, which is what sets you apart from others in your field or industry. It should be clear, engaging, and delivered with confidence to make a lasting impression on the listener.

Here's how to create an impactful elevator pitch.

1. **Define your audience:** Consider who your audience will be. Are you crafting the pitch for a potential employer, a networking event, or a business meeting? Tailor your pitch to address their needs and interests.

2. **Introduce yourself:** Start by introducing yourself with your name and your current role or profession. Keep the introduction simple and clear.

   Example: "Hi. I'm Sarah Johnson, a digital marketing specialist with a passion for driving brand growth."

3. **State your USP:** Highlight your USP, which sets you apart from others in your field. Focus on what makes you special and valuable.

   Example: "I specialize in creating data-driven marketing strategies that have consistently resulted in a 30% increase in online sales for my clients."

4. **Communicate your value:** Explain the value you bring and how your skills can solve a problem or fulfill a need for your audience.

   Example: "My ability to analyze consumer behavior and trends allows me to design targeted campaigns that generate tangible ROI."

5. **Showcase your achievements:** Mention any notable achievements or accomplishments to add credibility and demonstrate your expertise.

   Example: "In the past year, I successfully launched a social media campaign that reached over a million impressions and boosted brand awareness by 40%."

6. **Be conversational:** Craft your pitch to sound natural and conversational. Avoid using jargon or technical terms that may confuse your audience.

   Example: "I've always been fascinated by the power of storytelling in marketing, and I love finding creative ways to connect brands with their audiences."

7. **Practice, practice, practice:** Rehearse your elevator pitch until it flows smoothly and sounds confident. Practice in front of a mirror or with friends, or record yourself to evaluate your delivery.

8. **Customize for different situations:** Adjust your elevator pitch depending on the context and audience. Tailor it to specific events, industries, or networking opportunities.

9. **End with a call to action:** Wrap up your elevator pitch with a call to action (CTA), inviting further conversation or expressing your interest in connecting.

   Example: "I would love to learn more about your company's marketing goals and explore how I can contribute to your success."

TIP

Be yourself and let your passion and enthusiasm shine through. Authenticity leaves a lasting impression and builds genuine connections.

An elevator pitch isn't set in stone. Feel free to refine and adjust it as needed based on feedback and the outcomes of your interactions. A well-crafted elevator pitch can open doors and lead to exciting opportunities in your personal and professional journey.

REMEMBER

An elevator pitch should last no longer than 30 to 60 seconds. Keep it concise and impactful.

Creating a Strong Online Presence

In the digital age, having a strong online presence has become essential for individuals and businesses alike. The internet has transformed the way people connect, communicate, and engage with others, making it a powerful platform to showcase expertise, talents, and passions. Whether you're an aspiring entrepreneur, a creative professional, or someone looking to advance their career, establishing a compelling online presence can open doors to new opportunities, collaborations, and success.

Creating a strong online presence goes beyond merely having a social media account or a basic website. It involves strategically crafting your personal brand, curating your online image, and effectively communicating your value to your target audience. This chapter helps you explore the key components of building a powerful online presence and guides you through the steps to ensure you leave a lasting impression in the digital world.

From developing an authentic personal brand statement to leveraging various digital platforms, this chapter equips you with the knowledge and tools you need to establish yourself online and stand out in a crowded virtual landscape. Whether you're an entrepreneur, artist, professional, or simply looking to share your passions with the world, the principles shared here help you unlock the full potential of your online presence and build a strong foundation for your personal and professional growth. Let's embark on this journey together and discover how to make your mark in the vast digital universe.

Examining the art of online branding

The internet has become an integral part of everyday life. The digital landscape offers endless opportunities for personal and professional growth, which means establishing a strong online branding presence has never been more crucial. Online branding refers to the process of crafting a consistent and compelling image of yourself or your business in the virtual realm. It goes beyond having a website or social media profile; it involves curating an authentic and memorable identity that resonates with your target audience.

The significance of online branding lies in its ability to leave a lasting impression on those who come across your digital presence. With billions of internet users and countless websites, social media accounts, and online businesses, standing out from the crowd is a formidable challenge. A well-crafted online brand sets you apart, showcasing your unique strengths, skills, and passions in a way that captures the attention and interest of others.

A robust online brand not only helps you attract potential clients, customers, or employers but also enables you to build trust and credibility. When people encounter a consistent and professional online presence, they're more likely to perceive you as an expert in your field and feel confident in engaging with you. This increased trust can lead to new opportunities, collaborations, and a loyal following.

In the digital era, information spreads rapidly, and online reputation matters more than ever. With a strong online brand, you can take control of your narrative and shape the way others perceive you. By strategically managing your online presence, you can ensure that your key messages and values are communicated effectively, leaving no room for misconceptions or misinterpretations.

Furthermore, a well-established online brand can open doors to new horizons. It's a platform for networking and connecting with like-minded individuals, potential partners, and mentors. It can also showcase your work, allowing you to reach a global audience and gain recognition far beyond your local community.

Remember, the importance of online branding in today's digital world can't be overstated. It's a powerful tool that can elevate your personal or professional endeavors and pave the way for success in a highly competitive landscape. By investing time and effort into crafting an authentic and compelling online presence, you position yourself for growth, opportunity, and influence in the vast and ever-evolving virtual realm.

Crafting a compelling bio

Crafting a compelling bio is crucial for creating a strong online presence and leaving a lasting impression on your audience. Here's a step-by-step guide to help you write an engaging and impactful bio:

1. **Start with a hook:** Begin your bio with a captivating opening that grabs the reader's attention. This could be a thought-provoking question, an intriguing statement, or a memorable quote that reflects your personality or brand.

2. **Introduce yourself:** Provide a brief introduction that includes your name and a concise description of who you are and what you do. Keep it clear and straightforward.

3. **Highlight your achievements:** Share your key achievements, experiences, or credentials. Focus on the accomplishments most relevant to your audience and the purpose of your bio.

4. **Showcase your expertise:** Emphasize your expertise and highlight your USP. Explain what sets you apart and makes you the go-to person in your field.

5. **Share your passion and purpose:** Communicate your passion for what you do and the purpose behind your work. Connect with your audience on an emotional level by expressing why you're passionate about your field.

6. **Use a friendly tone:** Write your bio in a friendly and approachable tone. Avoid using jargon or technical language that may confuse your readers.

7. **Be concise:** Keep your bio short and to the point. Aim for a length of around 150 to 250 words, depending on the platform or purpose of your bio.

8. **Include relevant keywords:** Incorporate keywords related to your expertise and industry. This enhances your bio's visibility in search engines and helps your target audience find you.

9. **Add personal touches:** Share some personal details or hobbies that humanize you and make your bio more relatable. However, only include information that aligns with your brand and professional image.

10. **Use a CTA:** End your bio with a clear and compelling CTA, inviting readers to take the next step, such as visiting your website, subscribing to your newsletter, or connecting on social media.

11. **Edit and revise:** After writing your bio, review and edit it to ensure clarity, coherence, and grammar. Get feedback from friends, colleagues, or mentors to fine-tune your bio further.

12. **Tailor for different platforms:** Customize your bio for different platforms, considering the audience and character limitations. For instance, social media bios may be shorter than bios on a personal website.

Your bio is often the first impression you make on potential connections, clients, or employers. Craft a compelling and authentic bio that showcases your strengths and reflects your true personality and expertise.

Creating a professional social media profile

In the digital age, having a strong online presence is essential for building and promoting your personal brand. A well-designed website and engaging social media profiles can help you showcase your expertise, connect with your target audience, and expand your network. This section guides you through the process of creating a professional website and optimizing your social media profiles to strengthen your online brand.

- » **Use consistency across platforms:** Use the same profile photo and handle across all social media platforms. Maintain a consistent brand voice and messaging.

- » **Complete your profiles:** Fill out all relevant sections of your social media profiles. Provide a clear and concise bio that represents your expertise.

- » **Showcase your work:** Share samples of your work, projects, or achievements on social media. Use visuals and multimedia to make your content engaging.

- » **Engage with your audience:** Respond to comments, messages, and mentions promptly. Engage in conversations and discussions related to your field.

- » **Follow influencers and connect with peers:** Follow influencers and industry leaders to stay updated on trends and insights. Connect with peers and colleagues to expand your professional network.

- » **Utilize social media analytics:** Use social media analytics to track your engagement and reach. Analyze data to identify what content resonates most with your audience.

- » **Be mindful of your content:** Post thoughtfully and avoid controversial or unprofessional content. Remember that your social media presence contributes to your personal brand.

REMEMBER

Consistency and authenticity are key to building a strong online presence. By creating a professional website and optimizing your social media profiles, you can effectively showcase your expertise, connect with your audience, and enhance your personal brand's visibility in the digital world.

Developing a content strategy and engaging with your audience

Content strategy is a comprehensive plan that outlines how an individual or organization will create, publish, distribute, and manage content to achieve specific goals. It involves the thoughtful and strategic planning of content to ensure that it aligns with the brand's objectives and resonates with the target audience. Content strategy considers various aspects, such as content formats, topics, tone of voice, distribution channels, and publishing schedules, to deliver valuable and relevant content consistently.

A well-defined content strategy serves as a roadmap to guide content creators in producing high-quality, engaging, and valuable content that meets the needs of the audience. It also maintains brand consistency, enhances online visibility, builds trust and credibility, and ultimately drives desired actions from the audience, such as increased website traffic, lead generation, and conversions.

An effective content strategy takes into account the unique characteristics of the brand, the interests and preferences of the target audience, and the competitive landscape. It involves continuous analysis and optimization to ensure that the content remains relevant and resonates with the changing needs of the audience.

Content strategy is the foundation of a successful content marketing approach, ensuring that content efforts are purposeful, cohesive, and aligned with the overall goals of the brand or individual. It empowers content creators to deliver valuable content that establishes their expertise, builds brand authority, and strengthens their online presence.

Creating valuable and relevant content is a powerful way to establish yourself as an authority in your field, attract a loyal following, and build meaningful connections with your audience. An effective content strategy involves careful planning, consistent delivery, and active engagement with your followers. You can develop a content strategy and engage with your audience to strengthen your online brand by following these guidelines:

>> **Define your content goals:** Clarify your content objectives, whether it's to educate, inspire, entertain, or promote your services. Identify your target audience and understand their needs and preferences.

>> **Produce a variety of content formats and topics:** Diversify your content formats, including blog posts, videos, infographics, and podcasts. Choose topics that align with your expertise and resonate with your audience.

>> **Create a content calendar:** Create a content calendar to plan and organize your content publishing schedule. Consistency in posting establishes your online presence.

>> **Prioritize quality over quantity:** Prioritize quality over quantity when creating content. Ensure your content is well researched, valuable, and well presented.

>> **Write engaging headlines and introductions:** Craft compelling headlines and introductions to capture your audience's attention. Use storytelling or thought-provoking questions to draw readers in.

>> **Use visual appeal:** Use visually appealing graphics and images to enhance your content. Visuals can significantly improve engagement.

>> **Include a CTA:** Include a clear and actionable CTA at the end of your content. Encourage your audience to engage further, such as subscribing, sharing, or commenting.

>> **Strategize social media promotion:** Share your content across your social media platforms. Use hashtags and engage with your audience through comments and replies.

>> **Respond to comments and messages:** Engage with your audience by responding to comments and messages promptly. Encourage dialogue, and build relationships with your followers.

>> **Analyze performance:** Use analytics tools to measure the performance of your content. Analyze data to understand what content resonates most with your audience.

>> **Adapt and improve:** Continuously adapt your content strategy based on audience feedback and data. Seek ways to improve and refine your content to meet your audience's needs.

>> **Collaborate and network:** Collaborate with other influencers or brands to reach new audiences. Networking with peers and industry leaders can bring about new opportunities.

REMEMBER

Consistency and relevance are crucial in content creation. By developing a thoughtful content strategy and actively engaging with your audience, you can foster a strong and loyal community around your personal brand.

Knowing the Importance of Storytelling in Branding

Storytelling is an age-old human tradition, and throughout history, stories have played a fundamental role in shaping cultures, conveying values, and connecting people emotionally. In the realm of branding, storytelling serves as the heart and soul of a brand, providing it with a unique identity and making it stand out in a crowded marketplace.

Stories have an unparalleled ability to evoke emotions, spark curiosity, and create a lasting impact. When brands utilize storytelling effectively, they can inspire, motivate, and build meaningful relationships with their audience. Through storytelling, brands can showcase their values, beliefs, and purpose, creating an authentic and relatable image that resonates with consumers.

Understanding the power of storytelling in personal branding can help you create a unique narrative that aligns with your values, goals, and vision. By sharing your journey, your experiences, and the purpose behind your work, you can forge genuine connections with your audience and differentiate yourself in a competitive landscape.

Crafting your personal brand story requires introspection and a genuine willingness to share your authentic self. Identify the moments in your life that have shaped your values, beliefs, and passions. Reflect on your challenges and triumphs, and consider how they've contributed to your growth and expertise. Embrace vulnerability because it can be a powerful tool in building trust and relatability.

A compelling brand story is a powerful tool that can leave a lasting impression on your audience and create a strong emotional connection with them. Here are the key elements that contribute to crafting such a story.

» **Authenticity:** A compelling brand story is authentic and genuine. It reflects your true values, beliefs, and experiences. Being honest and transparent in your storytelling builds trust and credibility with your audience.

» **Emotion:** Emotions are at the core of a compelling brand story. Your story should evoke feelings of inspiration, empathy, or excitement in your audience. Emotionally resonating stories are more memorable and can lead to stronger connections.

» **Clarity:** Your brand story should be clear and concise. It should communicate who you are, what you stand for, and what makes you unique. Avoid unnecessary jargon or complexities that can confuse your audience.

» **Relevance:** A compelling brand story is relevant to your audience's needs and desires. It should address their pain points and aspirations, showing them how your brand can provide solutions or fulfill their desires.

» **Consistency:** Consistency is crucial in maintaining a strong brand identity. Your story should align with your actions and values across all touchpoints, from your website and social media to customer interactions.

» **Uniqueness:** Highlight what sets you apart from the competition. Showcase your unique strengths, experiences, or approach to solving problems. Being distinctive helps your brand stand out in a crowded market.

» **Visuals:** Visual elements, such as images and videos, can enhance your brand story and make it more engaging. Use visuals that align with your brand's tone and message to create a cohesive narrative.

» **Heroes and journey:** Every compelling brand story has a hero — the brand or the customer. Narrate the journey of how your brand or customers overcome challenges and achieve success. This makes your story more relatable and inspiring.

» **Impact:** Showcase the positive impact your brand has on people's lives or the community. Demonstrating the value you bring to others can strengthen your brand's reputation and foster loyalty.

>> **Evolution:** Your brand story shouldn't be static; rather, it should reflect growth and evolution over time. Share how your brand has evolved and adapted to meet changing needs and challenges.

>> **CTA:** A compelling brand story should have a clear CTA. Whether it's encouraging people to visit your website, sign up for a newsletter, or take part in a social cause, guide your audience toward the next step.

>> **Authenticity:** People connect with authentic stories. Be true to yourself and your brand, and avoid exaggerations or false claims. Let your story reflect who you genuinely are.

A compelling brand story is more than just a marketing tactic; it's a way to express your brand's essence and purpose. Invest time in crafting a story that truly represents your brand and resonates with your target audience.

Developing your personal story and message

Developing your personal story and message is a crucial aspect of building a strong personal brand. Your story is the foundation of your brand, creating an emotional connection with your audience. Here's how you can develop a compelling personal story and message:

1. **Self-reflect:** Begin by reflecting on your life journey, experiences, and key turning points that have shaped who you are today. Consider the challenges you've faced, the lessons you've learned, and the values that guide you.

2. **Identify core themes:** Look for common themes in your life story that align with your passion, values, and interests. These themes serve as the backbone of your personal brand message.

3. **Know your audience:** Understand the audience you want to connect with. Identify their needs, aspirations, and pain points. Tailor your story and message to resonate with them and address their specific concerns.

4. **Craft a compelling story:** Craft your personal story in a way that engages your audience emotionally. Use descriptive language, vivid details, and authentic anecdotes to bring your journey to life.

5. **Highlight your USP:** Your USP sets you apart from others. Identify the unique qualities, skills, or experiences that make you stand out. Emphasize how your USP aligns with your audience's needs.

6. **Be vulnerable and genuine:** Share your successes and failures with honesty and vulnerability. People connect with authenticity, and sharing your challenges and how you've overcome them can inspire others.

7. **Keep it concise:** Although your personal story should be meaningful, it's essential to keep it concise and focused. Avoid overwhelming your audience with unnecessary details.

8. **Align with your brand values:** Ensure that your personal story and message align with the values and mission of your personal brand. Consistency in messaging builds trust and credibility.

9. **Practice your delivery:** Rehearse telling your story in a confident and engaging manner. Practice in front of a mirror or with friends, or record yourself to refine your delivery.

10. **Adapt to your platform:** Tailor your personal story and message to suit different platforms. Whether it's a bio on your website, a social media post, or a networking event, adapt your story to fit the context.

11. **Inspire action:** End your personal story with a call to action. Encourage your audience to engage with you, follow your journey, or take a specific step toward your shared goals.

12. **Evolve and adapt:** Your personal story isn't set in stone. As you grow and evolve, your story may evolve too. Be open to adapting it as needed while staying true to your brand's essence.

3
Setting Yourself Up for Success

Develop a mindset for growth.

Practice time management and priority setting.

Rise above fear and risk aversion.

Secure yourself with a support system.

Chapter **12**

Understanding the Growth Mindset

In the pursuit of passion and personal growth, one of the most influential concepts that can shape your journey is the *growth mindset*. Coined by psychologist Carol Dweck, the growth mindset is a belief system that fundamentally influences how you approach challenges, setbacks, and opportunities for development. Embracing a growth mindset can have a transformative impact on how you navigate your passions, goals, and aspirations.

At its core, the growth mindset revolves around the belief that your abilities, talents, and intelligence aren't fixed traits but rather qualities that you can develop and improve over time. This contrasts with a *fixed mindset*, whereby you believe that your qualities are innate and unchangeable, leading to a fear of failure and resistance to taking on new challenges.

This section covers the concept of the growth mindset and explores its significance in pursuing passion and personal development. It examines the core principles of the growth mindset so that you can understand how it influences your behavior and choices and discover practical strategies to foster a growth mindset in your daily life. By embracing a growth mindset, you can unlock your full potential, embrace learning opportunities, and embark on a journey of continuous growth in your pursuit of passion and purpose.

Defining the "Growth Mindset"

The growth mindset is a powerful belief system that shapes your approach to challenges, learning, and personal development. Coined by psychologist Carol Dweck, this concept centers on the belief that you can cultivate and improve your abilities and intelligence over time through dedication, effort, and learning. In essence, having a growth mindset means understanding that your potential isn't fixed; you believe you can develop your skills and talents through perseverance and hard work.

Unlike a fixed mindset, which assumes that qualities are innate and unchangeable, a growth mindset encourages a more optimistic and proactive approach to life. With a growth mindset, you embrace challenges as opportunities for growth, view failures as part of the path to success, and actively seek out learning experiences to expand your knowledge and skills.

In the context of pursuing passion and personal development, the growth mindset is an essential tool. It encourages you to step out of your comfort zone, take on new challenges, and continuously improve yourself. By recognizing that your abilities can be developed, you're more willing to put in the effort required to achieve your goals and overcome obstacles along the way.

Ultimately, adopting a growth mindset empowers you to become a lifelong learner, navigate your passions with resilience, and reach new heights of personal and professional fulfillment. It's a mindset that can lead to remarkable achievements and a greater sense of purpose in your life.

Identifying the growth mindset characteristics

The growth mindset plays a pivotal role in finding and pursuing your passion. It's characterized by certain attitudes and beliefs that influence how you approach challenges, setbacks, and learning opportunities. You embrace the idea that you can develop your abilities and intelligence through effort, dedication, and learning from experiences. Table 12-1 shows some key characteristics of a growth mindset.

TABLE 12-1   Key Characteristics of a Growth Mindset

Characteristic	Explanation
Embracing challenges	You see challenges as opportunities for growth and learning. Instead of avoiding difficult tasks, you willingly take them on, knowing that effort and persistence can lead to improvement.
Persistence and effort	You understand that achieving mastery or success often requires sustained effort and hard work. You're willing to put in the time and energy you need to achieve your goals.
Viewing failure as learning	Instead of fearing failure, you view it as an essential part of the learning process. You see setbacks as opportunities to learn, adapt, and improve.
Openness to feedback	You're open to receiving feedback from others because you see it as valuable input for your growth and development. You use feedback to identify areas of improvement and make positive changes.
Inspiration from others' success	Rather than feeling threatened by others' accomplishments, you feel inspired and motivated by them. You see others' success as evidence that growth and improvement are achievable through effort and learning.
Desire for continuous learning	You have a strong desire for continuous learning and personal development. You seek out new knowledge and skills to expand your abilities and understanding.
Resilience	When faced with obstacles or setbacks, you bounce back quickly. You maintain your enthusiasm and determination to overcome challenges and reach your goals.
Seeing effort as the path to mastery	You believe that mastery comes through continuous effort and practice. You recognize that even the most accomplished individuals had to work hard to achieve their level of expertise.
Redefining "failure"	Instead of seeing failure as a reflection of your worth or abilities, you view it as a temporary setback or a steppingstone to future success.
Belief in development	You believe that personal development and improvement are possible for anyone. This conviction empowers you to take on new challenges and push beyond your comfort zone.

Developing a growth mindset is an ongoing process that requires self-awareness and intentional effort. It's an ongoing journey. Even small changes in your beliefs and attitudes can have a significant impact on your personal and professional growth.

By cultivating these characteristics, you can create a mindset that fosters resilience, adaptability, and continuous learning, which are essential qualities for finding passion and achieving success in all aspects of life.

GROWTH MINDSET SELF-CHECKLIST

The following checklist is designed to help you assess the presence of growth mindset characteristics in your beliefs and attitudes. Use it as a tool for self-reflection and as a starting point for cultivating a growth mindset in various areas of your life. Read each statement and mark the box that best represents your level of agreement.

❑ I view challenges as opportunities for growth and learning.

❑ I believe that I can develop my abilities through effort and dedication.

❑ I embrace failure as a valuable learning experience.

❑ I seek out feedback from others to improve and grow.

❑ I'm inspired by the success of others and see it as a source of motivation.

❑ I'm open to trying new things and taking on challenges outside my comfort zone.

❑ I see effort as a path to mastery and success.

❑ I believe that my intelligence and abilities can improve with practice.

❑ I view setbacks as temporary and believe that I can overcome them with effort.

❑ I enjoy learning and seek out new knowledge and skills.

❑ I'm resilient and bounce back quickly from setbacks.

❑ I see mistakes as opportunities to learn and grow.

❑ I believe that my potential isn't fixed and can be developed over time.

❑ I'm not afraid to ask for help and see it as a way to improve.

❑ I focus on the process and effort rather than just the outcome.

❑ I believe that I can improve in areas where I currently struggle.

❑ I'm not discouraged by criticism and use it to improve.

❑ I see challenges as a chance to discover new strategies and approaches.

Scoring: Add up the number of checked boxes to determine your score.

0–5: You may have more of a fixed mindset. Consider exploring ways to develop a growth mindset.

6–12: You have some growth mindset characteristics, but there's room for improvement.

13–18: You demonstrate a strong growth mindset. Keep fostering these beliefs and attitudes to continue growing and learning.

Embracing challenges of the growth mindset

With a growth mindset, you see challenges as opportunities for learning and growth. When it comes to finding your passion, you're more likely to explore diverse interests and step outside your comfort zone to discover what truly excites you. Instead of shying away from new experiences, you approach them with curiosity and openness, which can lead to unexpected passions and opportunities.

Resilience in the face of setbacks

Pursuing passion often involves encountering obstacles and setbacks. A growth mindset equips you with the mental fortitude to bounce back from failures and disappointments. You don't view setbacks as indications of your inadequacy but as a foothold on your journey toward passion. This resilience keeps you motivated and determined to explore until you find what truly resonates with you.

Continuous learning

You have a thirst for knowledge and continuous learning. In the context of passion, this translates to a willingness to expand your understanding of different fields, industries, or activities. You seek out information and actively engage in learning experiences that contribute to your personal growth and align with your evolving passions.

Experimentation and adaptability

A growth mindset encourages experimentation and adaptation. It allows you to try out different paths, experiences, and opportunities without fear of failure or judgment. This flexibility enables you to pivot and adjust your course as you gain more clarity about your passions and how you want to pursue them.

Empowerment to overcome limiting beliefs

Many people hold limiting beliefs that prevent them from fully exploring their passions. But with a growth mindset, you challenge these limiting beliefs and replace them with a belief in your potential to learn and grow. As a result, you become more willing to challenge societal norms, overcome self-doubt, and break free from the constraints that can hinder your passion pursuit.

Joy in the process

The journey of finding your passion isn't always straightforward. It involves ups and downs, exploration, and self-discovery. With a growth mindset, you find joy in this process rather than solely focusing on the end goal. You appreciate the growth and learning that occur along the way, making the pursuit of passion a fulfilling and enriching experience.

The growth mindset builds a powerful foundation for exploring, embracing, and nurturing passion. It fosters resilience, curiosity, and adaptability, empowering you to overcome challenges and obstacles as you embark on a fulfilling journey to find your true passions in life.

Recognizing a Growth versus Fixed Mindset

Understanding the difference between a growth mindset and a fixed mindset is crucial in understanding how your beliefs can influence your ability to find and pursue your passions. Here's a breakdown of the key distinctions between the two mindsets.

Beliefs about abilities

Having a growth mindset means believing that you can develop your abilities and intelligence through effort, dedication, and learning. You see challenges as opportunities to learn and improve, and you're not afraid to take on new tasks even if you're not yet an expert in the field.

In contrast, if you have a fixed mindset, you believe that your abilities and intelligence are static and can't be changed. You may avoid challenges to avoid failure and stick to what you're already good at because you fear that trying something new might reveal your limitations.

Recognizing these differences can help you cultivate a growth mindset, which is essential in the pursuit of passion and personal growth. Embracing a growth mindset opens up opportunities, fosters resilience, and empowers you to explore and nurture your passions.

Response to effort and failure

If you have a growth mindset, you see effort as a pathway to mastery. You embrace failure as a natural part of the learning process and use it as an opportunity to grow and improve. You view setbacks as just a natural part of the success journey.

If you have a fixed mindset, you may avoid putting in effort because you believe that your abilities are fixed. You may fear failure and be more likely to give up on tasks or passions if you don't immediately excel at them.

Response to feedback

If you have a growth mindset, you value feedback as a way to learn and grow. You see constructive criticism as a means to improve and are open to seeking feedback from others to enhance your skills and knowledge.

On the flip side, if you have a fixed mindset, you may feel threatened by feedback because you perceive it as a judgment on your inherent abilities. You may avoid seeking feedback or become defensive when receiving it.

Comparison with others

Having a growth mindset entails viewing the success of others as an inspiration. You see it as evidence that with effort and dedication, you too can achieve your goals and passions.

In contrast, having a fixed mindset may make you feel threatened by the success of others. You may view others' accomplishments as a reflection of your own inadequacy and may become discouraged from pursuing your passions.

Approach to learning

If you have a growth mindset, you're more likely to actively seek out learning opportunities and challenges. You believe that continuous learning and improvement are essential to achieving your passions.

On the other hand, if you have a fixed mindset, you may avoid learning experiences that challenge your existing beliefs about your abilities.

DO YOU HAVE A GROWTH OR A FIXED MINDSET?

Here's a short quiz to help identify whether you tend to have a growth mindset or a fixed mindset. Read each statement and choose the option that best represents your response:

1. When faced with a difficult task or challenge, I tend to:

    a. Avoid it because it might be too hard for me.

    b. Embrace it because it's an opportunity to learn and improve.

2. I believe that my intelligence and abilities are:

    a. Fixed and can't be changed significantly.

    b. Developable with effort and dedication.

3. Feedback from others:

    a. Makes me feel defensive and uncomfortable.

    b. Helps me identify areas for improvement and growth.

4. When I encounter failure, I:

    a. Feel discouraged and defeated, and it affects my confidence.

    b. See it as a chance to learn, regroup, and try again.

5. I often compare my skills and achievements to others, and when others succeed:

    a. I feel envious or threatened.

    b. I'm inspired and motivated to improve myself.

6. I believe that my personality and talents are:

    a. Set in stone and can't be changed.

    b. Capable of growth and development.

7. I tend to take on new challenges and tasks that:

    a. I'm already good at and comfortable with.

    b. Stretch my abilities and provide opportunities for growth.

8. When I encounter obstacles or setbacks, I:

    a. Give up easily and feel that it's a sign of my limitations.

    b. View them as opportunities to learn and find new solutions.

9. Learning new skills and gaining knowledge:

   a. Seems intimidating and unnecessary.

   b. Excites me and opens up possibilities for personal growth.

10. When I see someone achieving something I want, I think:

   a. They must be naturally talented or lucky.

   b. If I work hard and stay dedicated, I can achieve it too.

Scoring: Count the number of "b" responses you selected. The higher the number of "b" responses, the more likely you have a growth mindset.

Keep in mind that your mindset can vary in different situations, and no response is right or wrong. This quiz serves as a self-awareness tool to understand your predominant mindset and identify areas where you can cultivate a growth mindset further.

Developing a Growth Mindset to Succeed in Your Passion

The mindset you adopt can significantly influence your outcomes when pursuing your passion (or doing anything, for that matter). Embracing a growth mindset can be a transformative and empowering approach that opens doors to new possibilities, fuels perseverance, and fosters continuous learning and development. This section delves into the numerous advantages of cultivating a growth mindset when searching for and nurturing your passions.

A growth mindset, as coined by psychologist Carol Dweck, revolves around the belief that your abilities and intelligence aren't fixed traits but can be developed and improved through dedication, effort, and learning from challenges. Individuals with this mindset view setbacks as opportunities for growth and value the process over outcomes.

Adopting a growth mindset can be a powerful tool to overcome obstacles, build resilience, and uncover your true potential. By fostering a mindset that thrives on curiosity, learning, and adaptability, you set yourself on a path of self-discovery, purpose, and fulfillment.

This section explores the manifold benefits of a growth mindset in the context of finding passion. From recognizing the difference between a growth and a fixed mindset to understanding how it shapes your perception of challenges, it delves into the transformative impact a growth mindset can have on your pursuit of passion.

With the principles of the growth mindset in your arsenal, you can embark on a journey of exploration and self-improvement, paving the way for discovering and nurturing your passions in ways you never thought possible. Unveil the boundless potential it holds for your quest to find meaning and purpose in life.

Overcoming obstacles and taking risks

The advantages of a growth mindset in overcoming obstacles and taking risks are substantial and can lead to significant personal and professional growth. Table 12-2 lists some key advantages of cultivating a growth mindset when facing challenges and taking risks.

TABLE 12-2 **Advantages of a Growth Mindset When Facing Challenges**

Characteristic	Advantages
Resilience and perseverance	You're more resilient in the face of obstacles and setbacks. You understand that failure and setbacks are natural parts of the learning process and are less likely to be discouraged by temporary setbacks. Instead, you use these challenges as opportunities to learn and improve, enabling you to bounce back and continue moving forward.
Embracing change and adaptability	You show a willingness to embrace change and take calculated risks. Rather than sticking to your comfort zone, you're more open to new experiences and challenges. This adaptability allows you to thrive in dynamic and uncertain environments, where taking risks and trying new approaches can lead to innovation and success.
Increased learning and skill development	You actively seek opportunities to learn and develop your skills. You're more likely to take on new challenges that push your boundaries and provide opportunities for growth. As a result, you continuously acquire new knowledge and competencies, making you better equipped to overcome obstacles and take on more significant risks.
Greater problem-solving abilities	You approach problems with a solutions-oriented mindset. Rather than seeing problems as insurmountable barriers, you view them as puzzles to be solved. This mindset enables you to approach challenges with creativity and resourcefulness, leading to more effective problem-solving and a higher likelihood of success.
Increased self-confidence	As you continuously learn and develop your skills, you build greater self-confidence. This self-assurance empowers you to take on more significant challenges and risks, knowing that you have the capacity to learn, adapt, and grow.
Willingness to learn from failure	You view failure as an opportunity for learning and improvement rather than a reflection of your worth or abilities. You're more likely to analyze your failures, extract valuable lessons from them, and use that knowledge to enhance your future efforts.
Courage to take calculated risks	You have the courage to take calculated risks. You understand that taking risks is an inherent part of achieving meaningful goals and pursuing your passions. You're more willing to step outside your comfort zone and seize opportunities that align with your long-term aspirations.

A growth mindset empowers you to embrace challenges, learn from setbacks, and continuously develop your skills. This mindset fosters resilience, adaptability, problem-solving abilities, and the confidence to tackle ambitious goals and pursue passions. By cultivating this mindset, you can unlock your full potential and embark on a journey of continuous growth and success.

One of the key advantages of adopting a growth mindset in the pursuit of passion is its transformative impact on how you approach and overcome obstacles and take risks. When you embrace a growth mindset, you see challenges as opportunities for learning and growth rather than as insurmountable barriers. This shift in perspective empowers you to tackle obstacles with resilience, creativity, and determination. Read on for how a growth mindset can lead to successful outcomes in the face of challenges.

Achieving successful outcomes

The advantages of a growth mindset in overcoming obstacles and taking risks are profound. By embracing challenges, emphasizing effort and resilience, and seeing failure as an opportunity for growth, you can unleash your true potential and achieve remarkable success in your pursuit of passion. There are many examples of successful individuals who have demonstrated the power of a growth mindset in turning adversity into opportunities and setting the stage for incredible achievements, some of which I describe in the following sections.

Embracing challenges as opportunities

With a growth mindset, you view challenges as chances to expand your abilities and knowledge. Rather than shying away from difficult tasks, you lean into them, recognizing that overcoming obstacles is an essential part of the learning and growth process. By seeing challenges as opportunities for self-improvement, you remain motivated and determined to keep pushing forward.

Emphasizing effort and resilience

A growth mindset emphasizes the value of effort and resilience. Rather than being deterred by initial setbacks, you understand that progress often involves consistent effort and the ability to bounce back from failures. You see setbacks as part of the journey, not as indicators of your inherent limitations.

Embracing risks and learning from failure

A growth mindset encourages you to take calculated risks and view failure as an opportunity to learn and grow. You must be willing to step out of your comfort zone, try new things, and learn from both your successes and your failures.

Pursuing Continuous Learning and Development

Continuous learning and development refers to the ongoing process of acquiring new knowledge, skills, and abilities throughout your life or career. It involves actively seeking out opportunities for learning and improvement, both formally and informally, to stay relevant, adapt to changes, and reach personal and professional goals. Continuous learning isn't limited to formal education; it encompasses a wide range of activities, such as attending workshops, participating in training programs, reading books, taking online courses, seeking feedback, and engaging in experiential learning.

Continuous learning is characterized by a mindset that values growth and sees learning as a lifelong journey rather than a destination. It involves being open to new ideas, staying curious, and embracing challenges as opportunities for growth. Prioritizing continuous learning means being committed to self-improvement and understanding that developing new skills and knowledge enhances your overall effectiveness and value in the workforce and society.

In today's fast-paced and ever-changing world, continuous learning has become essential for personal and professional success. As industries evolve, technologies advance, and societal demands shift, engaging in continuous learning means being better equipped to adapt to these changes and thrive in your career. Additionally, continuous learning helps you remain competitive, enhances your problem-solving abilities, and fosters a growth mindset, which is crucial for overcoming challenges and achieving long-term success.

Overall, continuous learning and development play a fundamental role in shaping you into a lifelong learner, allowing you to stay relevant, innovative, and fulfilled throughout your life. By embracing continuous learning, you can unlock your full potential, embrace new opportunities, and make meaningful contributions to your field and community.

The role of a growth mindset in continuous learning and development is pivotal and can significantly affect your personal and professional growth. Embracing a growth mindset fosters a strong desire for ongoing learning and improvement, enabling you to continually expand your knowledge, skills, and capabilities. Here are some key aspects of how a growth mindset plays a crucial role in continuous learning and development:

>> **Embracing learning as a lifelong journey:** Having a growth mindset entails viewing learning as an ongoing and lifelong journey. It means understanding that there's always room for improvement and that your abilities aren't fixed. This mindset encourages you to seek out learning opportunities, whether through formal education, training programs, workshops, or self-directed learning.

» **Openness to new experiences and challenges:** A growth mindset promotes a willingness to step out of your comfort zone and explore new experiences. This openness to new challenges and opportunities allows you to learn from diverse situations and gain valuable insights that contribute to your personal and professional growth.

» **Persistence in the face of difficulties:** Continuous learning and development often involve facing complex challenges and setbacks. A growth mindset enables you to persevere through difficulties, seeing them as opportunities to learn and improve rather than as insurmountable barriers. This resilience helps you stay committed to your learning journey and overcome obstacles along the way.

» **Embracing feedback for growth:** Having a growth mindset means being open to receiving constructive feedback and using it as a catalyst for improvement. Rather than viewing feedback as criticism, you see it as valuable information that can help you enhance your skills and performance. This receptivity to feedback accelerates your learning and development process.

» **Nurturing a culture of curiosity:** A growth mindset fosters curiosity and a thirst for knowledge. Embracing this mindset means actively seeking out new information, exploring different perspectives, and engaging in discussions with others to expand your understanding. This curiosity-driven approach fuels your continuous learning journey.

» **Adaptability to change:** In today's rapidly changing world, adaptability is crucial for staying relevant and competitive. A growth mindset equips you with the flexibility to adapt to evolving circumstances and technologies. As you embrace change as an opportunity for growth, you can readily acquire new skills and knowledge to remain ahead of the curve.

» **Pursuit of mastery:** With a growth mindset, you aim to achieve mastery in your areas of interest or expertise. You recognize that true expertise requires ongoing learning and refinement of skills. This pursuit of mastery drives you to invest time and effort in continuous learning and development.

A growth mindset is a powerful driver of continuous learning and development. It fuels the desire to learn, adapt, and improve throughout your life, enabling you to reach your full potential and find fulfillment in your personal and professional pursuits. By cultivating a growth mindset, you can embrace the journey of lifelong learning and experience the numerous benefits it brings to your life.

The impact of a growth mindset on resilience

Resilience is the ability to bounce back and adapt in the face of adversity, challenges, or significant life changes. It's the capacity to cope with and recover from difficult or stressful situations, maintaining mental and emotional well-being. Resilience doesn't mean avoiding or denying difficult circumstances; instead, it involves facing them with a positive and proactive mindset.

Resilience is a dynamic and multifaceted trait that you can develop and strengthen over time. It allows you to maintain a sense of balance, control, and hope even in the face of setbacks or traumatic events. Resilience makes you better equipped to manage stress, handle uncertainty, and persevere through difficult times. Table 12-3 details the qualities that make up resilience.

TABLE 12-3   **Key Components of Resilience**

Component	How It Shows Up
Adaptability	You're flexible and can adjust your approach when faced with new challenges or changing circumstances. You're open to learning and trying new strategies.
Positive thinking	You maintain a positive outlook and focus on solutions rather than dwell on problems. You reframe negative thoughts and find silver linings in difficult situations.
Emotional regulation	You can effectively manage your emotions, even during challenging times. You practice self-awareness and self-regulation to avoid being overwhelmed by negative emotions.
Social support	You have a strong support system of family, friends, or colleagues who offer encouragement, understanding, and practical assistance during tough times.
Problem-solving skills	You have the ability to analyze problems, set goals, and take effective action to address challenges. You approach obstacles with a solution-oriented mindset.
Self-compassion	You're kind and understanding toward yourself, especially during difficult times. Self-compassion allows you to bounce back from setbacks without self-criticism.
Sense of purpose	You have a clear sense of purpose or meaning in life that enables you to keep moving forward and helps you find motivation during tough times.

Resilience isn't about being invincible or avoiding stress altogether; it's about developing the ability to navigate adversity and grow stronger from the experience. It's an essential quality for personal growth, well-being, and success in various aspects of life.

The impact of a growth mindset on perseverance

Perseverance is the quality of persisting in the pursuit of a goal or objective despite facing challenges, obstacles, or setbacks. It's the determination to keep going, even when things get difficult, and the willingness to stay committed to achieving your desired outcomes. Perseverance is often associated with a strong sense of purpose and the willingness to endure hardships and difficulties in the pursuit of success. Table 12-4 details the qualities that make up perseverance.

TABLE 12-4   **Key Components of Perseverance**

Component	How It Shows Up
Resilience	You can bounce back from failures and setbacks. You view challenges as opportunities for growth and learning, which helps you maintain your motivation and continue moving forward.
Tenacity	You have tenacity and a steadfast resolve to stay on course, especially when faced with obstacles that may tempt you to give up.
Self-discipline	You demonstrate self-discipline and the ability to stay focused and committed to your goals, even when distractions or temptations arise.
Patience	You're patient and understand that progress may not be immediate.
Adaptability	You're adaptable and willing to adjust strategies when necessary to overcome challenges.
Optimism	You have a positive and optimistic mindset. You're more likely to view setbacks as temporary and believe in your ability to succeed in the long run.
Belief in your abilities	You have a strong belief in your own capabilities and the confidence that you can overcome obstacles and achieve the desired outcome.

Perseverance is a valuable trait that can lead to personal growth, achievement, and success in various areas of life, whether in academics, career, sports, or personal pursuits. It's an essential quality if you want to reach your full potential and make a lasting impact on your life and the lives of others.

Cultivating a Growth Mindset: Principles and Strategies

This chapter has looked at the many ways in which having a growth mindset is helpful (if not essential) to finding your passion and succeeding in its pursuit. Read on to explore the principles and strategies for developing a growth mindset. By understanding and integrating these principles into your daily life, you can unlock your full potential and pave the way for a more fulfilling and purposeful journey in pursuit of your passions.

This section delves into the characteristics of a growth mindset, its benefits in overcoming obstacles and taking risks, and its role in fostering resilience and perseverance. It shows how a growth mindset can enhance your learning, development, and overall sense of fulfillment. It's time to embark on this transformative journey of cultivating a growth mindset and harness its power to shape a brighter and more purpose-driven future.

Developing a positive and open mindset

Developing a positive and open mindset is at the heart of cultivating a growth mindset. It involves consciously choosing to adopt a positive outlook on life and being open to new ideas, challenges, and experiences. This mindset shift allows you to embrace change, see failures as opportunities for learning, and maintain a sense of optimism even in the face of adversity.

One of the key elements of developing a positive and open mindset is self-awareness. By becoming aware of your thought patterns and beliefs, you can identify any negative or limiting thoughts that may be holding you back. Through self-reflection and introspection, you can challenge these thoughts and replace them with more constructive and empowering beliefs.

Another important aspect is practicing mindfulness. Mindfulness helps you stay present and fully engaged in the moment, allowing you to appreciate the journey and savor each step of the process. By being mindful, you can reduce stress and anxiety, enhance your focus, and make better decisions that align with your passions and goals.

Moreover, surrounding yourself with positive influences and supportive people can significantly influence your mindset. Building a strong support network of like-minded individuals can provide encouragement, motivation, and constructive feedback that fosters growth.

Additionally, seeking out new challenges and stepping outside of your comfort zone can expand your perspective and capabilities. Embracing a growth mindset means seeing challenges as opportunities to stretch yourself and develop new skills.

Practicing gratitude is another powerful tool for developing a positive mindset. By regularly acknowledging and appreciating the blessings and opportunities in your life, you shift your focus from what you lack to what you have. This shift in perspective can lead to greater contentment and a sense of abundance.

In conclusion, developing a positive and open mindset is an ongoing journey of self-awareness, mindfulness, supportive connections, embracing challenges, and practicing gratitude. By nurturing this mindset, you can unlock your full potential and embrace a growth-oriented approach to life, finding passion and fulfillment in every step of your journey.

Understanding yourself through self-awareness

Self-awareness is the ability to recognize and understand your own thoughts, emotions, and behaviors. It involves being in tune with your inner world, including your values, beliefs, strengths, weaknesses, and motivations. Self-awareness allows you to have a clear understanding of who you are and how you interact with the world around you.

When you're self-aware, you can recognize your emotional reactions and understand why you feel a certain way in particular situations. This awareness enables you to respond more effectively to challenges and make conscious choices rather than reacting impulsively. It also helps you identify patterns of behavior that may be hindering your personal growth or preventing you from pursuing your passions.

Self-awareness is a foundational skill for personal and professional development. It allows you to identify areas for improvement and take steps to enhance your skills and abilities. Moreover, self-awareness is essential for building meaningful relationships and understanding how your actions may affect others.

Cultivating self-awareness involves self-reflection, introspection, and seeking feedback from others. It requires a willingness to explore your thoughts and emotions with honesty and without judgment. Through self-awareness, you gain insights into your authentic self, which can lead to greater self-acceptance and a clearer sense of purpose and direction in life.

One of the key benefits of self-awareness is that it allows you to better understand your strengths and weaknesses. When you're aware of your strengths, you can leverage them to pursue activities and opportunities that align with your natural abilities and passions. On the other hand, being aware of your weaknesses enables you to identify areas for improvement and take proactive steps to develop new skills.

Self-awareness also helps you recognize your values and beliefs. Understanding what truly matters to you on a deep level allows you to make decisions that align with your values, leading to a greater sense of fulfillment and purpose in life.

Self-reflecting to gain insight

Self-reflection is the process of examining and analyzing your own thoughts, feelings, and actions in a thoughtful and introspective manner. It involves taking a step back from your daily activities and experiences to deeply consider your beliefs, values, goals, and behaviors. Through self-reflection, you gain insight into your emotions, motivations, and responses to various situations, allowing you to better understand yourself and your experiences.

Self-reflection is an essential tool for personal growth and development. It helps you become more self-aware, which in turn enables you to make more intentional and informed decisions in your life. By reflecting on your past experiences and actions, you can identify patterns, strengths, and areas for improvement. It also allows you to recognize the impact of your actions on yourself and others.

In the context of finding passion, self-reflection can be particularly valuable. It enables you to explore your interests, values, and strengths and understand what truly resonates with you. By engaging in self-reflection, you can uncover your passions and align your actions with your authentic self.

Self-reflection can take many forms, such as journaling, meditation, or simply taking time to think deeply about your experiences and emotions. It requires creating a space for quiet introspection, free from distractions, where you can delve into your thoughts and feelings honestly and openly. Through regular self-reflection, you can gain a deeper understanding of yourself, leading to personal growth, fulfillment, and a stronger sense of purpose.

In the pursuit of passion, self-reflection is a powerful tool for exploring your interests and understanding what brings you joy and fulfillment. By looking back on your experiences, examining your feelings and reactions, and contemplating what truly excites you, you can uncover your authentic passions.

TIPS FOR PRACTICING SELF-AWARENESS AND SELF-REFLECTION

Practicing both self-awareness and self-reflection is a fundamental aspect of personal development and finding passion. It involves becoming attuned to your thoughts, emotions, behaviors, and motivations and objectively observing yourself without judgment. By cultivating self-awareness and engaging in regular self-reflection, you can gain valuable insights into your inner world and make meaningful changes in your life.

Journaling, meditation, and mindfulness exercises are some practical ways to develop these skills. Through these practices, you can cultivate a deeper connection with yourself and lay the foundation for a more meaningful and purpose-driven life.

Here are some tips to help you develop these essential skills.

Mindfulness meditation: Dedicate some time each day to practice mindfulness meditation. This involves focusing on your breath and being fully present in the moment. It allows you to observe your thoughts and emotions without judgment.

Keep a journal: Maintain a journal to write down your thoughts, feelings, and experiences regularly. This can help you gain insights into patterns of behavior and identify areas where you can grow and improve.

Ask for feedback: Seek feedback from trusted friends, family members, or colleagues. Honest feedback from others can provide valuable perspectives on your strengths and areas for development.

Pause and reflect: Take moments throughout the day to pause and reflect on your experiences. Ask yourself how you feel and what may be influencing your emotions and actions.

Practice active listening: When engaging in conversations, practice active listening. Pay attention to what others are saying without interrupting or jumping to conclusions. This fosters empathy and understanding.

Challenge your assumptions: Question your beliefs and assumptions about yourself and the world. Are limiting beliefs holding you back? Can you explore new perspectives?

Set intentions: Before starting your day, set intentions for how you want to show up and what you want to accomplish. At the end of the day, reflect on how well you lived up to those intentions.

Use reflection prompts: Use reflective questions or prompts to guide your self-reflection. Examples include "What did I learn from today's challenges?" and "What am I most proud of accomplishing this week?"

Practice empathy: Try to understand the perspectives and feelings of others. Developing empathy can enhance your self-awareness by showing you how your actions affect those around you.

Celebrate progress: Celebrate your successes and growth, no matter how small. Acknowledging your progress can boost your motivation and confidence.

Be kind to yourself: Be gentle and compassionate with yourself. Avoid self-criticism, and remember that self-awareness is a skill that develops over time.

Remember, self-awareness and self-reflection are ongoing practices. Embrace the process, stay curious about yourself, and be open to continuous learning and growth. Over time, these habits will lead to a deeper understanding of yourself and pave the way to a more fulfilled and purposeful life.

Building a Growth-Oriented Community

A growth-oriented community is a supportive and empowering environment that encourages cultivating a growth mindset and pursuing continuous learning and personal development. In such a community, the focus is on nurturing the potential of its members, fostering resilience, and creating opportunities for growth.

Key characteristics of a growth-oriented community include:

>> **Shared values:** In a growth-oriented community, you often share common values with other members. These values might include a commitment to learning, personal growth, and supporting one another's aspirations.

>> **Supportive environment:** The community provides a safe and nonjudgmental space where you can express yourself, share your experiences, and seek guidance without fear of criticism.

>> **Collaboration and networking:** Collaboration and networking are actively encouraged, allowing you to connect with others, share knowledge, and learn from each other's journeys.

>> **Emphasis on growth mindset:** The community promotes the importance of adopting a growth mindset, which embraces challenges, sees failures as opportunities to learn, and believes in the potential for continuous improvement.

>> **Mentorship and coaching:** Mentorship and coaching opportunities are often available within the community. Experienced individuals can support and guide you if you're just starting your growth journey.

>> **Learning opportunities:** The community may organize workshops, seminars, webinars, or courses to provide valuable learning experiences and promote skill development.

>> **Recognition of achievements:** As a member, your accomplishments and milestones are celebrated and acknowledged, creating a positive and encouraging atmosphere.

>> **Accountability:** A growth-oriented community fosters a sense of accountability. Members encourage each other to set and achieve their goals.

>> **Diverse perspectives:** As part of the community, you welcome individuals from diverse backgrounds, disciplines, and experiences. A wealth of perspectives enrich the learning and growth process.

>> **Emphasis on well-being:** Although growth is a central theme, as part of the community, you also recognize the importance of well-being and self-care as essential components of personal development.

>> **Opportunities for reflection:** Regular opportunities for self-reflection are encouraged. This way you gain deeper insights into your experiences and progress.

Overall, a growth-oriented community serves as a supportive ecosystem that nourishes and inspires you to reach your full potential, find your passion, and navigate challenges with resilience. It creates an environment where personal growth isn't just encouraged but celebrated as a shared goal for everyone involved.

Building a growth-oriented community requires careful planning, dedication, and a focus on creating an environment that fosters continuous learning and personal development. Here are some tasks to help you get started:

>> **Identify your purpose:** Clarify the purpose and vision of the community. Determine what specific areas of growth and learning you want to focus on and what values will guide the community.

>> **Define your target audience:** Identify the individuals you want to attract to the community. Consider their interests, needs, and goals to ensure you create a relevant and engaging platform for them.

>> **Choose the right platform:** Decide on the best platform for your community. It could be a physical space, an online forum, a social media group, or a combination of different platforms.

>> **Create engaging content:** Develop valuable and engaging content that aligns with your community's purpose. This might include articles, videos, webinars, workshops, or any other form of educational material.

>> **Encourage collaboration:** Foster a collaborative environment where members can interact, share experiences, and support one another. Encourage discussions, ask questions, and promote networking opportunities.

>> **Promote learning opportunities:** Offer various learning opportunities such as workshops, webinars, guest speaker sessions, or book clubs. Provide resources that empower members to explore new topics and skills.

>> **Facilitate mentorship and coaching:** Encourage experienced members to mentor and coach those who are seeking guidance. Facilitate connections between mentors and mentees to create valuable learning relationships.

>> **Create a safe space:** Ensure the community is a safe and inclusive space where members feel comfortable expressing their thoughts and sharing their experiences without fear of judgment.

>> **Recognize and celebrate achievements:** Celebrate achievements and milestones to create a positive and encouraging atmosphere within the community.

>> **Encourage accountability:** Motivate members to set goals and hold each other accountable for their progress. Regularly check in on each other's growth journeys and provide support when needed.

>> **Promote feedback and reflection:** Encourage members to provide feedback on community activities and events. Promote regular self-reflection and encourage sharing of insights and lessons learned.

>> **Be consistent:** Consistency is key to building a thriving community. Regularly engage with members, post new content, and ensure the community remains active and vibrant.

>> **Build partnerships:** Collaborate with other organizations, institutions, or communities that share similar values and goals. Building partnerships can expand your reach and provide additional resources.

>> **Stay open to growth and evolution:** Be open to feedback, and be willing to adapt and evolve the community based on the needs and preferences of the members.

By following these steps and continuously fostering a supportive and growth-oriented environment, you can create a thriving community that empowers individuals to reach their full potential and find passion in their personal and professional lives.

Building a growth-oriented community requires dedication, active involvement, and a commitment to fostering an environment where members can thrive, learn, and find their passion. Use this steps as a guide to create a supportive and enriching community experience.

IN THIS CHAPTER

» **Understanding the value of time management**

» **Looking at the finite nature of time**

» **Setting priorities**

» **Using delegation and automation**

» **Maximizing efficiency**

Chapter **13**

Managing Your Time and Priorities

Time is a precious and finite resource, and how you choose to use it can significantly affect your journey to finding passion and purpose in life. In this fast-paced and demanding world, the ability to manage time effectively is more critical than ever. Time management goes beyond simply scheduling tasks and activities; it plays a vital role in helping you explore, pursue, and ultimately discover your true passions.

This chapter delves into the significance of time management in the context of finding passion. It explores how efficiently utilizing your time can lead to a more fulfilling and purpose-driven life. By mastering time management skills, you empower yourself to make intentional choices, set priorities, and allocate time to activities that resonate with your interests and values.

The next several pages examine practical strategies and techniques to help you make the most of your time. From setting clear goals and priorities to developing healthy habits and routines, this chapter uncovers the tools needed to strike a harmonious balance between exploring your passions and fulfilling other responsibilities.

The journey to discovering your passion can be both exciting and challenging. Time management acts as a guiding compass, steering you toward opportunities for growth, personal development, and meaningful experiences. As you begin this exploration, remember that every moment counts, and how you invest your time can shape the course of your life. Embark on the journey and unlock the boundless potential that lies within you.

Why Managing Your Time Matters

Time management is a critical factor in the pursuit of one's passion, often serving as the compass that guides individuals through the labyrinth of life. It's the art of allocating your most precious resource, time, in a way that maximizes productivity, minimizes distractions, and allows for the focused exploration of your interests. Understanding and embracing effective time management can significantly impact your journey in finding your passion for several reasons:

>> **Prioritization of exploration:** The process of discovering one's passion often requires exploration and experimentation. Time management helps you allocate dedicated blocks of time for self-discovery. It allows you to prioritize activities that bring you closer to your passion, whether it's trying out new hobbies, attending relevant events, or embarking on educational pursuits.

>> **Elimination of procrastination:** Procrastination is a formidable foe on the path to passion. Effective time management techniques, such as the Pomodoro Technique, the two-minute rule, or time blocking, can help you conquer procrastination. By breaking tasks into manageable time intervals, you reduce the allure of delay and increase your productivity.

>> **Consistency and skill development:** Passion often requires honing skills or gaining expertise in a particular area. Time management ensures you set aside regular, consistent periods for skill development. This habitual approach fosters mastery and enables you to make meaningful progress towards your passion.

>> **Balancing multiple interests:** It's common to have various interests and responsibilities. Effective time management allows you to strike a balance between these diverse aspects of your life. By allocating time to each interest, you avoid neglecting one area in pursuit of another, ensuring a holistic and fulfilling life.

>> **Avoiding burnout:** The journey to discovering and pursuing your passion can be exhilarating, but it's also easy to become consumed by it. Time management ensures you maintain a healthy work-life balance, preventing burnout. This balance is crucial for sustaining your passion in the long run.

>> **Opportunities for reflection:** Time management creates space for reflection. Regularly setting aside moments to review your progress, reassess your goals, and adjust your course ensures that you remain aligned with your evolving passions.

>> **Effective decision-making:** By managing your time wisely, you have the mental bandwidth to make informed decisions about the direction of your passion. It allows you to weigh the pros and cons, evaluate opportunities, and make choices that align with your deepest interests.

Time management is the guardian of your journey to finding and pursuing your passion. It ensures that you use your time purposefully, allocate it to activities that resonate with your aspirations, and maintain a balanced and sustainable approach. By mastering the art of time management, you not only enhance your productivity but also empower yourself to embark on a passionate, purpose-driven life with clarity and determination.

Recognizing the impact of time management on your well-being

Time management plays a pivotal role in productivity and overall well-being. When you effectively manage your time, you're better equipped to accomplish tasks efficiently, reduce stress, and enhance your sense of satisfaction and fulfillment.

>> **Boosting productivity:** Effective time management enables you to prioritize tasks, set clear goals, and allocate appropriate time for each activity. By organizing your days and establishing a well-structured routine, you can avoid procrastination and stay focused on the most important tasks. As a result, you become more productive and accomplish more in less time.

>> **Reducing stress:** One of the main sources of stress in modern life is feeling overwhelmed by the demands on your time. Poor time management can lead to missed deadlines, last-minute rushes, and a perpetual sense of rushing. On the contrary, when you manage your time wisely, you can complete tasks in a calm and organized manner, reducing stress and improving your mental well-being.

>> **Enhancing decision-making:** Time management allows you to evaluate your commitments and make informed decisions about how you spend your time. By understanding the impact of your choices, you can align your actions with your values and passions, leading to a more fulfilling and purpose-driven life.

>> **Fostering work-life balance:** Effective time management helps you strike a healthy balance between your personal and your professional life. By

allocating time for family, hobbies, self-care, and relaxation, you can avoid burnout and maintain your overall well-being.

» **Creating space for self-development:** Time management opens up opportunities for continuous learning and personal growth. When you allocate time for self-improvement, such as reading, taking courses, or developing new skills, you invest in your long-term success and fulfillment.

» **Improving relationships:** When you manage your time effectively, you can be present and fully engaged in your interactions with others. Quality time spent with loved ones and colleagues strengthens relationships, deepens connections, and fosters a sense of community.

» **Boosting confidence:** Accomplishing tasks and reaching goals within set timeframes boosts your confidence and self-esteem. Each successful achievement reinforces your belief in your capabilities, motivating you to take on new challenges with enthusiasm and optimism.

Identifying common time management challenges and barriers

Despite the numerous benefits of time management, many individuals face challenges and barriers that hinder their ability to effectively manage their time. Even the most successful individuals face time management challenges. However, by adopting effective strategies, setting clear priorities, and maintaining discipline, you can overcome these barriers and achieve extraordinary success in your personal and professional life.

Following are some common time management challenges and the experiences of successful individuals who have overcome them.

» **Procrastination:** Procrastination is a common time management challenge that affects people across all walks of life.

» **Distractions and multitasking:** Distractions in the form of smartphones, social media, and interruptions from colleagues or family members can disrupt focus and productivity.

» **Overcommitment:** Many individuals struggle with overcommitting themselves, leading to a lack of time for personal passions and well-being.

» **Lack of prioritization:** Without clear priorities, it's challenging to allocate time effectively.

» **Ineffective planning:** Without proper planning, you may find yourself overwhelmed or struggling to meet deadlines.

>> **Lack of boundaries:** Setting boundaries with work, social commitments, and technology is vital for effective time management.

>> **Failure to delegate:** You might struggle to delegate tasks, fearing that others may not complete them to your standards.

Managing Your Time and Priorities Effectively

Recognizing that time management isn't without its challenges, it's important to address common obstacles that you may encounter while trying to manage your time efficiently. Drawing insights from successful individuals who have faced similar hurdles, this section looks at how they overcame these challenges and honed their time management skills to achieve remarkable success.

If you struggle with time management, don't despair: Several practical tips and techniques are at your disposal so you can manage your time more effectively. From setting clear priorities and creating realistic schedules to employing productivity tools and techniques, a wealth of strategies can optimize your time and energy.

Self-awareness and self-reflection are also big factors in time management. By understanding your strengths, weaknesses, and natural rhythms, you can tailor your time management approach to suit your unique needs and preferences.

Keep in mind that effective time management isn't about squeezing more tasks into your day but rather about making conscious choices that align with your passions and values. By developing the art of time management, you're better equipped to pursue your passions, achieve your goals, and lead a more fulfilling life. Buckle up. It's time to dive in and unlock the secrets to managing your time and priorities effectively!

Setting goals and priorities based on your values and interests

Setting goals and priorities based on your values and interests is a foundational aspect of effective time management. When your goals align with your core values and passions, you're more likely to stay motivated, focused, and fulfilled throughout your journey.

TIP

One way to start is by conducting a personal values assessment. Reflect on what truly matters to you, what principles guide your decisions, and what brings you a sense of purpose and fulfillment.

If you value creativity and innovation, setting a goal to explore new hobbies or start a creative project could be highly rewarding. On the other hand, if making a positive impact on others is a top priority, pursuing volunteer opportunities or engaging in philanthropic activities might resonate with you.

Once you have a clear understanding of your values and interests, it becomes easier to prioritize your goals. Consider which goals have the most significant impact on your personal growth, career advancement, or overall well-being. As you set your priorities, keep in mind that not all goals are equally urgent or essential. Allocate your time and resources accordingly to focus on what matters most to you.

For example, if one of your values is work-life balance, prioritize spending quality time with family and friends over nonessential work tasks. Similarly, if career growth is a priority, allocate time for professional development, networking events, and skill-building activities that align with your aspirations.

Developing a schedule and routine that aligns with your goals

Developing a schedule and routine that aligns with your goals is an essential component of effective time management. When your daily activities align with your long-term aspirations, you become more focused, productive, and ultimately successful in pursuing your passions.

By prioritizing tasks, staying consistent, and embracing flexibility, you can create a structured framework that supports your passion and purpose. Remember that time is a valuable resource, and how you use it will significantly influence your journey toward finding fulfillment and success in your endeavors.

To start, clearly define your goals and priorities. Take the time to reflect on what lights your fire and what you want to achieve in the short and long term. Once you have a clear vision of your objectives, break them down into smaller, manageable tasks.

Next, organize these tasks into a daily or weekly schedule. Consider the time and effort required for each task, and allocate sufficient time to work on them. Be realistic about your capacity, and avoid overloading your schedule because that may lead to burnout and reduced productivity.

Keep in mind your natural energy levels and when you feel most productive. If you're a morning person, consider scheduling your most challenging and important tasks during that time. If you're more alert and creative in the afternoon or evening, plan your work accordingly.

Consistency is the key to creating a successful routine. Try to establish set times for specific activities, such as waking up and going to bed at the same time each day, designating certain hours for work, and setting aside time for relaxation and leisure. Following a consistent routine can help you stay focused and avoid procrastination.

Flexibility is also important in crafting your schedule. Life is unpredictable, and unexpected events often arise. Allow some buffer time in your daily plan to accommodate unforeseen circumstances. Embrace the ability to adapt to changes while staying committed to your overall goals.

Moreover, use productivity tools and apps to stay organized and on track. Utilize calendars, task managers, and reminders to keep you aware of deadlines and upcoming commitments. These tools can help you maintain a clear overview of your tasks and ensure that you don't miss important deadlines.

REMEMBER

Prioritize self-care in your schedule. Taking care of your physical and mental well-being is crucial for sustaining long-term passion and productivity. Include time for exercise, relaxation, and spending quality moments with loved ones to recharge and rejuvenate.

Review and adjust your schedule regularly. Regularly assess how well your routine aligns with your goals, and make necessary adjustments. If you find that certain tasks are taking longer than expected or you need more time for personal pursuits, tweak your schedule accordingly.

Practicing self-discipline and avoiding distractions

Practicing self-discipline and avoiding distractions are vital skills to master when managing your time effectively. With the abundance of digital devices and constant demands for attention, staying focused on your goals can be challenging. However, with the right strategies and mindset, you can develop self-discipline and focus on what matters.

One essential step in practicing self-discipline is to set clear boundaries. Identify potential distractions in your environment, and take proactive measures to minimize them. If you find that social media or certain websites consume much of your time, consider using website blockers or apps that limit your access during work hours.

Create a designated workspace that's conducive to productivity. This could be a quiet corner in your home or a coworking space. When you step into this area, your brain will associate it with work, making it easier to focus and avoid distractions.

Another valuable technique is time blocking. Allocate specific time intervals for different tasks, and commit to working solely on those tasks during those periods. By immersing yourself in one task at a time, you can maintain focus and achieve higher productivity.

Eliminating multitasking is crucial to staying disciplined and focused. Contrary to popular belief, attempting to juggle multiple tasks simultaneously can reduce productivity and lead to errors. Instead, concentrate on completing one task before moving on to the next.

Self-discipline also involves creating a healthy work-life balance. Avoid the temptation to overwork because burnout can hinder your progress and passion pursuit. Make time for relaxation, hobbies, and spending time with loved ones to recharge and maintain overall well-being.

Finally, consider finding an accountability partner or joining a group with similar goals. Having someone to share your progress and setbacks with can be a source of additional motivation and encouragement.

Keeping in Mind the Role of Delegation and Automation in Time Management

In this hectic world, managing time efficiently is crucial for pursuing your passions and achieving your goals. As you continue on your journey to optimize time management, you come across the powerful concepts of delegation and automation. These two practices can significantly enhance your productivity and free up your time for the important stuff.

This section dives into the role that delegation and automation play in time management. Delegation involves entrusting tasks and responsibilities to others, whereas automation refers to the use of technology and tools to streamline repetitive tasks. Both practices are essential in today's dynamic landscape, where efficiency and effectiveness are keys to success.

Freeing up time with delegation and automation

Delegation is the process of assigning specific tasks or responsibilities to others who have the necessary skills and expertise to handle them effectively. It involves transferring authority and accountability for completing certain tasks, projects, or decisions to individuals or teams within an organization or group. Delegation is a fundamental aspect of effective leadership and time management because it allows leaders and individuals to focus on higher-level tasks and strategic activities while empowering others to contribute their strengths and skills to the overall goal.

In a professional setting, delegation involves understanding the strengths and capabilities of team members and assigning tasks that align with their skills and expertise. By delegating tasks, leaders can distribute workloads evenly, improve efficiency, and foster a sense of empowerment and ownership among team members. Delegation also develops and nurtures the talents of team members by offering them opportunities to take on new challenges and grow professionally.

Effective delegation requires clear communication, expectations, and the necessary resources and support to ensure the successful completion of delegated tasks. It also involves regular follow-up and feedback to ensure that the delegated tasks are on track and meet the desired outcomes.

Delegation can also be applied in your personal life, such as at home or in volunteer activities. By sharing responsibilities and tasks with family members or community members, you can create more time and energy for pursuing your passions, achieving personal growth, and finding a better work-life balance.

Delegation is a powerful tool that enables you to maximize your time and resources by entrusting tasks to others while focusing on activities that align with your passions and expertise. It promotes collaboration, efficiency, and growth, leading to improved productivity and overall satisfaction in both personal and professional spheres.

Automation refers to the use of technology and software to perform tasks and processes with minimal human intervention. It involves streamlining and mechanizing repetitive or manual tasks, often using computer programs, artificial intelligence, or robotic systems. The primary goals of automation are to increase efficiency, reduce human error, and save time and resources.

In the context of time management, automation plays a crucial role in simplifying complex processes and eliminating time-consuming tasks. It allows you to focus on more strategic and high-value activities so that you can be more productive and achieve your goals.

You can apply automation to various areas:

>> **Email automation:** Setting up email filters, templates, and autoresponders to manage incoming emails efficiently and respond promptly.

>> **Task automation:** Using task management tools and software to automate reminders, deadlines, and task assignments.

>> **Data entry and processing:** Employing software to automate data entry and processing, reducing the need for manual input and potential errors.

>> **Social media management:** Using automation tools to schedule and publish social media posts, track engagements, and analyze performance.

>> **Financial management:** Utilizing automation for bill payments, invoice generation, and budget tracking.

>> **Customer support:** Implementing chatbots or automated responses to handle routine customer inquiries.

>> **File organization:** Using automated file and folder organization systems to keep digital documents orderly and easily accessible.

By embracing automation, you can optimize your time and effort so that you can concentrate on more creative, strategic, and fulfilling tasks. Automation lets you stay ahead in a fast-paced and technology-driven world, making your pursuit of passion and achieving personal and professional goals more attainable.

Delegation and automation play significant roles in the art of time management. They offer a plethora of benefits that can significantly affect how you utilize your time and resources:

>> **Efficiency and productivity:** Delegation allows you to assign tasks to individuals with the appropriate skills and expertise, streamlining the workflow and ensuring that each task is completed efficiently. Automation, on the other hand, enables you to automate repetitive and time-consuming processes, reducing human error and increasing overall productivity.

>> **Focus on core activities:** By delegating tasks to capable individuals or automating them, you free up time to focus on activities that align with your passions and expertise. This ensures that you can dedicate yourself fully to the areas that matter most to you, resulting in greater satisfaction and fulfillment.

>> **Time for innovation and creativity:** When you delegate or automate routine tasks, you create space for innovative thinking and creative problem-solving. This allows you to explore new ideas and pursue your passions with a fresh perspective, leading to more meaningful and impactful outcomes.

>> **Reduced stress and overwhelm:** Delegation and automation can alleviate the feeling of being overwhelmed by an endless to-do list. By handing off certain responsibilities or automating repetitive tasks, you gain a sense of control over your time, reducing stress and improving your overall well-being.

>> **Optimal resource utilization:** Delegation enables you to leverage the expertise and skills of others, ensuring that tasks are assigned to the right people. Automation optimizes resource utilization by efficiently managing repetitive tasks without the need for excessive manual intervention.

>> **Enhanced decision-making:** Delegating certain tasks empowers you to focus on higher-level decision-making and strategic planning. It allows you to use your time wisely to make well-informed choices that align with your long-term goals and passions.

>> **Improved work-life balance:** By delegating or automating tasks that consume excessive time, you create more space for your personal life and self-care. This leads to a better work-life balance, contributing to your overall happiness and contentment.

Incorporating delegation and automation into your time management practices can be transformative. These powerful tools allow you to make the most of your time, ensuring that you invest it wisely in activities that bring you joy, satisfaction, and personal growth.

Identifying tasks that can be delegated or automated

Identifying tasks that you can delegate or automate is a crucial step in optimizing your time management and freeing up valuable resources for more important activities. Here are some steps to help you identify such tasks:

1. **Analyze your tasks:** Begin by analyzing all the tasks you regularly perform, both in your personal and your professional life. Make a list of these tasks to get a comprehensive overview.

2. **Assess their complexity and repetition:** Evaluate the complexity and frequency of each task. Tasks that are simple, repetitive, or time-consuming are good candidates for automation or delegation.

3. **Identify core competencies:** Identify tasks that require your unique expertise and skills. Focus on those tasks that align with your passion and contribute significantly to your goals.

4. **Consider resource allocation:** Determine the resources — including time, effort, and money — required to perform each task. If a task demands considerable resources but offers limited value, it might be a candidate for delegation or automation.

5. **Review technology and tools:** Research available technologies, software, and tools that can automate or streamline specific tasks. Numerous apps, software, and AI-driven solutions are designed to simplify certain processes.

6. **Consult with others:** In a professional setting, talk to your team or colleagues about their workload and identify areas where you can share or delegate tasks.

7. **Test and evaluate:** Automate or delegate a few selected tasks to gauge their impact and efficiency. Regularly review the results to ensure that the chosen approach is effective.

Depending on the work you do and the administrative and other tasks it requires, you can determine for yourself where you can save valuable time by executing these tasks in another way. Figure 13-1 is a tool for identifying such tasks. I've filled out the first row as an example, but you can customize such a worksheet to add more rows for each task you want to assess. Use the information you gather to make informed decisions on delegation and automation, ultimately streamlining your workflow and improving your time management.

Instructions:

Review your personal and professional tasks and identify those that you can delegate or automate. Use this worksheet to list the tasks and assess their suitability for delegation or automation. Consider the complexity, frequency, and resources required for each task. (One task has been added as an example.)

Task Description: Describe the task you want to assess for delegation or automation.

Complexity (Low/Medium/High): Rate the complexity of the task. Low-complexity tasks are simple and straightforward, whereas high-complexity tasks are intricate and require specialized skills.

Frequency (Daily/Weekly/Monthly): Indicate how often you need to perform the task. Tasks with higher frequency may be good candidates for automation.

Resources Required: Identify the resources (time, effort, money) you need to perform the task.

Value/Importance: Evaluate the value or importance of the task toward contributing to your goals.

Suitable for Delegation (Yes/No): Determine if you may delegate the task to others. Consider whether someone else has the required skills and capacity to handle the task effectively.

Suitable for Automation (Yes/No): Determine if you can automate the task using technology or tools.

Reasoning: Provide a brief explanation for why you believe the task is suitable for delegation or automation.

Task Description	Complexity	Frequency	Resources Required	Value/Importance
Email filtering	Low	Daily	Moderate (10 min/day)	High (Organizes work)

FIGURE 13-1: Choosing tasks to delegate or automate.

Developing Systems and Processes to Maximize Efficiency

Systems and processes are organized sets of actions designed to achieve specific objectives. They provide structure, consistency, and clarity in performing tasks, making it easier to tackle complex projects and responsibilities. When you have well-established systems and processes in place, you can easily replicate successful outcomes, identify and resolve inefficiencies, and maintain a sense of order in your daily routines.

Well-defined systems and processes allow you to complete tasks faster and with fewer errors, maximizing your productivity. They ensure that tasks are performed consistently and with a high level of quality. They also save time, allowing you to focus on more strategic or enjoyable activities. In addition, they reduce stress and uncertainty because you know how to approach tasks and have a clear plan in place. Moreover, efficient systems can accommodate growth and changing demands without sacrificing quality. Finally, by automating or simplifying repetitive tasks, you can devote more time to activities that align with your passion and goals.

Developing systems and processes is a strategic approach to managing your time and resources efficiently. By streamlining tasks and maximizing productivity, you create more space for pursuing your passion, achieving your goals, and experiencing greater fulfillment in both your personal and your professional life. Embrace the power of systems and processes, and witness the positive impact they have on your journey to finding and living your passion.

IN THIS CHAPTER

» Recognizing the many functions of fear

» Taking stock of what scares you

» Noticing when fear gets in your way

» Tackling your fears to transcend them

» Executing fear-defeating strategies

» Determining which risks to take

Chapter 14

Overcoming Fear and Taking Risks

F ear is a powerful emotion that can exert significant influence over your decisions and actions, including your pursuit of passions. On one hand, fear serves as a natural survival mechanism, alerting you to potential dangers and helping you avoid harm. In this context, fear is beneficial and protective. On the other hand, fear can be paralyzing, preventing you from taking risks and pursuing new opportunities. It can manifest in various ways, inhibiting you from taking the steps necessary to explore your true interests and talents. By understanding how fear can hold you back, you can identify these patterns in your life and work toward overcoming them.

Fear is an inherent part of the human experience, and it can significantly influence your pursuit of passion and fulfillment. When embarking on a journey to discover your true calling, you often encounter fears and uncertainties that can either propel you forward or hold you back. Understanding the role of fear in finding passion is essential because it enables you to navigate these emotions and make empowered choices.

This chapter explores the multifaceted nature of fear and its impact on your quest to uncover your passions. By acknowledging and addressing these fears, you can harness their potential as catalysts for personal growth and transformation.

Understanding the Role of Fear in Passion Pursuit

When it comes to discovering your passions, fear may arise from various sources. It might be a fear of failure, judgment, uncertainty, or even success. Recognizing this dual nature of fear is crucial in understanding its impact on your journey toward finding passion. Fear can be a formidable adversary on the path to pursuing your passions.

However, it isn't insurmountable. I offer real-life examples of people who overcame their fears, embraced their passions, and achieved greatness in their respective fields. By acknowledging and addressing your fears, you can move closer to realizing your passions and potential, unlocking a world of fulfillment and purpose.

Fear as an obstacle to passion

Fear can act as a significant barrier to exploring your passions. It may lead to self-doubt, hesitation, and a reluctance to step out of your comfort zone. Fear can convince you to settle for familiarity rather than pursuing your true desires, stifling your growth and potential. The fear of failure, in particular, can deter you from trying new things, taking risks, and discovering new passions and avenues for self-expression.

Fear as a catalyst for growth

Alternatively, fear can serve as a catalyst for growth and transformation. When you acknowledge and confront your fears, you create opportunities for self-discovery and personal development. Overcoming fear requires courage and resilience, both of which are essential qualities in your pursuit of passion. Embracing fear as a natural part of the process empowers you to push beyond your perceived limitations and explore uncharted territories, leading you to unexpected and fulfilling passions.

Navigating fear on the path to passion

Navigating fear in the pursuit of passion involves developing emotional intelligence and self-awareness. By recognizing and understanding your fears, you gain insight into their underlying causes and triggers. This awareness enables you to challenge limiting beliefs and thought patterns, freeing you to take bold steps toward your passions. Additionally, mentors, friends, or professionals can dispense valuable guidance and encouragement to help you overcome fear.

Fear plays a profound role in your quest to find passion and purpose. Although it can serve as an obstacle, it can also be a catalyst for personal growth and transformation. By acknowledging and addressing your fears, you gain the power to navigate through uncertainties, embrace opportunities, and discover your true passions. Embracing fear with resilience and self-compassion enables you to unlock the full potential of your journey and create a life of purpose, fulfillment, and meaning.

What Are You Afraid of? Looking at What Fears Can Hinder You

In the pursuit of passion and fulfillment, you're likely to encounter various types of fears that can act as significant barriers. Understanding these fears enables you to identify and address the specific challenges they present. Each fear has its unique impact on your journey toward finding passion, and recognizing them empowers you to develop strategies to overcome them.

This section discusses some common fears that can hinder passion pursuit and explores their effects on your personal growth and development.

Recognizing the different types of fear that hinder passion pursuit is a crucial step in your personal growth journey. Each fear presents unique challenges, but they're all opportunities for growth and transformation. By developing self-awareness and emotional intelligence, you can confront these fears with courage and resilience. Embracing your fears with compassion and openness allows you to transcend their limitations and embark on a fulfilling journey toward finding passion and purpose in life.

Fear of failure

One of the most common types of fear that hinders passion pursuit is the fear of failure. This fear can be paralyzing, preventing you from taking risks and exploring new opportunities. It often stems from a belief that failure leads to disappointment, judgment, or a loss of self-worth. The fear of failure can keep you trapped in your comfort zone, hindering your ability to embrace new challenges and discover your passions.

Fear of uncertainty

The fear of uncertainty revolves around the unknown and the lack of predictability in pursuing your passions. It may manifest as hesitation to make decisions because you fear the consequences of stepping into the unknown. Embracing passion often requires taking leaps of faith and venturing into unfamiliar territories, which can trigger this fear. Overcoming the fear of uncertainty involves cultivating a willingness to adapt and grow amidst life's unpredictability.

Fear of rejection and criticism

The fear of rejection and criticism revolves around the worry of being judged or disapproved of by others. This fear can stifle your authentic expression and creativity as you may seek to conform to societal expectations or avoid potential disapproval. The fear of rejection can prevent you from sharing your passions with the world and connecting with like-minded individuals and communities.

Fear of success

Surprisingly, the fear of success can also hinder passion pursuit. This fear may arise from concerns about increased responsibilities, the pressure to maintain success, or the fear of losing sight of your values amidst success. The fear of success can lead to self-sabotaging behaviors or a reluctance to fully commit to pursuing your passions.

Fear of change

Finding and following your passion often involves embracing change and stepping outside your comfort zone. The fear of change can be rooted in the familiarity of your current circumstances, leading to resistance toward exploring new possibilities. Overcoming this fear requires embracing adaptability and viewing change as an opportunity for growth and self-discovery.

Recognizing How Fear Gets in Your Way

Fear is an intrinsic part of the human experience, and you can't overlook its impact on your pursuit of passion. When it comes to seeking out your true purpose and following your dreams, fear can be both a driving force and a formidable obstacle.

Understanding the impact of fear on passion pursuit is essential. It brings valuable insights into your inner workings and allows you to navigate these emotions more effectively. This section covers the various ways fear can influence your journey toward finding passion and explores strategies to overcome its limitations.

REMEMBER

By recognizing the ways fear can manifest in your life, you can begin to challenge its grip on your aspirations. Embracing vulnerability, building resilience, and developing a growth mindset are essential steps toward liberating yourself from fear's limitations. When you confront fear head-on, you create space for your passions to thrive and lead a fulfilling life aligned with your deepest aspirations.

Inhibits exploration and risk-taking

Fear has the power to inhibit your sense of exploration and adventure. When you fear failure, rejection, or the unknown, you may hesitate to take risks and step outside your comfort zone. As a result, you may remain stuck in familiar and safe spaces, missing out on the opportunities that can lead you to discover your true passions.

Dampens creativity and authenticity

The fear of judgment or criticism can lead you to suppress your creativity and authenticity. You may hold back from expressing yourself fully, fearing that others may not accept or appreciate your true passions and talents. This self-censorship hinders your ability to embrace your uniqueness and share your genuine self with the world.

Undermines self-confidence

Fear can erode your self-confidence, leading to self-doubt and feelings of inadequacy. The fear of not being good enough or worthy of pursuing your passions can hold you back from even trying. Without self-confidence, you may struggle to take the necessary actions to move closer to your passions.

Creates limiting beliefs and mindsets

Fear can give rise to limiting beliefs and mindsets that hinder your progress. These beliefs, such as "I'm not talented enough" or "I'll never succeed," become self-fulfilling prophecies, preventing you from fully embracing your passions. These negative thought patterns can become ingrained, making it challenging to break free from their grip.

Hinders resilience and perseverance

The presence of fear can make it challenging to bounce back from setbacks and obstacles. Instead of viewing challenges as opportunities for growth, you may be disheartened by failures and setbacks. This lack of resilience and perseverance can dampen your commitment to pursuing your passions when faced with adversity.

Blocks meaningful connections

Fear can also hinder your ability to form meaningful connections and collaborations. When you fear rejection or judgment, you may avoid reaching out to like-minded individuals or potential mentors who can support your passion pursuit. Building a network of supportive individuals is essential for finding and nurturing your passions.

REMEMBER

Recognizing the impact of fear on passion pursuit is a significant step toward overcoming its limitations. By acknowledging your fears and understanding how they influence your thoughts and actions, you can take proactive steps to confront and manage them.

Embracing fear as a natural part of the journey toward finding passion allows you to develop the resilience, courage, and self-compassion needed to navigate the challenges that arise. As you work toward transcending fear, you can open yourself to a world of possibilities, unearthing your true passions and living a fulfilling life aligned with your authentic self.

Strategies to Overcome Fear and Take Risks

In the pursuit of your passions and dreams, fear can often become a formidable roadblock, hindering your progress and holding you back from reaching your full potential. The fear of failure, uncertainty, rejection, or stepping outside your comfort zone can be paralyzing, making it challenging to take the necessary risks to follow your true passions. However, overcoming fear is an essential aspect of personal growth and success. This section explores powerful strategies to conquer fear and embrace risk-taking, empowering you to move forward confidently on the path of passion pursuit.

Identifying and reframing limiting beliefs and negative self-talk

Limiting beliefs and negative self-talk are insidious barriers that can hold you back from pursuing your passions and achieving your true potential. These self-imposed limitations stem from past experiences, societal conditioning, and often irrational fears that undermine your confidence and self-belief. However, recognizing these thought patterns and learning to reframe them is a powerful way to break free from their grip and move forward fearlessly.

To begin this transformative process, engage in self-awareness and introspection. Take a moment to observe the thoughts and beliefs that arise when you contemplate pursuing your passion. Are there recurring negative thoughts like "I'm not good enough," "I don't have the skills," or "I'll never succeed"? These are indicators of limiting beliefs at play.

Next, challenge these beliefs with evidence to the contrary. Seek examples from your past where you demonstrated competence and perseverance, even in unrelated areas. Remind yourself of the times you achieved success in overcoming challenges. By doing so, you can reframe these limiting beliefs into more empowering and realistic statements.

For instance, if you find yourself thinking, "I don't have the skills to pursue my passion," remind yourself of the times you acquired new skills or learned quickly when faced with a new challenge. Shift the belief to, "I may not have all the skills now, but I can learn and grow along the way."

Another powerful tool is to replace negative self-talk with positive affirmations. Affirmations are statements that reinforce your strengths and potential. For example, repeat affirmations like, "I'm capable of achieving my dreams," "I'm resilient and can overcome any obstacles," and "I'm worthy of pursuing my passions."

Practicing mindfulness can also help in identifying and challenging limiting beliefs and negative self-talk. Observe your thoughts without judgment, and when you notice negative patterns, gently redirect your focus to positive and empowering thoughts.

It takes time and effort to reframe limiting beliefs and negative self-talk, but with persistence and self-compassion, you can create a new, empowering narrative that propels you forward in your passion pursuit. By challenging and transforming these beliefs, you develop a growth-oriented mindset that embraces challenges as opportunities for growth, ultimately allowing you to take calculated risks and follow your passions with renewed confidence.

Identifying the risks and rewards of pursuing your passion

Pursuing your passion can be a transformative and fulfilling journey, but like any endeavor, it comes with its share of risks and rewards. Understanding both sides of the equation is essential to making informed decisions and navigating the path to success.

Table 14-1 looks at some of the risks.

TABLE 14-1   **Risks of Pursuing Your Passion**

Risk	What It Entails
Financial insecurity	Depending on your passion, it might not always translate into immediate financial stability. Starting a business, pursuing a creative career, or switching industries can involve financial uncertainty, especially during the initial stages.
Fear of failure	Pursuing your passion often involves stepping into uncharted territory. The fear of failure and not living up to your own or others' expectations can be paralyzing and might hinder progress.
Time and commitment	Passion-driven endeavors can demand significant time and effort. Balancing personal life, work, and pursuing your passion can be challenging and might lead to burnout if you don't manage it effectively.
Lack of support	Some passions might not align with societal norms or family expectations, leading to a lack of support or discouragement from pursuing your dreams.

Table 14-2 lists some rewards.

TABLE 14-2   **Rewards of Pursuing Your Passion**

Reward	What It Brings
Fulfillment and satisfaction	Following your passion brings a sense of purpose and fulfillment that transcends monetary rewards. It allows you to align your life with what truly matters to you.
Personal growth	Pursuing your passion involves pushing boundaries, learning new skills, and overcoming obstacles. This journey of personal growth and self-discovery can be immensely rewarding.
Work-life alignment	Integrating your passion into your career or lifestyle can lead to a more balanced and fulfilling life, where work feels less like a chore and more like a meaningful pursuit.
Impact on others	Passion-driven endeavors often have a positive impact on others. Whether through inspiring others to pursue their dreams or making a difference in their lives, you can create a lasting impact.
Success and recognition	By dedicating yourself to your passion, you increase the likelihood of excelling in your chosen field. Success and recognition often follow when you become an expert in what you love.

Taking small steps toward your goals and building momentum

In the pursuit of your passions, it's easy to feel overwhelmed by the magnitude of your dreams. Whether it's starting a new business, writing a book, or embarking on a new creative endeavor, the sheer size of the goal can sometimes lead to inaction. However, the key to making significant progress and achieving your aspirations lies in taking small, consistent steps and building momentum along the way.

Read on to explore the power of taking small steps and how it helps in building momentum toward your goals.

Step 1. Breaking down the big picture

When you focus solely on the end goal, it can appear daunting and almost unattainable. By breaking down the bigger picture into smaller, manageable tasks, you create a clear roadmap toward success. Each small step becomes a milestone, propelling you forward and instilling a sense of accomplishment.

Step 2. Overcoming procrastination

Procrastination often stems from feeling overwhelmed by the enormity of the task at hand. Taking small steps creates a sense of urgency and motivation to act. Once you start, the momentum gained from completing one task encourages you to move on to the next.

Step 3. Building confidence

Success breeds confidence. As you consistently accomplish smaller tasks, you gain confidence in your abilities to handle more substantial challenges. This growing self-assurance propels you to take on more significant endeavors with determination.

Step 4. Embracing continuous improvement

The journey toward your passion is a continuous process of learning and refining your skills. Taking small steps allows you to learn from each experience, make adjustments, and improve over time. It's about progress, not perfection.

Step 5. Maintaining consistency

Consistency is the key to success. By taking small, consistent steps, you develop habits that keep you focused and on track. These habits build the discipline you need to see your goals through to fruition.

Step 6. Overcoming fear and resistance

Often, fear and resistance hold you back from pursuing your passions. However, taking small steps enables you to face your fears gradually. With each successful step, fear diminishes, and your capacity to take bolder actions increases.

Knowing When and How to Take Calculated Risks

In the pursuit of your passions and dreams, there inevitably comes a time when you need to step outside your comfort zone and take risks. While the prospect of taking risks can be intimidating, it's often a crucial catalyst for growth and achievement. However, not all risks are created equal. Knowing when and how to take calculated risks is an essential skill that can make the difference between success and failure.

Understanding the difference between calculated risks and reckless risks

In the pursuit of your passions, taking risks is inevitable. However, not all risks are created equal. There's a crucial distinction between calculated risks and reckless risks. Although both involve stepping into the unknown, the outcomes they yield can be vastly different.

Calculated risks are carefully assessed and analyzed before taking action. They involve a thoughtful evaluation of potential benefits and drawbacks, considering the probabilities of success and failure. When taking a calculated risk, you gather information, seek advice, and weigh the potential rewards against the possible consequences. This strategic approach empowers you to make informed decisions and embrace uncertainty with a sense of preparedness.

In contrast, reckless risks are impulsive and hasty actions taken without much consideration for the consequences. They often stem from emotions like fear or impulsiveness, leading to decisions that aren't well thought out. Reckless risks can be driven by a desire for instant gratification or a lack of understanding of the potential downsides.

Calculated risks are strategic decisions that are carefully analyzed and evaluated before taking action. They involve a thorough assessment of potential benefits and drawbacks, considering the probabilities of success and failure. When taking a calculated risk, you gather relevant information, seek advice from experts or mentors, and conduct a comprehensive analysis of the situation. The goal is to make an informed decision that maximizes the chances of achieving the desired outcome while minimizing potential negative consequences.

In the context of pursuing passion, calculated risks often involve stepping out of your comfort zone to seize opportunities for growth and personal development. They may include starting a new business venture, pursuing a career change, or embracing a creative endeavor. Taking calculated risks doesn't imply that there's no uncertainty or possibility of failure. Instead, it means approaching risk with a sense of preparedness and a willingness to learn from both successes and setbacks.

Those who embrace calculated risks are willing to invest time, effort, and resources in pursuit of their goals, recognizing that the potential rewards outweigh the risks. They use a rational and strategic approach to decision-making, ensuring that their actions align with their values and long-term objectives.

Ultimately, calculated risks are an essential part of the journey to finding passion and fulfillment. They enable individuals to explore new opportunities, challenge themselves, and unlock their true potential, all while navigating the uncertainties of life with a thoughtful and well-considered approach.

Reckless risks, in contrast to calculated risks, are impulsive and ill-considered actions that are taken without adequate evaluation of potential consequences. Reckless risk-takers often act on impulse, without properly assessing the likelihood of success or the potential negative outcomes. They may be driven by a desire for immediate gratification or driven by emotions such as excitement or impulsivity, without giving due thought to the potential repercussions of their actions.

Reckless risk-taking can lead to hasty decisions that may result in adverse consequences, such as financial loss, damaged relationships, or missed opportunities. Those who engage in reckless risks may ignore warning signs or disregard feedback from others, believing that they can overcome obstacles or that things will somehow work out in their favor.

In the context of pursuing passion, reckless risks can hinder progress and impede personal growth. Instead of taking measured steps toward their goals, reckless risk-takers may leap into ventures without proper planning or without fully understanding the challenges ahead. This approach can lead to disappointment and setbacks, hindering their ability to find true fulfillment and passion.

Taking risks, in general, is an inherent part of pursuing your passions and dreams. However, you need to distinguish between calculated risks and reckless risks. By approaching risk with a thoughtful and strategic mindset, you can increase your chances of success while minimizing unnecessary setbacks.

Understanding the difference between these two types of risks is vital in your passion pursuit. By cultivating the ability to discern calculated risks from reckless ones, you can navigate challenges with clarity, foresight, and confidence. This section covers the key elements that distinguish the two, empowering you to make wise choices and approach risk-taking with a discerning mindset.

Identifying factors that contribute to making informed decisions about taking risks

Identifying factors that contribute to making informed decisions about taking risks is essential when you're seeking to pursue your passions in a balanced and thoughtful manner. Following are some key factors to consider:

>> **Assessment of potential outcomes:** Evaluating the potential outcomes of a risk is crucial. Consider the best-case scenario, the worst-case scenario, and the likelihood of each. Weigh the potential benefits against the possible drawbacks to make an informed decision.

>> **Understanding personal goals and values:** Aligning the risks with your long-term goals and values can provide clarity on whether a risk is worth taking. Ensure that the risk is in harmony with your passions and aspirations.

>> **Gathering information:** Conduct thorough research to gather relevant information about the risk you're considering. This can involve conducting market research, consulting with experts, or seeking advice from trusted mentors.

>> **Analyzing past experiences:** Reflect on your past experiences with risk-taking. Identify patterns of success and failure, and use them to inform your decisions.

>> **Risk tolerance:** Understand your risk tolerance level, which varies from person to person. Assess how comfortable you are with taking risks, and tailor your decisions accordingly.

>> **Having a contingency plan:** Develop a contingency plan to address potential challenges or setbacks. Having a backup strategy can make you more confident and mitigate some of the fear associated with taking risks.

>> **Seeking advice and feedback:** Consult with others who have experience in the domain you're exploring. Seek feedback from mentors, colleagues, or peers to gain valuable insights and different perspectives.

>> **Trusting intuition and gut feelings:** Intuition can play a role in decision-making. Pay attention to your instincts and feelings, especially when they align with your values and knowledge.

>> **Avoiding hasty decisions:** Taking time to deliberate and avoiding impulsive decisions is vital. Rushing into risks without adequate consideration can lead to regrets.

>> **Balancing fear and courage:** Acknowledge that fear is a natural response when taking risks, but use courage and determination to overcome it and move forward.

By taking these factors into account, you can make informed decisions about taking risks, allowing you to pursue your passions in a manner that is both bold and calculated. Such an approach can lead to personal growth, learning experiences, and a more fulfilling journey toward finding your true passion.

Developing a risk management strategy and contingency plan

Developing a risk management strategy and contingency plan is a crucial aspect of taking calculated risks while pursuing your passion. Here are some steps to create an effective risk management strategy:

» **Risk identification:** Begin by identifying potential risks associated with your pursuit of passion. Consider both internal and external factors that can affect your journey.

» **Risk analysis:** Assess the likelihood and potential impact of each identified risk. Categorize risks as low, medium, or high in terms of their severity.

» **Risk mitigation:** Develop strategies to mitigate the identified risks. This may involve creating alternative paths, seeking partnerships, or obtaining relevant insurance or support.

» **Contingency planning:** Create a contingency plan for each major risk. Outline specific actions and responses you will implement if the risk becomes a reality.

» **Monitoring and evaluation:** Continuously monitor your progress and reevaluate the risks as your pursuit unfolds. Stay vigilant to any emerging risks, and be prepared to adapt your strategy as needed.

» **Building a safety net:** Establish a safety net of resources, support, or finances that can help you cope with potential setbacks. This safety net can be your source of security and confidence for taking more calculated risks.

» **Learning from setbacks:** Embrace setbacks as learning opportunities. Analyze the reasons behind any failures, and use the insights to refine your risk management strategy.

» **Seeking professional advice:** If you encounter complex risks or challenges, seek guidance from professionals who have expertise in relevant fields. They can offer valuable insights and help you navigate potential obstacles.

» **Maintaining flexibility:** Be open to adjusting your plans and strategies as circumstances change. A flexible approach allows you to pivot and make necessary adjustments when unforeseen challenges arise.

» **Cultivating resilience:** Cultivate resilience to bounce back from setbacks and stay committed to your pursuit. Remember that risks are an inherent part of any meaningful journey.

By developing a comprehensive risk management strategy and contingency plan, you can approach your passion pursuit with greater confidence and assurance.

REMEMBER

A well-thought-out risk management strategy and contingency plan empowers you to take calculated risks while pursuing your passion. Regularly revisit and update this worksheet as you progress on your journey. Stay committed, and embrace the challenges and opportunities that come your way!

Building Confidence and Resilience in Taking Risks

Confidence is a positive and assured belief in your own abilities, skills, and judgment. It involves trusting in yourself and your capacity to handle challenges, achieve goals, and overcome obstacles. Confidence isn't about being arrogant or boastful but rather about having a strong sense of self-assurance and a healthy level of self-esteem.

Table 14-3 lists some of the characteristics that confident individuals exhibit.

TABLE 14-3 **Characteristics of Confident Individuals**

Trait	How It Manifests
Self-belief	Faith in your own abilities; not easily discouraged by setbacks or failures.
Courage	Willingness to take on new challenges and step outside your comfort zone.
Positive outlook	Positive attitude; focused on opportunities and solutions rather than problems.
Resilience	Ability to bounce back from setbacks and use failures as learning opportunities.
Effective communication	Proficiency in expressing thoughts and ideas clearly and assertively.
Self-motivation	Ambition to achieve goals without waiting for external validation or approval.
Openness to learning	Acceptance of feedback and continuous pursuit of self-improvement.

Confidence plays a crucial role in personal and professional success. It empowers you to take risks, seize opportunities, and face challenges with determination. When you believe in yourself, you're more likely to pursue your passions and ambitions, leading to a fulfilling and meaningful life.

REMEMBER

Confidence isn't an inherent trait; you can develop and strengthen it through experiences, self-reflection, and personal growth. Building confidence involves challenging self-limiting beliefs, setting and achieving goals, and embracing a growth mindset. As you cultivate confidence, you'll find yourself better equipped to navigate life's challenges and pursue your passions with conviction.

Resilience is the ability to bounce back, adapt, and recover from adversity, challenges, or significant life changes. It's the capacity to maintain mental and emotional strength in the face of setbacks and difficult circumstances. Resilient individuals possess the inner resources and coping strategies that allow them to withstand and even grow stronger through adversity.

Table 14-4 lists some key characteristics of resilient individuals.

TABLE 14-4   **Characteristics of Resilient Individuals**

Trait	How It Manifests
Positive outlook	Optimistic perspective; focused on possibilities and solutions rather than problems.
Emotional regulation	Ability to manage and express emotions in a healthy and constructive manner, which helps navigate challenging situations effectively.
Problem-solving skills	Inventiveness and expertise at finding solutions to encountered issues.
Flexibility	Adaptiveness to change and new circumstances, remaining open-minded and willing to adjust an approach.
Social support	Strong support systems of friends, family, or mentors who offer a network to lean on during tough times.
Self-compassion	Adherence to self-compassion and avoidance of self-blame, acknowledging that setbacks are a normal part of life and not a reflection of worth.
Growth mindset	Acceptance of challenges as opportunities for learning and personal growth rather than as insurmountable obstacles.

Resilience isn't about avoiding difficult situations or emotions; it's about developing the capacity to cope with and bounce back from them. You may experience stress, failure, or loss, but you can navigate these experiences without being overwhelmed, and you emerge stronger on the other side.

Building resilience is an ongoing process that involves developing coping skills, fostering social connections, setting realistic expectations, and practicing self-care. By enhancing resilience, you can effectively manage the challenges you encounter in your pursuit of passion and personal growth.

Chapter **15**

Building a Support System

Pursuing your passion can be a transformative and challenging experience, and having a support system in place is akin to having a safety net to
catch you when you stumble. A well-structured support system consists of
friends, family, mentors, peers, and other individuals who share similar interests and values. They become cheerleaders, advisors, and collaborators, offering
encouragement during difficult times, valuable feedback to guide your growth,
and opportunities to expand your horizons.

In the pursuit of passion, a strong and reliable support system plays a vital role
in your journey. The path to discovering and following your passions can be both
exhilarating and challenging, and having a support system can make all the difference. Whether it's pursuing a new career, starting a business, or diving into a
creative endeavor, having people who believe in you, guide you, and offer emotional support can be transformative.

The importance of a support system lies in its ability to empower you, uplift you
during difficult times, and reinforce your commitment to your passions. A well-
built support system can supply invaluable benefits as you navigate the twists and
turns of your passion pursuit. It acts as a safety net during setbacks and celebrates
your successes, creating an environment of encouragement and inspiration.

This chapter explores the various aspects of building a support system, from identifying the right individuals to understanding the positive impact it has on your motivation and well-being. It dives into the significance of cultivating meaningful connections and embracing the power of a support system in your journey to finding and living your passion.

The Value of Social Support in Passion Pursuit

Social support plays a crucial role in passion pursuit, providing a network of individuals who give encouragement, understanding, and validation. These people can be family members, friends, mentors, or colleagues who share your enthusiasm and believe in your capabilities. Their presence can serve as a source of motivation and strength when you encounter challenges or self-doubt.

One of the primary functions of social support in passion pursuit is validation. When you share your passions with others, their encouragement and positive feedback validate your interests and give you the confidence to pursue them further. Social support can act as a sounding board for your ideas and aspirations, offering constructive feedback and helping you refine your goals.

Additionally, social support feeds your motivation during challenging times. Passion pursuit can be met with obstacles and self-doubt, and having a support system that believes in you can boost your resilience and determination. Knowing that you have people who genuinely care about your success can help you push through difficulties and stay committed to your passions.

Furthermore, social support can broaden your perspectives and expose you to new opportunities. Through interactions with supportive individuals, you may discover new interests, insights, and potential collaborations that enrich your passion pursuit. The exchange of ideas and experiences within a supportive network can open doors to previously unexplored paths.

Here's an example. Sarah is an aspiring writer with a passion for storytelling. Despite her love for writing, Sarah struggled to find the confidence to share her work with others. She felt vulnerable and worried about criticism. However, when she joined a local writing group, she discovered a community of like-minded individuals who offered constructive feedback and unwavering support. Through their encouragement, Sarah gained the confidence to pursue her writing dreams and eventually published her first novel.

When pursuing a passion, you might encounter obstacles and uncertainties that cloud your judgment. Having a support system allows you to gain fresh perspectives and brainstorm potential solutions. Additionally, receiving feedback from others can help you refine your ideas and approach, leading to a more focused and effective pursuit of your passions.

Moreover, social support plays a vital role in maintaining your emotional well-being throughout your passion pursuit. Pursuing your dreams can be emotionally taxing, with highs and lows that may affect your motivation and mental state. Having individuals who genuinely care about your well-being can be a buffer against stress and anxiety, fostering a sense of resilience and perseverance.

In another example, there's Mark, a young entrepreneur passionate about environmental conservation. He faced numerous setbacks while building his sustainable products company. However, the unwavering support from his family and friends kept him going during difficult times. Their belief in his mission and constant encouragement helped Mark navigate challenges and eventually create a successful business that aligned with his values.

Don't underestimate the role of social support in passion pursuit. It empowers you with the confidence to pursue your dreams, offers valuable insights and feedback, and nurtures your emotional well-being. The stories of individuals like Sarah and Mark exemplify how a strong support system can elevate your passion pursuit and drive you toward success and fulfillment.

Bolstering motivation and well-being

Having a support network means you're not alone in pursuing your goals. Isolation and lack of support can have a significant impact on motivation and well-being when pursuing your passions. Without a support system to lean on, you may feel disconnected and discouraged, leading to a decline in motivation and enthusiasm for your goals.

One of the key challenges of isolation is the absence of external validation and encouragement. When you share your passions with others, you seek validation and acknowledgment for your efforts. However, in isolation, there are limited opportunities to receive this validation, which can lead to self-doubt and a sense of inadequacy. As a result, your motivation to continue pursuing your passions may dwindle, and you might question whether your endeavors are worthwhile.

Additionally, isolation can create a sense of loneliness and alienation. Passion pursuit can be a lonely journey, especially if others around you don't share the same interests or fail to understand the significance of your goals. The lack of like-minded individuals to share experiences and ideas with can lead to feelings of isolation, further impacting your emotional well-being.

Consider the case of Alex, a musician who dedicated years to mastering the guitar and composing original songs. However, due to a lack of support from family and friends, Alex felt discouraged and began to doubt his musical abilities. The isolation he experienced hindered his progress, and he started to lose interest in pursuing his passion.

Furthermore, isolation can limit access to new perspectives and insights. When you're surrounded by a diverse group of individuals with different experiences and expertise, you have the opportunity to learn from each other and gain fresh perspectives. Without this external input, your growth and development may become stagnant.

In contrast, having a support system provides a sense of belonging and fosters a positive environment for passion pursuit. If you feel connected to a community of like-minded people, you're more likely to remain motivated and resilient, even in the face of challenges. You can draw strength from the encouragement and empathy of your support network, which bolsters your confidence and determination.

Recognizing the impact of isolation and lack of support on motivation and well-being is essential for pursuing your passion. The absence of a support system can lead to self-doubt, loneliness, and limited growth. On the other hand, having a strong support network can supply you with the validation, encouragement, and diverse perspectives necessary to sustain motivation and foster personal growth toward your passion pursuit.

Fostering personal and professional growth

A strong support system plays a crucial role in cultivating personal and professional growth, especially when pursuing your passion. The benefits of having a support system are multifaceted and can significantly affect your journey of growth and development.

First and foremost, a support system offers encouragement and motivation. When facing challenges and setbacks in the pursuit of passion, having people who believe in you and your abilities can make all the difference. Supportive friends, family members, mentors, and colleagues can offer valuable words of encouragement, reminding you of your strengths and accomplishments and pushing you forward during difficult times.

Moreover, a support system can serve as a source of valuable feedback and guidance. Trusted individuals within the support network can offer constructive criticism, share insights, and provide advice that can contribute to your personal and professional development. Their different perspectives can shed light on blind spots you may have missed on your own, helping you make better-informed decisions and grow from your experiences.

Another benefit of a support system is the access to resources and opportunities. Within a well-connected network, you can leverage your connections to access learning opportunities, workshops, networking events, and other resources that can further enhance your skills and knowledge in your chosen field. These opportunities can open doors to new experiences and avenues for personal growth.

Furthermore, a support system fosters a sense of belonging and community. Feeling connected to others who share similar passions or goals can alleviate feelings of loneliness and isolation. Being part of a supportive community means a safe space to share challenges, successes, and aspirations, and this sense of belonging can boost your confidence and self-esteem.

Consider the example of Melissa, a young entrepreneur with a passion for sustainable fashion. She joined a community of like-minded individuals in her city, where she found encouragement, valuable insights, and opportunities to collaborate with others. This support system not only boosted her confidence but gave her the guidance and resources to grow her business successfully.

A support system offers a multitude of benefits in personal and professional growth. It provides encouragement, feedback, and access to resources, while fostering a sense of belonging and community. If you're on the journey of pursuing your passion, building and maintaining a strong support network can be a transformative factor in your growth and success.

Building and Maintaining a Support System

Building and maintaining a strong support system is a vital aspect of any journey, especially when it comes to pursuing passion and personal growth. Although passion can be a powerful driving force, having a network of supportive and like-minded individuals can make the difference between wavering in uncertainty and confidently forging ahead. This section explores the strategies and insights needed to build a robust support system that nurtures, empowers, and sustains you on your quest to discover and embrace your passions.

Read about the art of building a support system that aligns with personal values and objectives. From identifying potential networking opportunities and nurturing professional relationships to seeking out mentors and role models, it covers various strategies that facilitate the creation of a community of like-minded individuals.

REMEMBER

Building and maintaining a support system isn't merely about seeking assistance, but about contributing to the growth of others. By actively participating in a community, you can provide mutual support and encouragement, creating a positive cycle of inspiration and empowerment.

Here's how you can build a diverse and inclusive support system:

>> **Be open to different perspectives:** Embrace the diversity of opinions, backgrounds, and experiences that people bring to the table. Approach conversations with an open mind, and be willing to learn from others' viewpoints.

>> **Seek out diverse networks:** Look for opportunities to connect with people from different cultural, ethnic, and social backgrounds. Attend events, workshops, and gatherings that attract a diverse group of individuals who share your passion.

>> **Create an inclusive environment:** In your interactions with others, make a conscious effort to be inclusive and welcoming. Encourage everyone to participate and contribute, regardless of their background or identity.

>> **Be respectful and empathetic:** Treat others with respect and empathy, recognizing that everyone has unique challenges and perspectives. Be mindful of cultural differences, and avoid making assumptions.

>> **Engage in intersectional conversations:** Intersectionality acknowledges the interconnected nature of various aspects of identity, such as race, gender, and socio-economic status. Engaging in conversations that consider these intersections can lead to deeper understanding and connection.

>> **Challenge biases and stereotypes:** Be aware of your own biases and stereotypes, and actively challenge them. Educate yourself about different cultures and identities to promote inclusivity.

>> **Promote inclusivity in your community:** If you're part of an organization or group related to your passion, advocate for inclusive practices and policies. Encourage diverse representation in leadership roles and decision-making processes.

>> **Support underrepresented voices:** Amplify the voices of individuals from underrepresented groups within your passion's community. Acknowledge and celebrate their contributions and achievements.

>> **Foster safe spaces:** Create safe and respectful spaces where individuals can express themselves without fear of judgment or discrimination. Encourage open dialogue and constructive feedback.

>> **Be mindful of language and communication:** Use language that's inclusive and avoids perpetuating stereotypes or exclusivity. Be mindful of the impact your words may have on others.

Building a diverse and inclusive support system not only enriches your passion pursuit but contributes to a more compassionate and understanding society. Embrace the richness of human diversity, and actively seek opportunities to connect with individuals from all walks of life. Embracing inclusivity leads to a more meaningful and impactful journey as you pursue your passion.

As you explore the importance of fostering meaningful connections, you'll discover the immense power of a support system in fueling your passions, overcoming challenges, and achieving personal and professional fulfillment.

Identifying the people and resources that can support you

Identifying the right people and resources to support your passion pursuit is a crucial step in building an effective support system. These individuals and assets play a significant role in encouraging, guiding, and amplifying your efforts toward realizing your dreams. Here are some key elements to consider while identifying your support network:

>> **Family and friends:** Your immediate circle of family and friends often forms the bedrock of your support system. They're the ones who know you intimately and can provide emotional support during challenging times. Consider the family members and friends who have shown genuine interest in your passions, listen to your ideas without judgment, and are ready to stand by your side through thick and thin. For example, if you have a passion for art, a supportive family member might encourage you to take up art classes or give you a dedicated space for creative endeavors.

>> **Mentors and role models:** Mentors and role models can offer invaluable insights and guidance based on their own experiences. Look for individuals who have achieved success in areas related to your passion and who are willing to share their knowledge and expertise. They can serve as a source of inspiration and help you navigate through the challenges that lie ahead. For instance, if you aspire to become an entrepreneur, connect with a successful business owner as a mentor because that person can offer invaluable advice and encouragement.

>> **Networking communities:** Seek out networking communities, both online and offline, that revolve around your area of interest. These communities can be professional associations, clubs, or online forums where people with similar passions come together to share ideas and collaborate. Joining such communities opens up opportunities to meet like-minded individuals who can offer support, collaboration, and constructive feedback. For instance, if you're passionate about sustainable living, joining a local environmental group can connect you with others who share your passion and ideas.

>> **Educational and skill development resources:** Look for resources that can enhance your skills and knowledge related to your passion. These may include workshops, courses, webinars, books, or online platforms. Continuous learning is crucial for personal growth, and having access to relevant educational resources not only empowers you but strengthens your credibility in your chosen field.

>> **Supportive work environment:** If you're pursuing your passion while holding a job, having a supportive work environment can make a significant difference. Seek out workplaces that encourage personal growth, creativity, and innovation. A supportive boss and understanding colleagues can create a positive atmosphere where you can thrive both professionally and personally.

TIP

Building a support system is an ongoing process, and it's essential to surround yourself with individuals who believe in your potential and support your journey. Keep an open mind, seek out opportunities to connect with others, and don't hesitate to reach out for help when needed. With the right support system in place, you're better equipped to face challenges, stay motivated, and make significant strides in your pursuit of passion.

Developing relationships and networks with like-minded individuals

Developing relationships and networks with like-minded individuals is a fundamental aspect of building a strong support system. When you connect with people who share your passions and interests, you create a sense of community and camaraderie that can be highly motivating and empowering. Here are some key steps to foster meaningful relationships with like-minded individuals:

>> **Attend events and workshops:** Look for events, workshops, seminars, or conferences related to your passion. These gatherings are excellent opportunities to meet people who share similar interests and goals. Engaging in discussions and sharing your experiences can lead to valuable connections.

>> **Join online communities:** The digital age offers various online platforms and social media groups centered around specific interests. Join relevant online

communities, and actively participate in discussions. Share your thoughts, seek advice, and connect with others who are equally passionate about the subject.

>> **Volunteer for causes:** Engaging in volunteer work related to your passion is a fantastic way to meet like-minded individuals while contributing to a cause you care about. Whether it's environmental conservation, animal welfare, or community service, volunteering brings people together who have shared values.

>> **Participate in collaborative projects:** Seek out opportunities to collaborate on projects or initiatives that align with your interests. Working together toward a common goal can strengthen bonds and open doors to new possibilities.

>> **Attend meetups and networking events:** Many cities organize meetups and networking events for specific interests or industries. Attend these gatherings to meet others who are enthusiastic about the same topics as you. Don't be afraid to initiate conversations and exchange contact information to stay connected.

>> **Engage in online discussions:** Actively participate in online forums and discussion boards that focus on your passion. Share your insights, and ask questions to engage with others and build relationships within the online community.

>> **Organize or host gatherings:** If you can't find local events that cater to your specific interests, consider organizing your own gatherings or meetups. By taking the initiative, you can attract like-minded individuals and foster a sense of community around your passion.

>> **Be a supportive listener:** Building relationships isn't just about expressing your own interests but about showing genuine interest in others' passions. Be a supportive listener, and learn from the experiences of those around you.

Remember, building meaningful relationships takes time and effort. Be patient and authentic in your interactions, and focus on nurturing connections that align with your values and interests. Like-minded individuals can be a tremendous source of inspiration, encouragement, and shared knowledge as you pursue your passion.

The Role of Accountability Partners and Peer Support

The support and encouragement of others can be a powerful catalyst for success. This is where accountability partners and peer support come into play, providing a crucial role in keeping you motivated, focused, and on track. As you navigate the challenges and triumphs of following your passions, having individuals who hold you accountable and share in your journey can make all the difference. This section explores the importance of accountability partners and peer support and how they can contribute to your growth, resilience, and ultimate success in pursuing your passions. Read on to discover how these meaningful connections can become pillars of strength in your pursuit of fulfillment and purpose.

Understanding the benefits of accountability in passion pursuit

Accountability plays a vital role in your journey to find passion. It acts as a powerful motivator that keeps you committed to your goals and aspirations. When you have someone to hold you accountable, you're more likely to stay on track, push through obstacles, and maintain your focus even when challenges arise. Knowing that you're answerable to someone else, whether it's a friend, mentor, or colleague, creates a sense of responsibility and helps you avoid procrastination or complacency.

One of the significant benefits of accountability in passion pursuit is that it enhances your self-discipline. When you have someone who's aware of your objectives and progress, you feel a greater sense of obligation to stay consistent and disciplined in your actions. This can be particularly helpful when you encounter setbacks or face moments of self-doubt. An accountability partner can offer encouragement, remind you of your capabilities, and reinforce your commitment to the path you've chosen.

Accountability also fosters a sense of support and camaraderie. By sharing your aspirations with someone who genuinely cares about your success, you build a deeper connection and create a support system that boosts your morale during challenging times. This support system can result in valuable insights, ideas, and feedback that you might not have considered on your own.

Real-life examples abound of individuals who have benefited significantly from accountability in their passion pursuit. For instance, an aspiring writer joined a writing group where members shared their work and held each other accountable for regular writing sessions. As a result, the writer made consistent progress, completed a novel, and eventually got it published. Similarly, a fitness enthusiast partnered with a friend to achieve their fitness goals. The mutual support and shared commitment not only helped them stay motivated but made the journey more enjoyable.

In essence, accountability acts as a guiding force that keeps you on course and reminds you of the importance of your passions. It fuels your determination and reinforces the belief that your dreams are worth pursuing. When you embrace accountability, you open yourself to a world of possibilities and create a sense of responsibility that propels you forward on your quest to discover your true purpose.

Identifying potential accountability partners and peer support groups

Identifying the right accountability partners and peer support groups is crucial for effectively leveraging the power of accountability in passion pursuit. When selecting these individuals or groups, you need to seek those who share similar interests, values, and goals. Here are some steps to identify potential accountability partners and peer support groups:

>> **Assess your needs:** Start by reflecting on your specific goals and the areas where you feel you need the most support and accountability. Are you seeking someone to help you stay focused on your career aspirations, personal projects, or health and wellness goals? Understanding your needs can guide your search for the right individuals or groups.

>> **Look within your circle:** Begin your search for accountability partners among your existing network of friends, colleagues, or acquaintances. You may find individuals who share common interests and are eager to pursue their passions. A friend with a similar passion or a colleague looking to achieve similar goals can be an excellent starting point.

>> **Join online communities:** The internet offers a vast array of online communities and forums focused on various interests and passions. Platforms like Meetup, Facebook, and LinkedIn have groups that are great places to connect with like-minded individuals who are on a similar journey. Participate in discussions and events to get to know potential accountability partners.

>> **Attend workshops and events:** Look for workshops, seminars, or events related to your passion or area of interest. These gatherings often attract people with shared passions, making it easier to find individuals or groups that align with your goals.

>> **Reach out to professional networks:** If your passion pursuit is related to your career or professional development, consider reaching out to professional networks or industry associations. People who have similar career aspirations can lend you valuable support and insights.

>> **Online mastermind groups:** A mastermind group is a peer-to-peer mentoring group used to help members solve their problems with input and advice from the other group members. The concept was coined in 1925 by

author Napoleon Hill in his book *The Law of Success,* and described in more detail in his 1937 book *Think and Grow Rich.* Mastermind groups are designed to facilitate peer support, accountability, and knowledge sharing. Look for existing mastermind groups, or consider starting one with individuals who have complementary skills and aspirations.

>> **Attend meetups and networking events:** Attend local meetups and networking events related to your interests. These gatherings are an excellent opportunity to meet new people and explore potential accountability partnerships.

>> **Evaluate compatibility:** Once you've identified potential accountability partners or groups, take the time to evaluate compatibility. Look for individuals who are genuinely invested in their own growth and willing to offer meaningful support. Mutual respect and shared commitment are essential factors in a successful accountability partnership.

Remember that accountability partnerships and peer support groups can evolve over time, so it's okay to experiment and adjust until you find the right fit. Building a strong support system can be a transformative experience that propels you closer to your passions and fosters an environment of encouragement and growth.

Developing a plan for accountability and peer support

Developing a solid plan for accountability and peer support is essential to ensure that you and your partners stay on track and effectively support each other in your passion pursuit. Use these steps to create a robust plan:

1. **Set clear goals:** Begin by defining your specific passion-pursuit goals. Ensure that your objectives are specific, measurable, achievable, relevant, and time-bound (SMART). Share these goals with your accountability partners or group members so that everyone is on the same page.

2. **Establish regular check-ins:** Decide on the frequency and format of your accountability check-ins. It could be weekly, biweekly, or monthly meetings, depending on the nature of your goals and the availability of participants. Utilize video calls, phone calls, or in-person meetings to connect effectively.

3. **Define accountability measures:** Determine how you'll track and measure progress toward your goals. It might involve sharing updates, milestones, or metrics with each other. Accountability partners can provide constructive feedback and encouragement, which helps you stay motivated and focused.

4. **Create a supportive environment:** Foster an environment of trust and nonjudgment within your accountability partnership or peer support group. Make it safe for everyone to share their challenges and setbacks without fear of criticism. Supportive and empathetic feedback builds resilience and encourages continued effort.

5. **Establish consequences (if desired):** Some accountability partnerships choose to set consequences for not meeting agreed-upon goals. These consequences can serve as additional motivation to stay committed to your passions. However, ensure that the consequences are positive and not overly punitive.

6. **Celebrate achievements together:** Acknowledge and celebrate each other's successes, no matter how small. Positive reinforcement is a powerful tool for maintaining momentum and building a sense of accomplishment.

7. **Share resources and expertise:** Encourage open sharing of resources, insights, and expertise within the group. Everyone brings unique perspectives and knowledge that can benefit others in their passion pursuits.

8. **Be open to feedback:** Embrace feedback from your accountability partners with an open mind. Constructive criticism can offer valuable insights and fresh perspectives that may lead to breakthroughs.

9. **Stay committed and respectful:** Consistency is the key to making accountability partnerships effective. Respect each other's time and efforts by being punctual and committed to the agreed-upon schedule.

10. **Evaluate and adjust:** Regularly review the effectiveness of your accountability plan. If certain aspects aren't working, be open to making adjustments to better suit the group's needs.

REMEMBER

The success of your accountability and peer support plan relies on the active participation and dedication of all involved. Figure 15-1 can help you develop a plan for developing this type of support. Together, you can create a powerful support system that fuels your passion, keeps you motivated, and drives you toward achieving your dreams.

Your accountability and peer support plan is a dynamic process. It's essential to adapt and grow together as you pursue your passions. Stay committed to each other's success, and leverage the collective power of your support system to achieve remarkable outcomes.

Developing a Plan for Accountability and Peer Support

Step 1: Define your passion pursuit goals.

Write down your specific passion pursuit goals in clear and measurable terms.

Set a timeline for achieving each goal, specifying the target completion date.

Step 2: Identify your accountability partners or support group.

List potential individuals or groups who can serve as your accountability partners or peers.

Consider their availability, commitment level, and areas of expertise that align with your goals.

Step 3: Establish communication channels.

Decide on the frequency and mode of communication for your check-ins, such as weekly video calls or biweekly in-person meetings.

Choose a communication platform that works best for everyone. You might use Zoom, Skype, or in-person meetups.

Step 4: Outline accountability measures.

Determine the specific metrics or milestones you'll track and share with your partners.

Clarify how you'll provide updates and progress reports to each other.

Step 5: Create a supportive environment.

Discuss ground rules for the group, emphasizing trust, respect, and confidentiality.

Agree to provide constructive feedback and encouragement to foster a positive atmosphere.

Step 6: Set consequences (optional).

Decide if you want to set positive consequences for meeting goals or negative consequences for not meeting them.

Ensure that the consequences are motivational and agreed upon by all participants.

Step 7: Define celebration moments.

Determine how you'll celebrate achievements, both big and small.

Plan rewards or recognition for reaching milestones in your passion pursuit.

Step 8: Share resources and expertise.

Encourage open sharing of relevant resources, knowledge, and experiences among group members.

Explore how each member's unique expertise can benefit the entire group.

Step 9: Confirm commitment and schedule evaluations.

Confirm each participant's commitment to the group's agreed-upon schedule and expectations.

Schedule regular evaluations to assess the effectiveness of the accountability plan and make necessary adjustments.

Step 10: Reflect and revise.

Regularly reflect on the progress and challenges of your passion pursuit journey.

Revise the accountability plan, communication methods, or group members if needed for continuous improvement.

Step 11: Stay positive and motivated.

Keep a positive mindset, and encourage each other through ups and downs.

Support one another in overcoming obstacles and maintaining motivation.

FIGURE 15-1:
Continued

4

Practicing Well-Being and Self-Care

IN THIS PART . . .

Manage setbacks and letdowns.

Practice self-care to keep yourself going.

Keep burnout and stress at bay.

Build a safety net of supporters to catch you when you fall.

Turn failure into opportunity for growth.

Chapter **16**

Dealing with Setbacks and Rejection

I n the journey of finding and pursuing your passion, setbacks and rejections are almost inevitable companions. The path to discovering what truly ignites your soul can be filled with twists and turns, obstacles, and disappointments. Yet, don't view these experiences as roadblocks but rather as steppingstones that inch you forward on the path to your true calling.

This chapter explores the significance of setbacks and rejections in the pursuit of passion and how they can serve as valuable opportunities for growth, learning, and, ultimately, finding your true purpose in life.

Embracing setbacks and rejections as part of the process can transform the way you approach your journey, empowering you to become more resilient, persistent, and open to new possibilities. By embarking on this exploration, you begin to understand the role of setbacks and rejections in your quest to live a purposeful and fulfilling life.

Embracing — and Dealing With — Setbacks and Rejections Along Your Path

In the pursuit of your passions, it's not uncommon to encounter various setbacks and rejections that can momentarily shake your confidence and determination. These challenges can take various forms, each testing your resolve in unique ways. Following are some common ones you might face:

» **Initial failures:** Many successful individuals have faced initial failures and setbacks before reaching their goals. These setbacks may arise from trial and error, lack of experience, or unforeseen challenges in the early stages of pursuing a passion.

» **Negative feedback and criticism:** As you explore your passions, you may encounter individuals who doubt or criticize your ideas, plans, or work. This external feedback can sometimes dampen your spirits and lead to moments of self-doubt.

» **Self-doubt and uncertainty:** Finding your true passion often involves introspection and self-exploration, which can be accompanied by moments of doubt and uncertainty about your abilities, choices, or future path.

» **Unexpected roadblocks:** Throughout your journey, unexpected obstacles may arise, hindering your progress and requiring you to adapt and find alternative solutions.

» **Rejections:** In the pursuit of passion, you may face rejections, such as not being selected for opportunities or facing closed doors. These rejections can be disheartening, but they can teach valuable lessons and redirect you.

Although facing setbacks and rejections can be challenging, you need to recognize that they're a natural part of the growth process. Understanding and acknowledging these common setbacks and rejections can help you prepare for them and develop the resilience to navigate through them with grace and determination. Embracing these challenges as learning opportunities can ultimately strengthen your resolve and lead you closer to discovering your true passion.

Recognizing the impact of setbacks and rejection on motivation and confidence

Setbacks and rejection can have a significant impact on your motivation and confidence as you pursue your passions. They can be discouraging and may lead to a temporary loss of momentum or enthusiasm. When faced with challenges, it's natural to question yourself and your abilities.

Navigating setbacks and rejection requires inner strength and a growth mindset. By understanding that challenges are part of the journey and not the end of it, you can use these experiences to become more resilient, learn from your mistakes, and become more determined in the pursuit of your passions. Embracing setbacks as par for the course can lead you to remarkable achievements and fulfillment in your chosen endeavors.

REMEMBER

Setbacks and rejection can be disheartening, but they're not definitive judgments of your abilities or worth. Many successful individuals have faced challenges on their path to greatness, and their resilience and determination were instrumental in achieving their goals. By acknowledging the impact of setbacks and rejection, you can better understand your reactions and find ways to rebuild your motivation and confidence to continue pursuing your passion with renewed strength.

Read on for how setbacks and rejection can affect you and how some individuals have navigated through such experiences.

Impact on motivation

J. K. Rowling, the author of the *Harry Potter* series, faced numerous rejections from publishers before finding one that believed in her work. Despite the setbacks, she persisted, and her books went on to become one of the best-selling series of all time.

When faced with setbacks, your motivation can wane as you grapple with feelings of disappointment or frustration. An aspiring entrepreneur may face multiple rejections from potential investors, leading to doubts about the viability of their business idea.

Effect on confidence

Receiving negative feedback or criticism can erode your self-confidence, making you question your skills and abilities. This can be particularly challenging if you've invested time and effort into your passion projects.

Walt Disney faced multiple failures and rejections before creating the iconic Disney brand. Early in his career, he was fired from a job for lacking creativity and imagination, a stark contrast to the legacy he ultimately created.

Fear of future rejection

Oprah Winfrey, despite her enormous success, faced numerous challenges and setbacks in her journey. At various points in her career, she was told she wasn't fit for television and faced criticism for her talk show style. However, she persisted, became one of the most influential media personalities, and even launched a television network.

Setbacks and rejections may instill a fear of experiencing similar outcomes in the future. This fear can lead individuals to avoid taking risks or trying new opportunities to protect themselves from potential disappointment.

Fear of judgment

Setbacks and rejection can also trigger a fear of judgment from others. You may worry about what people will think of you or fear that they'll see you as a failure. This fear of judgment can be paralyzing and may prevent you from putting yourself out there again.

Thomas Edison, the inventor of the light bulb, faced thousands of failures before successfully creating a working prototype. When asked about his many unsuccessful attempts, he famously said, "I have not failed. I've just found 10,000 ways that won't work." His resilience and ability to embrace failure as part of the learning process ultimately led to his groundbreaking success.

Loss of direction

Vera Wang, a renowned fashion designer, initially pursued a career as a figure skater but faced setbacks that prevented her from making it to the Olympics. She later transitioned to the fashion industry and worked her way up from a fashion editor to a designer. Her ability to adapt and find her true passion in fashion led to her success in the industry.

Setbacks and rejection can sometimes leave you feeling lost or unsure about your next steps. You may question whether you're on the right path or if you should change course entirely.

Building resilience

Setbacks and rejection can be challenging, but they also offer valuable opportunities for growth and resilience. When you face adversity, you have a chance to learn from your experiences, improve your skills, and develop greater emotional strength.

Michael Jordan, widely regarded as one of the greatest basketball players of all time, faced numerous failures and setbacks in his career. He was cut from his high school basketball team, and even after becoming an NBA star, he faced defeat in critical games. However, he used these setbacks as fuel to work harder and eventually achieved unparalleled success in his sport.

Identifying the benefits of setbacks and rejection in personal and professional growth

Setbacks and rejection, though challenging, can actually bring about several benefits in both personal and professional growth.

Embracing setbacks and rejection as part of the growth process allows you to cultivate strength, resilience, and a deeper understanding of yourself. By viewing these experiences as opportunities for learning and growth, you can transform challenges into catalysts for personal and professional development.

Facing these difficulties can have positive results:

>> **Resilience and strength:** Dealing with setbacks and rejection requires resilience, which is a valuable trait in facing life's obstacles. When you encounter difficult situations and find the strength to persevere, you develop emotional resilience that helps you handle future challenges with greater ease.

>> **Learning and adaptation:** Setbacks and rejections often offer valuable lessons. When you analyze what went wrong and learn from your mistakes, you gain insights that can help you make better decisions and improve your approach moving forward.

>> **Discovering true passions:** Sometimes experiencing rejection or failure in one area leads you to explore new avenues. As you pivot and try different paths, you may discover passions and interests you were previously unaware of, ultimately leading you to more fulfilling pursuits.

>> **Building character:** Adversity tests your character and pushes you to dig deep into your values and beliefs. Through this process, you develop a deeper understanding of yourself and what truly matters to you.

>> **Developing empathy:** Facing challenges can make you more empathetic toward others who are going through similar experiences. It allows you to connect with and support those around you who might be facing their own setbacks.

>> **Setting realistic expectations:** Rejection and setbacks can offer a reality check, prompting you to reassess your expectations and set more achievable goals. This can lead to more focused efforts and a clearer understanding of what you need to do to succeed.

>> **Increasing innovation and creativity:** Adversity often sparks innovation. When faced with roadblocks, you're pushed to think creatively and find unconventional solutions to overcome challenges.

>> **Building a growth mindset:** Embracing setbacks as learning opportunities contributes to developing a growth mindset. Rather than seeing failure as a dead end, you perceive it as a way forward to improvement and progress.

Identifying the benefits of resilience and perseverance in overcoming setbacks and rejection

Resilience and perseverance play pivotal roles in helping you overcome setbacks and rejection, empowering you to navigate through difficult times with determination and optimism.

By developing resilience and perseverance, you can cultivate the inner strength you need to overcome setbacks and rejection. These qualities foster personal growth, instill confidence, and source the resilience to thrive amidst life's uncertainties.

Oprah Winfrey faced multiple challenges and setbacks early in her career, including being fired from her first job as a news anchor and initially struggling with her talk show. However, she persisted, honed her skills, and embraced opportunities for growth. Today, she's one of the most influential media moguls in the world, illustrating the power of resilience and perseverance.

Cultivating resilience and perseverance in the face of adversity has numerous benefits, as detailed in Table 16-1.

TABLE 16-1   Benefits of Cultivating Resilience and Perseverance

Benefit	What It Allows
Mental and emotional well-being	Resilience enables you to bounce back from disappointments and failures, preventing you from falling into a downward spiral of negativity. It enhances emotional well-being by promoting a positive outlook and the ability to manage stress effectively.
Maintaining focus on goals	Perseverance allows you to stay committed to your goals despite obstacles. Instead of being derailed by setbacks, you learn from the experience and maintain your focus on what you want to achieve.
Increased problem-solving skills	Resilience fosters an adaptive and solution-oriented mindset. When faced with challenges, you're more likely to seek creative solutions and approach problems from various angles.
Bolstered self-confidence	Overcoming setbacks and rejection bolsters self-confidence. Each time you successfully handle a challenging situation, you gain greater faith in your abilities and become more self-assured.

Benefit	What It Allows
Enhanced coping mechanisms	Resilience equips you with effective coping mechanisms to deal with stress and anxiety. Rather than feeling overwhelmed, you're better equipped to manage emotions and cope with difficult circumstances.
Positive mindset and attitude	Perseverance fosters a positive mindset and attitude, even when faced with failure. It encourages you to view setbacks as learning opportunities rather than as insurmountable obstacles.
Adapting to change	Resilience and perseverance facilitate adaptability to change. In a dynamic world, being able to adjust and remain flexible is crucial for continued growth and success.
Long-term success	The ability to rebound from setbacks and rejection is a key factor in achieving long-term success. Resiliency allows you to view failure as a starting point, not as a final destination. You're more likely to persevere until you achieve your objectives.

Strategies for Dealing with Rejection and Setbacks

In the pursuit of passion and personal growth, setbacks and rejection are inevitable. They're part of the journey toward success, providing invaluable opportunities for learning and self-discovery. This section explores effective strategies to navigate through these challenging moments, helping you build resilience and overcome obstacles with grace and determination.

Dealing with rejection and setbacks can be emotionally taxing and disheartening. Just know that everyone faces these challenges at some point in their lives, including some of the most successful individuals in history. The key lies in how you respond to these setbacks and what you choose to learn from them.

By adopting the strategies and tools presented in this section, you're better equipped to embrace rejection and setbacks as bridges to growth rather than as stumbling blocks. Each strategy is designed to empower you with the resilience you need to face adversity head-on, strengthen your resolve, and ultimately propel you forward on your path to pursuing your passions. Explore how to transform setbacks into opportunities for growth and success.

Practicing self-compassion and reframing negative self-talk

Self-compassion is the practice of treating yourself with kindness, understanding, and acceptance, especially in moments of difficulty, failure, or suffering. It involves offering the same level of care and support to yourself that you naturally extend to a friend or loved one who's going through a challenging time. Self-compassion acknowledges that everyone experiences hardships and setbacks. It's a way to respond to these experiences with empathy and nonjudgmental understanding.

Psychologist Kristin Neff introduced the concept of self-compassion. She identified three key components of this approach: self-kindness, common humanity, and mindfulness.

Self-kindness means being warm and understanding toward yourself in times of struggle, rather than being critical and harsh. It involves being nurturing and supportive, recognizing that you're only human and not perfect.

Common humanity is a way of recognizing that everyone faces difficulties and hardships in life. It's the understanding that you're not alone in your challenges, and your experiences are part of the shared human experience.

Mindfulness is holding your struggles with a balanced and nonjudgmental awareness. It allows you to acknowledge and accept your feelings and experiences without getting carried away by them or avoiding them.

Practicing self-compassion isn't about dismissing or ignoring your mistakes or shortcomings. Instead, it's about treating yourself with the same care and kindness you offer to others, promoting emotional well-being and resilience. Self-compassion helps you build a healthier relationship with yourself, fostering a sense of self-worth and inner peace, which can have a positive impact on your overall mental and emotional health. It can also be a valuable tool in dealing with stress, anxiety, and self-criticism, making it an essential skill in promoting personal growth and self-improvement.

Negative self-talk refers to the inner dialogue or thoughts you have about yourself that are critical, self-critical, pessimistic, and judgmental. It's the voice in your head that focuses on your weaknesses, mistakes, and perceived shortcomings, often leading to feelings of inadequacy, self-doubt, and low self-esteem. Negative self-talk can be subtle and automatic, becoming a habitual pattern of thinking that influences how you perceive yourself and interpret events in your life.

Common examples of negative self-talk include phrases like these:

"I'm not good enough."

"I always mess things up."

"I'll never be able to do this."

"I'm such a failure."

"Nobody likes me."

Negative self-talk can have a significant impact on your mental and emotional well-being. It can lead to increased stress, anxiety, and feelings of hopelessness, hindering your ability to cope with challenges and pursue your passions. When you consistently criticize yourself and focus on your weaknesses, it becomes challenging to build confidence and take risks in life.

Recognizing and challenging negative self-talk is an important step in promoting self-compassion and building a growth mindset. By becoming aware of these negative thought patterns, you can begin to challenge their validity and replace them with more realistic and positive affirmations.

Practicing self-compassion, reframing negative thoughts, and cultivating a positive and supportive inner dialogue can lead to improved self-esteem, resilience, and a more positive outlook on life.

In the face of rejection and setbacks, it's common for negative self-talk to creep in and cloud your perspective. You often become your own harshest critic, feeding yourself with self-doubt and self-blame. However, practicing self-compassion is a powerful tool to counter these negative thoughts and nurture a more positive mindset.

Self-compassion involves treating yourself with the same kindness and understanding you offer to a friend facing a similar challenge. It means acknowledging that setbacks and rejection are a natural part of life that don't define your worth or potential. Instead of berating yourself for not meeting your expectations, self-compassion allows you to embrace your imperfections with understanding and gentleness.

To cultivate self-compassion, begin by challenging your negative self-talk and replacing it with kinder, more empowering thoughts. When you encounter setbacks, instead of dwelling on what went wrong, focus on the effort and courage you put forth in pursuing your passions. This shift in mindset can help you view setbacks as learning opportunities rather than as personal failures.

Moreover, reframing negative self-talk involves consciously questioning the accuracy of your self-critical thoughts. For example, if you catch yourself thinking, "I'm just not good enough," you can ask yourself if this thought is based on solid evidence or if it's an unfounded assumption. Challenging these negative thoughts allows you to gain a more balanced and realistic perspective of your abilities and potential.

By practicing self-compassion and reframing negative self-talk, you create a nurturing internal environment that supports you during challenging times. This, in turn, fosters resilience and enables you to bounce back stronger after setbacks and rejection, ultimately fueling your pursuit of passion and success. Remember, being kind to yourself isn't a sign of weakness but a demonstration of strength and self-awareness, laying the foundation for a more fulfilling and empowered life journey.

Seeking support, feedback, and advice from mentors and peers

Seeking support, feedback, and advice from mentors and peers is a valuable strategy for dealing with rejection and setbacks. When faced with challenges and disappointments, it can be helpful to share your experiences with others who can offer guidance and encouragement. Mentors, in particular, play a crucial role in providing valuable insights based on their own experiences and expertise. They can offer constructive feedback, share their own stories of overcoming obstacles, and assist you in navigating difficult situations.

Peers, too, can be a valuable source of support and understanding. Sharing your setbacks with others who are going through similar experiences can create a sense of camaraderie and a reminder that you're not alone in facing challenges. Peers can offer empathy, encouragement, and practical advice on how to cope with setbacks and move forward.

Support from mentors and peers can also contribute an outside perspective on your situation, helping you gain new insights and alternative approaches to problem-solving. They can offer constructive criticism without judgment, helping you identify areas for improvement and growth.

Moreover, having a support system of mentors and peers can boost your motivation and resilience. They can remind you of your strengths, potential, and past successes, which can help you bounce back from setbacks and maintain a positive outlook.

Seek support, feedback, and advice with an open mind and a willingness to learn from others. By embracing the wisdom and guidance of mentors and peers, you can turn setbacks into opportunities for growth and continue pursuing your passion with renewed determination and confidence.

Identifying lessons learned and growth opportunities from setbacks and rejection

Identifying lessons learned and growth opportunities from setbacks and rejection is a crucial step in turning these experiences into valuable learning opportunities. Although setbacks and rejections can be disheartening, they also allow self-reflection and growth. By taking a proactive approach to analyze these experiences, you can extract valuable insights and use these challenges to your advantage.

One way to identify lessons learned is to engage in self-reflection. Ask yourself what went wrong. Were there any warning signs you overlooked? What could you have done differently? Through this process, you can pinpoint specific areas for improvement and identify patterns that may have contributed to the setback.

Approach this self-reflection with self-compassion and without self-blame. Instead of dwelling on perceived shortcomings, focus on the actionable steps you can take to enhance your skills, knowledge, and approach.

Moreover, setbacks and rejections can reveal areas of your passion that you may not have explored fully or challenges you hadn't anticipated. Embrace these opportunities for growth, and be open to adjusting your goals or strategies accordingly. Remember that resilience and adaptability are key traits in the pursuit of passion.

In addition to personal reflection, others can shine light on valuable insights. Ask for feedback from mentors, peers, or colleagues who have a different perspective on the situation. They can help you identify blind spots.

Once you've identified the lessons learned, create an actionable plan for growth and improvement. Set specific goals to address the areas that need development, and commit to continuous learning and skill-building. By approaching setbacks as learning experiences, you can transform them into springboards toward achieving your passion with greater wisdom and strength.

Turning Setbacks into Opportunities

Turning setbacks into opportunities is a powerful skill that can make a significant difference in the pursuit of your passions. Life is full of twists and turns, and setbacks are inevitable. However, the way you respond to these challenges can determine whether you get stuck in disappointment or find a catalyst for growth. This section explores strategies and insights on how to transform setbacks into opportunities, allowing you to emerge stronger, wiser, and more resilient in your journey to pursue your passions.

Embracing setbacks as opportunities for growth requires a shift in mindset. Instead of viewing them as failures or roadblocks, you can reframe setbacks as valuable first steps on the path to success. By doing so, you create a mindset that's open to learning from every experience, both positive and challenging. This perspective empowers you to navigate setbacks with resilience and optimism, recognizing that they provide unique chances to refine your approach and uncover new possibilities.

This section covers the transformative power of self-reflection and how it can help you identify valuable lessons from setbacks. It explores the role of perseverance and resilience in bouncing back from adversity, as well as practical steps to build these essential traits. By leveraging the wisdom gained from setbacks, you can seize new opportunities, make informed decisions, and continuously evolve toward a more purposeful and passionate life. Empower yourself to embrace challenges as a natural part of your growth and fulfillment.

Developing a growth mindset and embracing challenges as opportunities for growth

A growth mindset is the belief that your abilities and intelligence can be developed and improved over time through effort, learning, and perseverance. Coined by psychologist Carol Dweck, the concept of a growth mindset contrasts with a fixed mindset, where you believe your qualities, skills, and intelligence are innate and unchangeable.

Individuals with a growth mindset see challenges, failures, and setbacks as opportunities for learning and growth. They understand that abilities can be cultivated through hard work, dedication, and the willingness to take on new challenges. Instead of being discouraged by obstacles, they view them as pathways to progress and view failure as a natural part of the learning process.

Those with a growth mindset embrace effort as a necessary part of achieving success, and they see criticism and feedback as valuable tools for improvement. They're more likely to take risks, set ambitious goals, and persist in the face of setbacks. This mindset fosters resilience and a love for learning, as individuals continuously seek out opportunities for self-improvement and personal development.

Having a growth mindset is particularly beneficial in both personal and professional realms. In personal life, it can lead to increased self-confidence, motivation, and adaptability. In the workplace, it can drive innovation, creativity, and collaboration, as individuals are more open to taking on new challenges and exploring unconventional solutions.

Overall, a growth mindset is a powerful belief system that empowers you to embrace your potential for growth and self-improvement. It enables you to approach life with curiosity, determination, and a willingness to learn, ultimately unlocking new opportunities and helping you achieve your goals and pursue your passions.

Developing a growth mindset and embracing challenges as opportunities for growth is a fundamental aspect of turning setbacks into opportunities. A growth mindset is the belief that you can develop your abilities and intelligence through dedication, hard work, and learning. This perspective allows you to approach challenges with curiosity and enthusiasm, knowing that you can improve and overcome obstacles with effort and determination.

To cultivate a growth mindset, you need to recognize and challenge your fixed beliefs about your abilities and potential. Instead of viewing setbacks as indicators of your limitations, view them as chances to learn, adapt, and grow. Embracing challenges with a growth mindset means reframing negative thoughts into constructive ones, such as seeing mistakes as learning opportunities or setbacks as ways to improve.

When you embrace challenges as opportunities for growth, you become more resilient in the face of adversity. Rather than being discouraged by setbacks, you see them as essential parts of the learning process. By seeking out challenges and pushing yourself outside your comfort zone, you gain valuable experience and knowledge that ultimately propels you forward in your journey.

Moreover, viewing challenges as growth opportunities allows you to approach them with a sense of empowerment rather than fear. Instead of avoiding difficult situations, you embrace them, knowing that each challenge presents an occasion to test your skills, discover new strengths, and unlock your full potential.

A growth mindset also fosters a love for learning and improvement. You become more open to feedback and constructive criticism because you see them as valuable insights that can help you grow. This continuous drive to improve and evolve contributes to your personal and professional development, enabling you to pursue your passions with greater confidence and enthusiasm.

Developing a growth mindset and embracing challenges as opportunities for growth is a transformative approach to turning setbacks into starting points. By cultivating this mindset, you harness the power of resilience, curiosity, and self-belief, empowering you to navigate setbacks with grace and embrace the growth they bring. With this mindset, you're better equipped to transform life's challenges into opportunities and move forward on your path to finding and pursuing your passions.

Reframing setbacks as opportunities for learning and growth

Reframing setbacks as opportunities for learning and growth is a key aspect of adopting a growth mindset. When you encounter challenges or experience setbacks, your immediate reaction might be disappointment, frustration, or even self-doubt. However, by reframing these experiences, you can transform them into valuable learning opportunities and catalysts for personal growth.

Instead of viewing setbacks as failures or dead ends, individuals with a growth mindset see them as rungs on their ladder of success. They understand that setbacks are natural and inevitable and can offer important insights and lessons. Embracing setbacks has its benefits, as spelled out in Table 16-2.

TABLE 16-2   Benefits of Viewing Setbacks as Natural and Inevitable

Benefit	Insight
Learn from mistakes	Rather than dwelling on mistakes, those with a growth mindset analyze what went wrong and why. They identify the areas where improvement is needed and use this knowledge to adjust their approach in the future.
Develop resilience	Viewing setbacks as opportunities for growth builds resilience. When faced with challenges, individuals with a growth mindset bounce back stronger and more determined to overcome the obstacles in their way.
Adopt a solution-oriented approach	A growth mindset encourages problem-solving. Rather than getting stuck in self-blame or negativity, individuals look for solutions and strategies to address the challenges they face.
Stay motivated	Reframing setbacks helps maintain motivation and commitment to goals. These individuals see each setback as a step toward improvement, reinforcing their determination to succeed.
Cultivate a learning attitude	Those with a growth mindset actively seek new knowledge and skills. They embrace continuous learning and see every experience as an opportunity to grow and expand their capabilities.
Enhance self-confidence	By viewing setbacks as temporary hurdles, not as reflections of their worth or abilities, individuals maintain their self-confidence. This positive self-perception enables them to face future challenges with greater self-assurance.

REMEMBER

Reframing setbacks as opportunities for learning and growth is a fundamental mindset shift that enables you to harness the power of adversity. By embracing setbacks, you unlock their potential to propel you forward, build resilience, and continuously improve as you pursue your passions and strive for success. Figure 16-1 is a tool for embracing perceived setbacks as opportunities to reset your path.

Reframing Setbacks as Opportunities for Learning and Growth: Self-Planning Worksheet

Setback identification: Describe the recent setback or challenge you encountered in your pursuit of passion.

Initial reaction: Reflect on your initial emotional response to the setback. How did it make you feel, and what thoughts went through your mind?

Reframed setback: Consider how you can reframe this setback as an opportunity for learning and growth. Write down a positive and constructive way to view the situation.

Lesson learned: Identify the lessons or insights you can gain from this setback. What valuable information can you take away from this experience?

Adjusted approach: Based on what you've learned, think about how you can adjust your approach or strategy moving forward. What changes can you make to improve your chances of success?

Strengths and resilience: Recognize your strengths and resilience in facing this setback. What qualities did you demonstrate that helped you handle the situation?

Positive self-talk: Write down a positive affirmation or statement to remind yourself of your ability to overcome challenges and grow from setbacks.

Growth action plan: Outline specific actions to embrace the learning opportunities from this setback. What steps can you implement to apply your new insights?

Source of support: Consider who you can reach out to for support, advice, or mentorship during this time. How can they help you reframe setbacks positively?

Progress acknowledgment: Acknowledge and celebrate every step forward, no matter how small. Write down ways you can reward yourself for your efforts in reframing setbacks and pursuing your passion.

Reflection and adaptation: Regularly review your progress and experiences with reframing setbacks. Adapt your strategies as needed, and continue to cultivate a growth mindset.

FIGURE 16-1:
Reframing
setbacks
worksheet.

REMEMBER

Setbacks are part of the journey toward success. By reframing them, you can turn them into powerful opportunities for learning, resilience, and growth. Embrace the process, and stay committed to your personal and professional development.

Identifying alternative paths and opportunities that setbacks present

Setbacks and challenges are an inevitable part of any journey, including the pursuit of your passions. Although they can be discouraging at first, setbacks often open the door to new opportunities and alternative paths that you might not have considered before. Table 16-3 shows that by adopting a positive mindset and being open to change, you can transform setbacks into springboards for growth and exploration.

TABLE 16-3   **Pathways to Opportunity**

Action	Opportunity
Remain open-minded	When facing a setback, resist the urge to become fixated on a single predetermined path. Instead, stay open-minded and willing to explore different directions. Sometimes the best opportunities emerge when you're willing to adapt and embrace change.
Reflect on your interests and strengths	Use setbacks as opportunities to reevaluate your passions, interests, and strengths. Do new paths align better with who you are and what you love? Take time to reflect on what truly drives you and how you can channel your strengths in different ways.
Seek feedback and input	Reach out to mentors, colleagues, or friends for feedback on your situation. They might provide insights, suggestions, or connections that lead to new opportunities you hadn't considered.
Embrace skill diversification	A setback can prompt you to develop a broader skill set. Consider how you can expand your knowledge and expertise to explore different industries or roles that interest you.
Network and collaborate	Engage with a diverse network of individuals, and collaborate with others who share your passions. New connections can expose you to unique opportunities or collaborative projects you hadn't anticipated.
Pivot with purpose	If your initial path is blocked, consider pivoting your approach with a clear purpose in mind. A setback can be a chance to redefine your goals and the means to achieve them.
Take calculated risks	With a growth mindset, be willing to take calculated risks that align with your passions. Step outside your comfort zone and explore new opportunities that can lead to meaningful growth.
Learn from setbacks	Analyze the reasons behind setbacks and use them as learning opportunities. Each setback can equip you with valuable knowledge and experience that may benefit you in unforeseen ways down the road.
Stay patient and persistent	Resilience and perseverance are key traits to navigate alternative paths. Stay patient with yourself, and persistently pursue opportunities that resonate with your passions.
Stay positive and adaptable	Maintaining a positive attitude and embracing adaptability enables you to see setbacks as opportunities for personal and professional growth.

REMEMBER

Setbacks aren't the end of the road, but rather crossroads that present new possibilities. By approaching setbacks with an open mind and a growth-oriented mindset, you can uncover alternative paths and opportunities that lead you closer to realizing your passions and aspirations. Embrace change, and remain committed to finding fulfillment in your journey.

Building resilience and perseverance

Building resilience and perseverance are essential attributes that enable you to bounce back from setbacks, rejections, and challenges with renewed determination. They serve as the bedrock of personal growth and success in the pursuit of passions.

Building resilience and perseverance is an ongoing process that requires patience and dedication. It involves developing a strong sense of self-belief and a willingness to learn and grow from every experience. By cultivating these traits, you can navigate setbacks and rejections with greater confidence and continue your pursuit of passion with unwavering determination.

To develop these qualities, consider implementing the following strategies:

>> **Develop a growth mindset:** Embrace the belief that setbacks and rejections are opportunities for learning and growth. Cultivate a growth mindset that views challenges as detours rather than roadblocks. This shift in perspective allows you to approach difficulties with curiosity and openness, enabling you to extract valuable lessons from every experience.

>> **Practice self-compassion:** Treat yourself with kindness and understanding during difficult times. Acknowledge that setbacks are a natural part of the journey, and be gentle with yourself as you navigate through them. Self-compassion involves recognizing that everyone faces obstacles and imperfections and being kind to yourself in the face of adversity.

>> **Maintain perspective:** When facing setbacks, try to maintain a broader perspective. Reflect on the progress you've made, the lessons you've learned, and the strengths you've developed. Remember that setbacks aren't defining moments but moments for growth. By focusing on the bigger picture, you can better understand how each experience contributes to your overall development.

>> **Stay adaptable:** Be open to adapting your strategies and plans when faced with challenges. Resilient individuals are flexible and can adjust their approach to better navigate obstacles. By being adaptable, you can find alternative routes to your goals when the original path is obstructed.

>> **Seek support:** Surround yourself with a supportive network of mentors, friends, and family who can offer encouragement and guidance during tough times. Their perspective and advice can be invaluable in helping you stay motivated and remind you of your capabilities.

>> **Set realistic goals:** Break your long-term goals into smaller, achievable milestones. Celebrate the milestones you achieve, and use them to propel you toward your overarching passion. Recognizing and celebrating progress, no matter how small, can keep you motivated and engaged.

>> **Learn from failure:** Embrace failure as a natural part of the process. Use it as an opportunity to gain insights, reevaluate your approach, and make necessary improvements for future endeavors. Each failure can lend valuable feedback that can lead to greater success in the future.

>> **Visualize success:** Cultivate a positive vision of your future success. Visualization can strengthen your resolve and motivation, even when you're faced with setbacks. By vividly imagining yourself achieving your goals, you create a powerful sense of determination to persist despite challenges.

>> **Practice perseverance:** Understand that passion-driven journeys often have ups and downs. Stay committed to your path, and persistently work toward your goals, even when the going gets tough. Perseverance allows you to push through difficult times with determination and tenacity.

>> **Take care of yourself:** Prioritize self-care to maintain physical and emotional well-being. A healthy mind and body are better equipped to handle challenges and maintain resilience. Regular exercise, sufficient rest, and participation in activities that bring you joy can bolster your ability to cope with adversity.

Chapter **17**

The Role of Self-Care in Finding Passion

I n the journey of finding passion, one crucial aspect that's often overlooked is self-care. As you strive to explore your interests, set goals, and overcome challenges, it's vital to prioritize your well-being and mental health.

Self-care plays a fundamental role in fostering a healthy and sustainable pursuit of passion. This chapter digs into the significance of self-care, its impact on the pursuit of passion, and various strategies to incorporate self-care into your daily life. By nurturing and replenishing yourself, you can navigate the path of passion with resilience, balance, and an unwavering commitment to personal growth and fulfillment.

Understanding the importance of self-care is essential in maintaining motivation and overall well-being as you embark on the journey of pursuing your passion. The pursuit of passion can be both rewarding and challenging, and it's easy to become consumed by the drive to achieve your goals. However, neglecting self-care can lead to burnout, fatigue, and decreased motivation.

Self-care involves taking intentional and mindful actions to nourish your physical, emotional, and mental health. It allows you to recharge and rejuvenate, ensuring that you have the energy and focus needed to stay committed to your passion. When you prioritize self-care, you create a foundation of resilience, enabling you to bounce back from setbacks and face obstacles with greater determination.

In this chapter, we will explore the essence of self-care in staying on course while trying to find and pursue our passion

Understanding the Importance of Self-Care in Maintaining Motivation and Well-Being

Maintaining a healthy balance between your passion pursuits and self-care routines can lead to improved overall well-being. Taking time for activities that bring you joy and relaxation, such as hobbies, exercise, time with loved ones, and mindfulness practices, reduces stress and anxiety. By managing stress levels effectively, you can stay focused and motivated to keep pushing forward on your path to passion.

Moreover, self-care fosters self-awareness, allowing you to understand your boundaries and limitations. This awareness empowers you to set realistic goals, prioritize your time effectively, and make necessary adjustments to your plans. It prevents you from overextending yourself and feeling overwhelmed, ensuring a sustainable and fulfilling pursuit of your passions.

Self-care is a foundational pillar in the pursuit of passion. By understanding its role in maintaining motivation and well-being, you can cultivate a sustainable and fulfilling journey toward your goals. Making time for self-care activities and nurturing yourself holistically doesn't only contribute to your personal growth but enhances your ability to thrive in your passion pursuits.

Neglecting self-care can have a significant impact on your passion pursuit and overall well-being. When you become overly consumed by your goals and neglect to prioritize self-care, several negative consequences can arise.

First, neglecting self-care can lead to burnout. Passion pursuit often involves putting in long hours and intense effort, which can leave you physically and emotionally exhausted. Without adequate rest and time for rejuvenation, you may find yourself losing motivation, feeling fatigued, and experiencing a decline in the quality of your work. Burnout can erode your passion, making it challenging to sustain your enthusiasm and drive.

Second, neglecting self-care can lead to increased stress and anxiety. Pursuing your passions can be inherently stressful, especially when you're facing challenges and uncertainties. Failing to manage stress effectively can lead to poor concentration, irritability, and even physical health issues. High levels of stress can negatively influence your ability to perform at your best and may hinder your progress toward your goals.

Furthermore, neglecting self-care can strain your relationships and support systems. Passion pursuit may require a significant amount of time and energy, and if you neglect self-care, you may inadvertently neglect the people who are important to you. This can lead to feelings of isolation and disconnection, which can further affect your emotional well-being and motivation.

WARNING

Another consequence of neglecting self-care is decreased creativity and innovation. When you're constantly in "work" mode without taking time for relaxation and creative exploration, your mind can become stagnant and less receptive to new ideas. Self-care activities, such as engaging in hobbies or spending time in nature, offers the mental space you need to spark creativity and generate fresh perspectives on your passion pursuits.

Recognizing the impact of neglecting self-care is crucial in maintaining a healthy and sustainable passion pursuit. Prioritizing self-care not only enhances your well-being but fuels your motivation, creativity, and resilience to overcome obstacles in your path. By taking the time to nurture yourself, you can better navigate the challenges of passion pursuit and find greater fulfillment in your journey.

Identifying Common Self-Care Practices that Can Enhance Passion Pursuit

Identifying and incorporating self-care practices into your daily life is essential to enhancing passion pursuit and overall well-being. By incorporating these self-care practices into your life, you can create a foundation of well-being and resilience that supports your passion pursuit. Regularly nurturing yourself helps you stay focused, motivated, and better equipped to overcome challenges on the path to fulfilling your dreams.

Here are some common self-care practices that can positively influence your journey toward fulfilling your passions.

>> **Mindfulness and meditation:** Practicing mindfulness and meditation can help you stay present, reduce stress, and enhance focus. Taking a few minutes each day to meditate or practice deep breathing can improve your emotional regulation and mental clarity, making it easier to navigate challenges and stay connected to your passions.

>> **Physical exercise:** Regular physical activity not only benefits your physical health but also has a significant impact on your mental well-being. Engaging in exercises you enjoy, such as jogging, yoga, or dancing, can release endorphins and boost your energy levels, keeping you motivated and focused on your goals.

>> **Adequate sleep:** Prioritizing rest and ensuring you get enough quality sleep is crucial for overall health and optimal cognitive function. When you're well rested, you're better equipped to face challenges and make sound decisions in pursuit of your passions.

>> **Time in nature:** Spending time outdoors and connecting with nature can be rejuvenating and inspiring. Nature has a way of calming your mind and fostering creativity, providing a refreshing break from your passion pursuits and opening up new perspectives.

>> **Nurturing hobbies:** Engaging in hobbies that bring you joy and relaxation can be an excellent form of self-care. Whether it's painting, gardening, cooking, or playing a musical instrument, hobbies are an opportunity to unwind and recharge, enhancing your overall well-being and passion pursuit.

>> **Healthy nutrition:** Paying attention to your diet and consuming nourishing foods can play a big role in your physical and mental health. Eating well-balanced meals can boost your energy levels, improve focus, and offer the stamina you need to stay dedicated to your passions.

>> **Setting boundaries:** Establishing healthy boundaries is vital in preventing burnout and maintaining work-life balance. Learning to say no to excessive demands and carving out time for yourself allows you to recharge and approach your passions with renewed energy.

>> **Social connections:** Maintaining meaningful relationships and a strong support network is essential for emotional well-being. Connecting with friends, family, or like-minded individuals who share your passions can provision you with encouragement, feedback, and camaraderie on your journey.

>> **Journaling:** Keeping a journal can be a powerful self-care practice. Writing down thoughts, emotions, and reflections can bring clarity, aid in problem-solving, and help you process setbacks or obstacles on your path to passion pursuit.

The Benefits of Self-Care for Your Well-Being and Success

In this fast-paced and demanding world, prioritizing self-care is more important than ever. As you strive to pursue your passions and achieve success, taking care of your well-being is a fundamental aspect of your journey. This section explores the significant benefits of self-care and how it contributes not only to your overall well-being but also to your success in various areas of life.

Self-care is more than just a trendy buzzword; it encompasses a holistic approach to nurturing yourself physically, emotionally, mentally, and spiritually. By engaging in practices that promote self-care, you equip yourself with the tools to navigate challenges, manage stress, and maintain a healthy work-life balance. Moreover, self-care plays a pivotal role in enhancing your focus, creativity, and productivity, enabling you to achieve your goals with clarity and determination.

Throughout, this chapter delves into the manifold advantages of self-care, backed by research and real-life examples of individuals who have experienced transformative changes by making self-care a priority. From improved mental health and increased resilience to better relationships and higher levels of productivity, the benefits of self-care extend far beyond your immediate well-being. Embracing self-care as an integral part of your journey to finding passion and success will empower you to thrive in all aspects of life, both personally and professionally. Read on for how self-care can contribute to a more fulfilling and successful life.

The advantages of self-care in managing stress and burnout

In today's fast-paced and demanding world, stress and burnout have become all too common, especially if you're passionately pursuing your goals. However, by incorporating self-care practices into your daily routine, you can effectively manage and even prevent stress and burnout, ensuring a more sustainable path toward your passions and aspirations.

>> **Reduced stress levels:** Self-care techniques, such as mindfulness, meditation, and deep breathing exercises, can reduce stress hormone levels in your body. Taking the time to engage in these practices allows you to calm your mind, gain perspective, and approach challenges with a clearer, more composed mindset.

>> **Enhanced resilience:** Regular self-care fosters emotional resilience, enabling you to bounce back more quickly from setbacks and challenges. When you

care for yourself, you build the emotional resources you need to withstand the pressures and uncertainties that come with pursuing your passions.

>> **Improved focus and productivity:** Chronic stress and burnout can hinder your ability to focus and be productive. By prioritizing self-care, you can recharge your mental energy, which enhances your concentration and efficiency in pursuing your goals.

>> **Better physical health:** Self-care encompasses taking care of your physical well-being through exercise, proper nutrition, and sufficient rest. By caring for your physical health, you boost your immune system and overall health so that you're better equipped to handle the demands of your passionate pursuits.

>> **Prevention of burnout:** Engaging in regular self-care can act as a buffer against burnout, a state of emotional, physical, and mental exhaustion resulting from prolonged stress. By recognizing and addressing your needs, you can avoid reaching a point of burnout, allowing you to stay dedicated and enthusiastic about your passions.

>> **Enhanced emotional well-being:** Self-care practices that nurture your emotional health, such as journaling, seeking support from loved ones, and spending time in nature, can improve your emotional well-being. This, in turn, enables you to navigate challenges with a more positive outlook and emotional balance.

>> **Balanced work-life integration:** Passion-driven individuals often find it challenging to strike a balance between their personal and professional lives. Self-care helps you set boundaries, prioritize your time, and create a healthier work-life integration, promoting sustainable passion pursuit.

>> **Increased creativity and innovation:** Taking breaks and engaging in activities that bring you joy can foster creativity and innovation. Self-care gives your mind space to rest, allowing you to return to your passions with fresh perspectives and new ideas.

By recognizing the advantages of self-care in managing stress and burnout, you empower yourself to sustainably pursue your passions and achieve success. Not only is incorporating self-care practices into your daily life essential for your well-being, but it enhances your ability to thrive and make a positive impact on the world around you.

The role of self-care in enhancing creativity and productivity

Self-care plays a pivotal role in enhancing creativity and productivity, particularly for individuals on a passionate pursuit. When you prioritize your well-being and take the time to care for yourself, you create a conducive environment for creativity to flourish and productivity to soar.

» **Reduced mental clutter:** Engaging in self-care activities like meditation, time in nature, and hobbies can clear mental clutter and make space for creative thoughts to emerge. By stepping away from the daily hustle, you allow your mind to wander and connect seemingly unrelated ideas, fostering creativity.

» **Renewed energy and focus:** Proper self-care, such as getting enough sleep, staying hydrated, and eating nutritious foods, replenishes your physical energy. This revitalization translates into increased focus and attentiveness, which are crucial for productivity.

» **Enhanced emotional resilience:** Embracing self-care practices, such as practicing gratitude and seeking support, bolsters emotional resilience. As you navigate the ups and downs of passionate pursuits, this emotional strength enables you to bounce back from setbacks and maintain motivation.

» **Mindful living:** Self-care encourages mindful living, allowing you to be fully present in your activities and experiences. By being attentive to the present moment, you can fully immerse yourself in your creative endeavors, leading to more profound insights and innovative ideas.

» **Stress reduction:** Chronic stress can stifle creativity and hinder productivity. Self-care practices, like deep breathing exercises and yoga, can significantly reduce stress levels, fostering a more relaxed and creative state of mind.

» **Cultivating a growth mindset:** Engaging in self-care can help you develop a growth mindset, where you see challenges as opportunities to learn and grow. This mindset boosts your confidence in tackling creative projects and encourages continuous improvement.

» **A clearer vision:** Taking time for self-reflection during self-care activities allows you to gain clarity on your passions and creative vision. When you align your self-care practices with your passions, you become more purposeful and focused in your pursuits.

» **Breaks and rest:** Self-care emphasizes the importance of taking breaks and allowing yourself to rest. Contrary to popular belief, breaks can reinvigorate creativity and productivity by giving your mind a chance to wander and recharge.

REMEMBER

Overall, self-care isn't a luxury; it's an essential component of fostering creativity and productivity. By valuing your well-being and making time for self-care, you unlock the potential for creativity to flourish and productivity to thrive in your passionate endeavors.

The impact of self-care on personal and professional relationships

Self-care goes beyond benefiting individual well-being; it also has a profound impact on personal and professional relationships. When you prioritize self-care, you're better equipped to cultivate healthy and meaningful connections with others.

>> **Enhanced empathy and understanding:** Self-care fosters a deeper understanding and connection with your own emotions and needs. This heightened self-awareness allows you to empathize better with the feelings and experiences of others, leading to more compassionate and understanding relationships.

>> **Effective communication:** Engaging in self-care practices can reduce stress and promote emotional balance. As a result, you're more likely to communicate calmly, openly, and effectively in your personal and professional interactions. Clear communication facilitates better understanding and promotes healthy relationships.

>> **Boundaries and self-respect:** Self-care empowers you to set and maintain healthy boundaries in both your personal and your professional life. By respecting your own needs and limits, you can establish and enforce boundaries that protect your well-being and promote respectful relationships with others.

>> **Reduced conflict:** When you prioritize self-care, you're better equipped to manage stress and emotions. This reduces the likelihood of reactive behavior and unnecessary conflicts in your relationships. Instead, you can approach conflicts with a calmer and more constructive mindset.

>> **Building trust:** Taking care of yourself sends a positive message to others about your self-worth and commitment to your own growth. This builds trust in your relationships, as others recognize that you're reliable and committed to being the best version of yourself.

>> **Increased presence:** Self-care practices often involve being present in the moment and fully engaging in the activities you enjoy. This presence extends to your interactions with others, allowing you to be more attentive, responsive, and supportive in your relationships.

>> **Strengthened support networks:** By investing time in self-care, you nurture your own well-being, which in turn enables you to be a source of support for others. When you're emotionally balanced and fulfilled, you can be more reliable and understanding of friends, family members, and colleagues.

>> **Modeling healthy behavior:** Prioritizing self-care sets an example for those around you. When you take care of yourself, you inspire others to do the same, creating a positive ripple effect in your personal and professional circles.

Overall, self-care is a vital foundation for building and maintaining healthy, meaningful relationships. By nurturing your own well-being, you can show up more authentically and compassionately in your interactions with others, leading to more fulfilling and supportive relationships in both personal and professional spheres.

Strategies for Practicing Self-Care

In this fast-paced and demanding world, practicing self-care is more crucial than ever. As you pursue your passions and work toward your goals, it's essential to prioritize your physical, emotional, and mental well-being. This section explores effective strategies for incorporating self-care into your daily life, ensuring that you have the energy, resilience, and focus to thrive in your personal and professional endeavors.

Self-care is a necessity for maintaining a healthy and balanced life. It involves intentionally engaging in activities that nourish your body, mind, and soul, allowing you to recharge, rejuvenate, and stay connected with yourself. By understanding the importance of self-care and the positive impact it can have on various aspects of your life, you can develop practical and sustainable self-care practices that align with your passions and goals.

The following sections cover specific self-care strategies, each tailored to address different aspects of well-being. From managing stress and enhancing creativity to fostering stronger relationships, self-care serves as the cornerstone of a fulfilling and purpose-driven life. Read on to explore the empowering strategies that will equip you to practice self-care effectively and embark on a journey of holistic well-being as you pursue your passions.

Developing a self-care routine that aligns with your values and interests

Developing a self-care routine that aligns with your values and interests is a powerful way to ensure that your well-being remains a top priority as you pursue your passions. This personalized approach allows you to integrate self-care seamlessly into your daily life, making it easier to maintain and sustain. Here are some key steps to help you create a self-care routine that resonates with your unique needs:

>> **Reflect on your values and interests:** Begin by identifying what truly matters to you and what brings you joy. Consider your core values and

passions because they play a significant role in shaping your self-care routine. For instance, if you value connection and nature, spending time with loved ones outdoors may be a meaningful self-care activity for you.

>> **Assess your daily schedule:** Take a close look at your daily activities and commitments. Determine how much time you can realistically dedicate to self-care each day. Even small moments of self-care can have a profound impact on your well-being, so find opportunities to weave self-care into your routine.

>> **Choose activities that nourish you:** Select self-care practices that resonate with you on a deep level. These activities should feel nourishing and fulfilling, not like a chore. It could be anything from meditation and journaling to engaging in a creative hobby or physical exercise.

>> **Create a balanced routine:** Aim for a well-rounded self-care routine that addresses different aspects of your well-being. Consider incorporating activities that support your physical health, emotional well-being, mental clarity, and spiritual growth.

>> **Be flexible and adaptive:** Life is dynamic, and so should be your self-care routine. Be open to adjusting and refining your practices as circumstances change. Embrace flexibility, and remember that self-care is a journey, not a rigid checklist.

>> **Set realistic goals:** Set achievable self-care goals that align with your current circumstances and priorities. Avoid overwhelming yourself with an overly ambitious routine. Start with manageable steps and gradually build upon them.

>> **Make self-care a priority:** Treat self-care as non-negotiable "me time." Just like you prioritize other responsibilities, give yourself the same level of attention and importance. By making self-care a priority, you demonstrate the value you place on your well-being.

>> **Create reminders and accountability:** Establish reminders or cues to engage in your self-care activities regularly. It could be as simple as setting calendar alerts or creating a daily checklist. Consider enlisting the support of a friend or loved one to hold you accountable.

>> **Celebrate progress:** Acknowledge your efforts and celebrate the progress you make in nurturing your well-being. Celebrating small wins can boost your motivation and reinforce the positive impact of self-care on your life.

REMEMBER

Your self-care routine is personal. What matters most is that it brings you joy, replenishes your energy, and helps you stay grounded as you pursue your passions and navigate life's challenges. Be kind to yourself, and embrace the transformative power of a self-care routine that aligns with your values and interests.

Prioritizing self-care activities that promote physical, emotional, and mental health

Prioritizing self-care activities that promote physical, emotional, and mental health is essential for maintaining overall well-being and fostering a strong foundation for pursuing your passions. Here are some effective strategies for integrating self-care practices that cater to each aspect of your health:

>> **Physical health:** Taking care of your physical well-being directly impacts your energy levels and ability to engage fully in your passions. Prioritize activities that support your physical health, such as regular exercise, a balanced diet, sufficient sleep, and proper hydration. Engaging in physical activities you enjoy, whether it's yoga, hiking, dancing, or any other form of exercise, can not only improve your physical health but also enhance your mood and reduce stress.

>> **Emotional health:** Emotional well-being is crucial for maintaining resilience and a positive mindset as you pursue your passions. Make time for self-compassion, mindfulness, and emotional processing. Journaling can be a valuable tool for expressing emotions, performing self-reflection, and gaining clarity. Additionally, support from friends, family, or a therapist can be an outlet for emotional release and understanding.

>> **Mental health:** A clear and focused mind is essential for creativity and problem-solving in your passion pursuits. Engage in activities that challenge your brain, such as reading, learning a new skill, and solving puzzles. Practice mindfulness and meditation to cultivate mental clarity and reduce stress. Minimize distractions, and create a conducive environment for concentration and productivity.

>> **Limiting screen time:** Although technology can be useful, excessive screen time can negatively affect your well-being. Set boundaries on your screen usage, especially during your self-care moments. Instead, use this time to engage in meaningful face-to-face interactions or enjoy activities that foster personal growth and relaxation.

>> **Incorporate mindful breaks:** Intentionally include breaks throughout your day for self-care. These pauses can be as short as a few minutes of deep breathing or taking a walk outdoors. Mindful breaks recharge your energy and reduce feelings of overwhelm.

>> **Set boundaries and say no:** Learn to say no to commitments or tasks that deplete your energy and hinder your self-care efforts. Setting healthy boundaries allows you to protect your time and focus on activities that genuinely nourish you.

>> **Practice gratitude:** Cultivate a habit of expressing gratitude daily. Focus on the positive aspects of your life, passions, and personal growth. Gratitude can shift your perspective and bring a sense of contentment, even during challenging times.

>> **Social connections:** Nurture meaningful relationships with friends and loved ones who support your well-being and passion pursuits. Engaging in social activities and fostering a sense of belonging positively influences your emotional and mental health.

Remember that self-care isn't a one-size-fits-all approach. Customize your self-care routine to fit your preferences, schedule, and specific needs. Consistency is key to reaping the full benefits of self-care, so make an effort to prioritize it in your daily life. By dedicating time and attention to promoting your physical, emotional, and mental health, you create a strong foundation for finding passion and living a fulfilling life.

Building habits and routines that support self-care

Building habits and routines that support self-care is essential to ensuring that self-care becomes an integral part of your daily life. By incorporating self-care practices into your routines, you create a sustainable and consistent approach to nurturing your well-being. Here are some strategies for building habits and routines that promote self-care:

>> **Start small:** Begin by incorporating one or two simple self-care activities into your daily routine. Starting small makes it easier to stick to the habit and prevents overwhelm. For example, you can start with a five-minute morning meditation or a brief walk during your lunch break.

>> **Be consistent:** Consistency is crucial in forming new habits. Set aside dedicated time for self-care activities each day or week and commit to following through with them. Consistency reinforces the habit and makes it more likely to become a natural part of your routine.

>> **Link self-care to existing habits:** Pair self-care activities with existing habits to make them easier to remember and incorporate. For instance, if you enjoy reading, you can make it a point to read a few pages of a book before going to bed each night.

>> **Create a schedule:** Plan and schedule your self-care activities in advance. Treat these appointments with yourself as non-negotiable, just like any other commitment on your calendar.

- **» Practice mindfulness:** Be present and intentional during your self-care activities. Engage fully in the experience and focus on the positive impact it has on your well-being. Avoid multitasking during self-care moments to fully reap the benefits.

- **» Use reminders and visual cues:** Set reminders on your phone or use visual cues, such as sticky notes or symbols, to prompt you to engage in self-care throughout the day.

- **» Be flexible:** Life can be unpredictable, and routines may need adjustments from time to time. Be flexible and adaptable in your approach to self-care, permitting yourself to make changes when necessary.

- **» Monitor your progress:** Keep track of your self-care habits and progress. A habit tracker or journal can help you visualize your efforts and celebrate your achievements.

- **» Involve others:** If possible, involve friends, family, or colleagues in your self-care routines. Engaging in self-care activities with others can enhance the experience and strengthen social connections.

- **» Celebrate small wins:** Acknowledge and celebrate your commitment to self-care, even when it seems insignificant. Every step, no matter how small, contributes to your overall well-being and personal growth.

Building new habits takes time and patience. Be kind to yourself throughout the process, and don't be discouraged by occasional slip-ups. Consistency and perseverance will ultimately help you build a solid foundation of self-care that supports your passion pursuit and enhances your overall quality of life.

Chapter **18**

Embracing Failure and Learning from Mistakes

I n the journey to discover and pursue your passion, the path is rarely free of obstacles. Failure and mistakes are integral parts of this pursuit, often acting as valuable signposts that guide you toward your true passions.

In the pursuit of passion, the path is often paved with both achievements and setbacks. Failure and mistakes, although seemingly negative, hold valuable lessons that can significantly influence your motivation and confidence. When things don't go as planned, it's easy to lose sight of your initial enthusiasm. The emotional toll of failure can make it challenging to maintain the drive required to chase your passions.

Maybe you're an aspiring artist who faces rejection from art galleries for your first exhibition. The disappointment can lead to a downward spiral of self-doubt, causing your motivation to dwindle. Confidence takes a hit as you internalize the rejection as a sign of your artistic inadequacy. These emotions can cast a shadow on your passion, making it difficult to summon the energy needed to keep creating.

Or perhaps you're an aspiring entrepreneur who starts a business venture with high hopes but encounters financial setbacks. As the business faces challenges, your confidence in your abilities may waver. The motivation to continue pushing forward may diminish as the weight of failure increases. The fear of making more mistakes can immobilize you, preventing you from taking necessary risks to nurture your passion.

The notion of failure can be daunting, but understanding its role as a catalyst for growth and self-discovery is essential. This chapter delves into the significance of failure and mistakes in the process of finding your passion and supplies insights on how to harness these experiences to fuel personal and professional growth. By accepting these setbacks as part of the process, you can unlock a world of potential and fulfillment in your quest for passion.

Maintaining Motivation and Confidence Despite Failure and Mistakes

Don't think of failures and mistakes as dead ends, but as essential components of the journey. When you embrace these experiences as opportunities for growth, you empower yourself to overcome setbacks and rekindle your motivation. Confidence, too, receives a boost as you recognize that resilience and a willingness to learn are the keys to success on the path of passion.

Failure isn't a reflection of intrinsic worth. Rather, it's a crucial aspect of growth and development. When you manage to reframe your perspective on failure as an opportunity for learning, you tend to bounce back stronger. Each setback becomes a steppingstone toward mastery. If you were the artist who faced gallery rejection, you might use this experience to refine your technique, create new artwork, and eventually secure a spot in another exhibition.

Acknowledge that failure and mistakes are natural aspects of any journey. When you don't properly understand them, they can have a debilitating effect on your sense of purpose and enthusiasm. But by recognizing that these experiences are part of the learning process, you can reframe your perspective. This change in mindset empowers you to regain your motivation and confidence, leading you to persevere in your pursuit of passion.

Failure and mistakes can cast a shadow over your motivation and confidence, making the pursuit of passion a daunting endeavor. When faced with setbacks, you might grapple with self-doubt and feelings of inadequacy. These emotions can create a sense of discouragement that dampens the fire of motivation that initially fueled the pursuit of passion. Confidence, too, can take a hit when you interpret failure as a personal shortcoming rather than as an opportunity for growth.

Recognizing the benefits of failure and mistakes in personal and professional growth

Failure and mistakes aren't endpoints, but catalysts for transformation and progress. In the pursuit of passion, these experiences offer unique advantages that contribute to personal and professional growth. Although they might seem discouraging at first, they have the power to shape you in profound ways.

Failure also fosters resilience. When you learn to adapt and persevere through adversity, you build the emotional muscle necessary to overcome future challenges. This resilience extends beyond the immediate endeavor, influencing how you approach new projects, face uncertainty, and handle setbacks. Mistakes, too, offer a rich landscape for growth. They force you to confront areas that need improvement, encouraging you to learn from missteps and innovate.

Recognizing the benefits of failure and mistakes in personal and professional growth is pivotal. Embracing these experiences builds resilience, fosters innovation, and nurtures a mindset that welcomes challenges as opportunities for improvement. It allows you to harness their transformative power to propel yourself closer to your passions and goals.

Accepting failure and learning as part of passion pursuit

Embracing failure and learning from mistakes is a crucial mindset for pursuing your passions. Although failure can be disheartening, viewing it as a valuable source of insight and growth is a game-changer. In the journey to find and nurture your passion, the role of failure and mistakes is profound.

First, failure reframes the concept of success. A setback provides a chance to pause, reflect, and assess what went wrong. This reflective process is an invaluable aspect of personal growth because it prompts you to delve deeper into your goals and motivations.

Take the story of Steve Jobs, the cofounder of Apple Inc. After his initial success, he faced a major setback when he was ousted from his own company. Instead of succumbing to defeat, Jobs embraced this failure as a turning point. He went on to found NeXT, a company that played a pivotal role in shaping his future successes. By learning from his mistakes, he refined his approach and ultimately returned to Apple, leading it to unparalleled heights.

Mistakes also pave the way for innovation. The process of trial and error encourages creative thinking and the exploration of new ideas. When a mistake is made, it often prompts the question: How can this be done differently? This fuels a cycle of improvement and innovation that directly contributes to the pursuit of your passions.

Moreover, learning from mistakes is essential for avoiding stagnation. It pushes you out of your comfort zone, encouraging you to tackle new challenges and learn new skills. It cultivates a sense of adaptability that's essential in an ever-changing world.

In essence, embracing failure and learning from mistakes is fundamental. It reframes setbacks as opportunities, fosters innovation, and fuels personal growth. By recognizing the value in these experiences, you can navigate your paths with resilience and an ever-improving skill set. Figure 18-1 is a worksheet that can guide you through gaining insights from mistakes you may make along the way.

Remember, mistakes are opportunities for growth. By approaching them with curiosity and a willingness to learn, you can transform your setbacks in a positive way.

Learning from Mistakes Worksheet

Step 1: Identify the mistake.

Describe the specific mistake you made.

What was the situation or context in which the mistake occurred?

Step 2: Reflect on the experience.

How did you feel immediately after making the mistake?

What were your initial thoughts and reactions?

Step 3: Analyze the cause.

What factors contributed to the mistake? (e.g., lack of preparation, miscommunication)

Were there external influences that played a role?

Step 4: Identify lessons learned.

What can you learn from this mistake?

How does this experience offer insights for future decisions?

Step 5: Explore alternatives.

What could you have done differently to avoid or mitigate the mistake?

How can you apply this knowledge to similar situations in the future?

Step 6: Plan for improvement.

How will you adjust your approach to prevent a similar mistake?

What strategies or steps will you take to enhance your performance the next time?

Step 7: Acknowledge growth.

Reflect on how this mistake has contributed to your personal and professional growth.

Embrace the opportunity to learn and evolve from challenges.

FIGURE 18-1:
Learning from
mistakes.

Step 8: Set a reminder.

Write down a key lesson or insight from this experience.

Place this reminder somewhere visible to help you remember the importance of the lesson.

Step 9: Track your progress.

Keep a journal to record how you've applied the lessons learned from this mistake.

Note any positive outcomes or improvements resulting from your changed approach.

Step 10: Celebrate small wins.

Acknowledge your efforts in learning from your mistakes.

Celebrate the positive changes and progress you've made.

FIGURE 18-1: *Continued.*

Strategies for Bouncing Back after Failure or Missteps

Embracing failure and learning from mistakes is an art that requires both courage and a growth-oriented mindset. In the pursuit of passions, setbacks are inevitable, but you can transform them into catalysts for growth and progress. This section covers actionable strategies that empower you to not only cope with failure but extract valuable lessons from it.

Navigating failure requires more than just a positive outlook; it demands a deliberate approach that enables you to move forward stronger than before. From entrepreneurs to artists, countless success stories are born from the ashes of failures. The strategies outlined here provide a roadmap.

Whether you're seeking guidance on reframing failures, leveraging mistakes for innovation, or cultivating resilience, this section is designed to equip you with the tools you need to transform failures into profound growth opportunities. By embracing failures and learning from mistakes, you're better equipped to journey toward your passions with renewed determination and a steadfast commitment to growth.

Practicing self-compassion and reframing negative self-talk

Self-compassion involves treating yourself with the same kindness and understanding that you would offer to a close friend who's struggling. Instead of engaging in harsh self-criticism or judgment, self-compassion encourages a nurturing and empathetic attitude toward yourself. This practice recognizes that failure and setbacks are part of the human experience and that they don't define your worth or potential.

When setbacks occur, it's easy to default to self-blame and negative self-talk. Practicing self-compassion involves acknowledging your struggles without judgment and offering yourself words of kindness and encouragement. This helps in creating a safe space for processing emotions and prevents self-criticism from spiraling into deeper feelings of inadequacy.

Self-compassion is a concept rooted in treating yourself with the same kindness, understanding, and empathy that you'd offer to a close friend in times of struggle or difficulty. It involves extending the same level of care to yourself that you give so easily to others. This practice encompasses three key elements:

>> **Self-kindness:** This involves approaching yourself with warmth and understanding, especially during moments of failure, setbacks, or challenges. Instead of being harshly self-critical, you respond with gentleness and patience.

>> **Common humanity:** Facing difficulties and making mistakes is a fundamental aspect of self-compassion. This perspective acknowledges that personal struggles are part of the shared human experience rather than unique flaws.

>> **Mindfulness:** Self-compassion involves acknowledging and accepting your thoughts and emotions without judgment. Mindfulness enables you to observe your feelings and reactions without being overly identified with them.

In essence, self-compassion encourages you to be your own source of comfort and support, offering understanding and reassurance during challenging times. It's a powerful tool for promoting mental and emotional well-being, building resilience, and fostering a healthier relationship with yourself.

Negative self-talk refers to the inner dialogue or thoughts that are self-critical, pessimistic, and damaging to your self-esteem and well-being. It involves the habit of interpreting situations, experiences, and your own abilities in a negative and unconstructive manner. Negative self-talk can manifest as thoughts that undermine self-confidence, reinforce self-doubt, and contribute to feelings of inadequacy.

Recognizing negative self-talk

Negative self-talk can be insidious and can quickly erode confidence and motivation. The key to combating negative self-talk is to challenge and reframe those thoughts. Instead of accepting self-defeating statements as truths, consciously evaluate their accuracy and explore alternative, more positive perspectives.

For example, if your inner dialogue after a setback is, "I'm a failure, and I'll never succeed," consciously reframe it to, "This setback is part of my growth journey. I can learn from this experience and come back stronger." This reframing shifts the focus from failure to growth.

The following are examples of negative self-talk:

>> **Catastrophizing:** Assuming the worst possible outcome in any situation and exaggerating the potential consequences.

>> **Personalization:** Blaming yourself for external events or circumstances that are beyond your control.

>> **Overgeneralization:** Drawing broad conclusions about yourself based on isolated incidents or mistakes.

>> **All-or-nothing thinking:** Seeing situations as either perfect or a complete failure, without recognizing any middle ground or progress.

>> **Discounting positives:** Dismissing or downplaying positive achievements, compliments, or feedback from others.

>> **Comparing:** Measuring yourself against others and feeling inadequate due to perceived shortcomings.

>> **Labeling:** Attaching negative labels or identities to yourself based on mistakes or perceived weaknesses.

Negative self-talk can have detrimental effects on your mental health, self-esteem, and overall well-being. It can lead to increased stress, anxiety, and feelings of hopelessness. Recognizing and challenging negative self-talk is an essential step toward cultivating a more positive and compassionate relationship with yourself.

In the pursuit of passion, setbacks and failures are inevitable. When you're faced with these challenges, it's natural for negative thoughts and self-criticism to arise. However, how you respond to these internal dialogues can significantly influence your ability to overcome obstacles and continue on your path with resilience. This is where the practices of self-compassion and reframing negative self-talk come into play.

Reframing negativity

Practicing self-compassion and reframing negative self-talk work hand in hand to cultivate resilience. By treating yourself with kindness and challenging negative thoughts, you build emotional strength and foster a growth mindset. These practices don't negate the reality of failures; rather, they equip you to navigate challenges with a more constructive and self-supportive approach.

Ultimately, embracing self-compassion and reframing negative self-talk requires practice and patience. As you integrate these practices into your daily life, setbacks become opportunities for growth rather than obstacles that hold you back. With self-compassion as your guide and a positive internal dialogue, you can transform failures into valuable lessons and continue pursuing your passions with unwavering determination.

Here are the steps for reframing negative self-talk so you don't lose confidence or motivation:

1. **Identify your negative thoughts:** Write down a recent situation or event that triggered negative self-talk. Describe the specific negative thoughts that arose from this situation.

2. **Recognize the patterns:** Do you notice recurring themes or patterns in your negative self-talk? List common triggers or situations that tend to lead to negative thoughts.

3. **Challenge your negative thoughts:** For each negative thought, ask yourself these questions: Does evidence support or contradict this thought? Would I say this to a friend in the same situation? How likely is the worst-case scenario I'm imagining? Write down more balanced and rational ways to view the situation.

4. **Replace your negative thoughts with positive affirmations:** Create positive and affirming statements that counteract your negative thoughts. Make sure these affirmations are realistic, encouraging, and empowering.

5. **Practice self-compassion:** Write a letter to yourself as if you were a supportive friend offering understanding and encouragement. Remind yourself that everyone makes mistakes, and failure is a part of growth.

6. **Develop a response plan:** For situations that often trigger negative self-talk, plan a positive response. Practice using your positive affirmations and self-compassionate thoughts in these moments.

7. **Track your progress:** Keep a journal where you note instances of negative self-talk and how you reframed them. Reflect on how your perspective and feelings change over time.

8. **Seek support:** Share your journey with a trusted friend, family member, or therapist. Discuss your progress and challenges in reframing negative self-talk.

Remember, reframing negative self-talk takes time and practice. Be patient with yourself, and celebrate even small steps of progress. Over time, cultivating a more positive and compassionate self-dialogue can lead to improved self-esteem, resilience, and overall well-being.

TIP

Developing a growth mindset, a psychological perspective that reflects the belief that you can develop and improve abilities, intelligence, and talents over time through dedication and effort, thwarts feelings of discouragement that can arise in times of failure. I cover how to cultivate a growth mindset in Chapter 12.

Identifying lessons learned and growth opportunities

Identifying lessons learned and growth opportunities from failure and mistakes is a crucial aspect of personal and professional development. Although failure can be disappointing and mistakes can feel discouraging, they also offer valuable insights that can lead to significant growth and improvement. Embracing failure as a learning experience requires a mindset shift that focuses on extracting wisdom from the situation rather than dwelling on the negative aspects.

1. **Reflect on the experience:** Take the time to reflect on what happened and why it led to failure or mistakes. What were the contributing factors? What decisions or actions could have been different? This self-reflection allows you to gain a deeper understanding of the situation and its complexities.

2. **Analyze the root causes:** Digging into the root causes of failures and mistakes helps you identify patterns or recurring issues that might need attention. Can you spot gaps in your skills, knowledge, or processes that contributed to the outcome? By addressing these root causes, you can prevent similar issues in the future.

3. **Extract the key insights:** Consider what you've learned from the experience. What worked well, and what could be improved? Identify the specific lessons that can guide you in future endeavors. These insights can range from tactical skills to broader concepts like decision-making and adaptability.

4. **Adjust your approach:** Armed with new insights, modify your approach. Failure and mistakes are prime for refining your strategies, adjusting your tactics, and making informed decisions. Applying the lessons learned can lead to better outcomes and increased efficiency.

5. **Embrace humility:** Acknowledging mistakes and seeking lessons from them requires humility. Recognize that everyone makes mistakes, and they're a natural part of growth. Embracing this reality fosters a growth mindset and openness to new experiences.

6. **Value persistence:** Learning from failure often involves persistence. It's easy to become disheartened, but staying committed to the process of improvement shows resilience and determination.

7. **Turn setbacks into strengths:** Use the knowledge you gain from failures to turn your weaknesses into strengths. These experiences are opportunities to develop resilience, problem-solving skills, and the ability to adapt to change.

8. **Apply insights to future goals:** Apply the lessons learned to your future endeavors. Incorporate the insights into your decision-making, problem-solving, and risk management processes. Each new project becomes a chance to demonstrate growth and improvement.

9. **Seek feedback:** Engage in open conversations with mentors, colleagues, or trusted individuals about your experiences. Their perspectives can offer fresh insights and alternative viewpoints that contribute to your personal growth journey.

10. **Embrace continuous learning:** Treat failure as a pathway to continuous learning. When you approach life with a growth mindset, you understand that failures are opportunities for growth, and mistakes are part of the journey toward mastery.

By following these steps, you're taking a proactive approach to personal and professional development that fuels your journey toward success and fulfillment.

Cultivating Resilience and Perseverance

Resilience is the ability to bounce back from adversity and adapt in the face of challenges, adversity, and setbacks. It's the capacity to maintain mental and emotional strength when confronted with difficult situations. If you're resilient, you have a strong sense of inner resourcefulness that enables you to withstand stress, overcome obstacles, and recover from disappointments.

Resilience involves a combination of mental attitudes, emotional strategies, and behavioral skills. It's not about avoiding difficulties but about navigating through them with a positive mindset. As a resilient person, you're able to maintain your composure, problem-solving abilities, and emotional well-being even when facing significant stressors.

Resilience isn't a fixed trait but one you can develop and strengthen over time. It's a dynamic process that involves learning from experiences, adapting to new situations, and building coping mechanisms. Building resilience involves cultivating skills like emotional regulation, effective communication, and problem-solving and seeking support when needed.

In the context of pursuing passion, resilience is crucial. The journey toward your passions is often accompanied by setbacks, failures, and challenges. Resilience enables you to stay committed, continue learning from mistakes, and keep moving forward despite difficulties. It shields you from succumbing to setbacks and allows you to adapt, learn, and grow in the face of adversity.

Perseverance, on the other hand, is the unwavering commitment to staying the course despite the challenges. It's the determination to persist despite obstacles. Perseverance refers to the steadfast determination and persistence to achieve a goal or overcome challenges, even in the face of difficulties, obstacles, or repeated failures. It's the ability to maintain your focus, effort, and commitment over an extended period, even when things get tough. Perseverance involves a strong belief in your ability to succeed and a willingness to keep pushing forward despite setbacks.

Perseverance is closely related to resilience but emphasizes the ongoing effort and dedication needed to reach a particular goal. It's not just about bouncing back from setbacks but about pushing through challenges with a resolute spirit. Persevering individuals don't give up easily; they keep trying different approaches, learning from mistakes, and adapting their strategies to achieve their desired outcomes.

In the pursuit of passion, perseverance is essential. Passionate endeavors often require time, effort, and a willingness to face uncertainties. Whether it's mastering a skill, starting a business, or achieving a personal goal, perseverance allows you to stay committed even when progress is slow or obstacles arise. It helps you maintain your motivation and enthusiasm in the face of challenges, enabling you to ultimately achieve your aspirations.

Both qualities are pivotal in transforming dreams into reality because they provide the inner strength to navigate through the unpredictable terrain of passion pursuit. They aren't mere traits; they're essential skills you can nurture and develop over time. They empower you to stay focused, overcome obstacles, and keep moving forward, even when the path ahead seems daunting.

In the pursuit of your passions, obstacles are like threads woven into the fabric of your journey. These challenges can take various forms, from external factors like financial constraints and societal expectations to internal struggles like self-doubt and fear of failure. Resilience and perseverance emerge as your steadfast companions, guiding you through the labyrinth of difficulties.

By embracing these qualities, you can not only overcome obstacles but emerge from them stronger, more experienced, and better prepared for the path ahead. Resilience and perseverance infuse passion pursuits with an indomitable spirit so that you can forge toward your dreams with confidence.

Failure and mistakes are often seen as roadblocks on the journey to success, but they can lead you to resilience and perseverance. When you navigate the landscape of setbacks with the right mindset, failure becomes a powerful teacher, and mistakes become valuable lessons. Mistakes hold hidden gems of learning. When you embrace mistakes as learning opportunities, you fuel perseverance and innovation.

Developing resilience and perseverance through failure and mistakes requires a growth-oriented mindset. When you approach these experiences with curiosity, view them as part of the learning process, and acknowledge that setbacks aren't the end of the road, you cultivate resilience. Perseverance, too, stems from the understanding that failure isn't a permanent state but a temporary setback.

Resilience and perseverance not only aid in overcoming setbacks but enhance the overall journey of passion pursuit, making it a more enriching and transformative experience.

Chapter **19**

Managing Stress and Burnout

I n the pursuit of your passions and goals, it's common to encounter challenges, setbacks, and moments of intense dedication. Although passion can fuel your drive and enthusiasm, the journey may also expose you to stress and even burnout. The pressure to excel and the weight of expectations can take a toll on your physical, emotional, and mental well-being.

This chapter dives into the crucial topic of stress and its role in finding and sustaining your passion. It covers how to recognize and prevent burnout, which is the state of emotional, physical, and mental exhaustion due to prolonged stress. Burnout can have severe consequences on your overall well-being. Read about how stress and burnout relate to one another yet are different in both characteristics and implications.

Understanding how stress and burnout can distress you is vital for maintaining a healthy and fulfilling pursuit of your passions. This chapter explores the signs of stress and burnout, the potential consequences they may have on your life, and most importantly, strategies to overcome and prevent them. By addressing stress and burnout proactively, you can create a more balanced and resilient approach to passionately following your dreams and finding fulfillment in the process.

Understanding How Stress and Burnout Are Different

According to Oxford, stress is "pressure or worry caused by problems in somebody's life or by having too much to do."

So, stress is the body's response to any physical, mental, or emotional demand. For example, your body releases hormones like adrenaline and cortisol when you perceive a threat. This "fight-or-flight" response is designed to help you deal with the perceived threat.

In moderation, it can be beneficial. It can improve your focus and performance and help you to stay motivated. However, when stress is constant and unmanageable, it can lead to burnout.

An example of stress is feeling overwhelmed by work. You might have too many deadlines or be expected to do more than what is humanly possible. This can lead to feeling anxious, irritable, and unable to focus.

Oxford defines burnout as "the state of being extremely tired or ill, either physically or mentally, because you have worked too hard."

Burnout is a state of mental, emotional, and physical exhaustion that is caused by excessive or extended stress. It appears when you feel overwhelmed, hopeless, and unable to meet the demands of your life.

Burnout can have severe consequences for your health, including depression, anxiety, heart disease, and even death. If you're dealing with chronic stress, seeking help is crucial before it leads to burnout.

An example of burnout is feeling so overwhelmed by work that you can't even get out of bed in the morning. Your entire life feels like one big to-do list, and you can't see a way to escape it. As a result, you might feel hopeless, helpless, and like you're just going through the motions.

The line between stress and burnout is a blurred one, and it's often difficult to see where one ends and the other begins. Burnout is the accumulation of unchecked and built up stress over a period of time. Think of burnout as the larger, meaner, older brother of stress. It requires stress to exist, but you can have stress without being burnt out.

The Impact of Stress and Burnout in Finding Passion

Passion is a powerful, driving force, but the journey toward achieving your goals can be demanding and intense. Stress can significantly sway your motivation and overall well-being when you're pursuing your passions. As you pour your time, energy, and resources into your goals, make sure you're aware of how stress and burnout can afflict you.

Stress can have a profound influence on your motivation. When stress levels are high, it can be challenging to stay focused and committed to your goals. The overwhelming pressure can lead to feelings of fatigue, demotivation, and even doubt in your abilities. As a result, the passion that initially ignited you might wane, and you may find yourself losing sight of the purpose behind your pursuits.

WARNING

Burnout — the result of prolonged stress — can manifest in feelings of cynicism, detachment, and a reduced sense of accomplishment. This emotional depletion can lead to a decline in your passion and enthusiasm for your goals, making it difficult to find joy and fulfillment in what you once loved.

STRESS ISN'T ALWAYS THE ENEMY

Stress, when managed properly, isn't always a bad thing. Although it's easily connected to panic and discomfort, stress is also associated with excitement, anticipation, and a positive outlook, which can contribute to a more enjoyable and engaging experience. In fact, there are several ways in which feeling stress can be a strong motivator and encouraging experience when pursuing your passions.

When you feel stress, you experience physiological shifts that can spring you to alertness and energize you. Stress can serve as a healthy call to action, and action perpetuates motivation. Here are some ways in which good stress can work in your favor:

- **Increased alertness and focus:** When you feel a healthy dose of stress, you experience heightened senses and bolstered your alertness, which are beneficial when you need to concentrate and perform well.

- **Enhanced performance:** A moderate level of stress can push you to work harder and perform at your best. This can give you the boost you need to meet deadlines, achieve goals, and excel in tasks that require extra effort.

(continued)

(continued)

- **Sense of achievement:** Successfully overcoming challenges that cause you stress can lead to a sense of accomplishment and boost your confidence.

- **Adaptation and growth:** You often experience stress when you feel out of your comfort zone. That kind of stress can lead to unexpected personal growth and the development of new skills and competencies you didn't know you had.

Moreover, stress and burnout can negatively disturb your physical health. The toll of constant pressure and inadequate self-care can lead to sleep disturbances, a weakened immune system, and a higher risk of developing health issues like anxiety and depression. When you aren't physically well, it becomes even more challenging to maintain the drive and energy you need to pursue your passions effectively.

WARNING

Unmanaged stress and burnout can also take a toll on your personal relationships. Feeling overwhelmed and exhausted can spill over into your interactions with loved ones, leading to misunderstandings and conflicts. Those, in turn, can create a cycle of additional stress and hinder your ability to find the support you need to navigate the challenges of pursuing your passions.

Understanding the impact of stress and burnout on your motivation and well-being is crucial for maintaining a healthy and sustainable approach to passion pursuit. By acknowledging the signs of stress and burnout and implementing effective coping strategies, you can protect your motivation and well-being and continue your journey toward your passions with resilience and fulfillment.

Identifying the benefits of managing stress and burnout in passion pursuit

Managing stress and burnout is crucial for maintaining a healthy and sustainable pursuit of your passions. By recognizing the benefits of effectively managing stress and burnout, you can create a positive and fulfilling journey toward your goals.

Consciously seeking effective ways to manage stress levels and prevent burnout is a vital aspect of passion pursuit. By recognizing the benefits of stress management, you can foster a positive and resilient mindset that allows you to fully embrace the journey and achieve success in your pursuits. Following are some of the benefits you can experience when you're able to keep a healthy level of stress.

>> **Sustained motivation:** When you manage stress and burnout, your motivation remains intact. You're better able to stay focused on your passions and persevere through challenges, even during difficult times.

» **Enhanced creativity:** Managing stress allows your mind to be more open to creative thinking. When you're not overwhelmed by stress, you can think more clearly and come up with innovative ideas to pursue your passions.

» **Improved productivity:** Reduced stress and burnout can lead to increased productivity. By maintaining a healthy work-life balance and avoiding the pitfalls of burnout, you can achieve more with greater efficiency.

» **Better decision-making:** Stress can cloud your judgment, making it difficult to make sound decisions. When you manage stress effectively, you can approach decision-making with clarity and confidence.

» **Enhanced physical health:** Chronic stress can have detrimental effects on your physical health. By managing stress, you promote better overall well-being, allowing you to stay physically healthy to pursue your passions with vigor.

» **Stronger resilience:** Effective stress management builds resilience. When you face obstacles, you can bounce back more quickly and continue pursuing your passions with determination.

» **Improved relationships:** Managing stress and burnout can positively bolster your relationships with others. You can communicate more effectively and avoid unnecessary conflicts, making it easier to collaborate with others who share your passions.

» **Increased satisfaction:** A healthy balance between passion pursuit and self-care results in increased satisfaction and fulfillment. You enjoy the journey and find joy in the process of reaching your goals.

» **Long-term sustainability:** By managing stress and burnout, you increase the sustainability of your passion pursuit. You can maintain your dedication and enthusiasm for the long haul without succumbing to exhaustion.

» **Personal growth:** Overcoming stress and burnout requires personal growth. Through this process, you learn valuable lessons about yourself and build a stronger foundation for pursuing your passions.

Recognizing the warning signs and symptoms of stress and burnout

Recognizing the warning signs and symptoms of stress and burnout is essential for taking proactive steps to address these challenges and protect your well-being while pursuing your passions. Stress and burnout can manifest in various ways, but being aware of these signs can help you identify when you might be at risk of experiencing these negative effects.

Recognizing these warning signs allows you to take proactive measures to address stress and burnout. Engaging in self-care, setting boundaries, seeking support from mentors or loved ones, and practicing stress-reduction techniques like mindfulness or meditation can contribute to managing and reducing the impact of stress and burnout in your pursuit of passion. By paying attention to these signs, you can maintain your motivation, well-being, and resilience as you continue on your journey of passion pursuit.

>> **Physical symptoms:** Stress and burnout can lead to physical manifestations such as frequent headaches, fatigue, muscle tension, and digestive issues. Feeling constantly fatigued and run-down, despite adequate rest, can be a red flag for burnout.

>> **Emotional exhaustion:** Persistent feelings of emotional exhaustion and over-whelm are common signs of stress and burnout. It might feel challenging to cope with everyday tasks. Even the thought of pursuing passions can seem draining.

>> **Reduced productivity and concentration:** Stress and burnout can hamper your ability to stay focused and productive. You might find it difficult to concentrate on tasks, leading to a decline in the quality of your work and progress toward your goals.

>> **Detachment and cynicism:** Developing a cynical or negative outlook toward your passions and goals is a potential sign of burnout. You might start to feel detached from your aspirations and lose the enthusiasm that once drove you forward.

>> **Increased irritability and mood swings:** Stress and burnout can lead to heightened irritability and mood swings. You might find yourself becoming more reactive or short-tempered in your interactions with others.

>> **Neglecting self-care:** A decline in self-care practices — such as neglecting exercise, healthy eating, or spending time with loved ones — can indicate that stress and burnout are taking a toll on your overall well-being.

>> **Withdrawal from social interactions:** Avoiding social interactions and isolating yourself can be a sign of emotional exhaustion and the need for support.

>> **Sleep disturbances:** Difficulty falling asleep, staying asleep, or experiencing restless nights can be related to stress and burnout.

Strategies for Managing Stress and Burnout

In the pursuit of your passions, managing stress and avoiding burnout are essential to maintain your well-being and sustain your motivation. As you encounter challenges and immerse yourself in your endeavors, make sure you have effective strategies in place to handle stress and prevent burnout. This section delves into a variety of practical and proven techniques to help you navigate the demanding aspects of your passion pursuit while preserving your mental, emotional, and physical health.

The strategies discussed in this section can empower you to understand and address stress and burnout effectively. From building resilience to implementing self-care practices, each strategy serves as a valuable tool in your arsenal, enabling you to strike a balance between your ambitious pursuit and personal well-being.

By delving into these strategies, you can cultivate a deeper understanding of your personal boundaries, develop coping mechanisms, and foster a more sustainable approach to achieving your passions. Embracing these techniques will not only enhance your ability to cope with the inevitable stressors but also empower you to find joy and fulfillment in the journey, ensuring that your passion pursuit remains purposeful and rewarding.

Practicing stress management techniques such as mindfulness, meditation, and exercise

Practicing stress management techniques is a crucial aspect of maintaining your well-being while pursuing your passions. Mindfulness, meditation, and exercise are powerful tools that can significantly reduce stress and enhance your ability to cope with challenges.

Mindfulness involves being fully present in the moment, observing your thoughts and feelings without judgment. By cultivating mindfulness, you become more aware of your stress triggers and can respond to them in a balanced manner. Regular mindfulness practices, such as deep breathing exercises or mindful meditation, can calm your mind, reduce anxiety, and improve your overall emotional resilience.

Meditation is another effective technique for managing stress. Through meditation, you can quiet your mind, enhance focus, and achieve a sense of inner peace. Taking a few minutes each day to meditate can benefit your mental clarity and emotional well-being. Moreover, meditation allows you to detach from the pressures of your passion pursuit temporarily, giving you a fresh perspective and renewed energy.

Engaging in regular physical exercise is not only beneficial for your physical health but plays a pivotal role in managing stress. When you exercise, your body releases endorphins, which are natural mood enhancers. This chemical boost combats stress and promotes a sense of relaxation and positivity. Whether it's going for a brisk walk, practicing yoga, or participating in a sport you enjoy, incorporating physical activity into your routine can be a powerful stress-relief tool.

By incorporating these stress management techniques into your daily life, you can build emotional resilience, reduce the negative impact of stress, and maintain a more balanced and fulfilling pursuit of your passions. These practices empower you to approach challenges with greater clarity and focus, enhancing your overall well-being and ability to thrive on your journey toward living your passions to the fullest.

Developing a self-care plan that prioritizes rest, relaxation, and rejuvenation

Developing a well-rounded self-care plan that prioritizes rest, relaxation, and rejuvenation is essential for effectively managing stress and preventing burnout. A self-care plan is so important to pursuing passion that Chapter 17 is entirely dedicated to it. But in a nutshell, this plan should be personalized to suit individual preferences and needs, ensuring that it encompasses various self-care practices that cater to physical, emotional, and mental well-being.

Rest and adequate sleep are fundamental components of a self-care plan. Getting enough quality sleep is crucial for restoring your body and mind, improving cognitive functions, and boosting overall mood and productivity. Incorporating a consistent sleep schedule and creating a relaxing bedtime routine can enhance the quality of your rest and rejuvenation.

Taking time for relaxation is equally important. Engaging in activities that bring joy and peace, such as reading a book, spending time in nature, and pursuing a hobby, helps you recharge and disconnect from stressors. Incorporating relaxation techniques, like deep breathing exercises and progressive muscle relaxation, can alleviate tension and promote a sense of calm.

Additionally, taking regular breaks throughout the day is vital. Building short moments of rest and rejuvenation into your daily schedule can prevent feelings of overwhelm and increase your overall efficiency. Stepping away from work or other commitments for a few minutes to stretch, meditate, or simply take a mindful pause can decrease your stress levels and increase your mental clarity.

Incorporating rejuvenation practices, such as spending quality time with loved ones, cultivating positive relationships, and engaging in creative pursuits, further enhances your self-care plan. Social connections and creative outlets contribute to emotional well-being and foster a sense of fulfillment.

Designing a self-care plan is an ongoing process, and it may require adjustments as your needs evolve. Make self-care a non-negotiable priority, and commit to implementing the plan consistently. By nourishing your physical, emotional, and mental health through rest, relaxation, and rejuvenation, you can effectively manage stress and burnout and remain resilient and focused on your journey to pursuing your passions wholeheartedly.

Setting boundaries to prevent burnout

Boundaries can take many forms. They can range from being rigid and strict to appearing almost nonexistent. If you have more rigid boundaries, you might:

» Keep others at a distance

» Seem detached, even with intimate partners

» Have few close relationships

» Avoid close relationships

If you have more loose or open boundaries, you might:

» Get too involved with others' problems

» Find it difficult to say "no" to others' requests

» Overshare personal information with others

» Seek to please others for fear of rejection

A person with healthy boundaries understands that making their expectations clear helps in two ways: It establishes what behavior you will accept from other people, and it establishes what behavior other people can expect from you. If you have healthy boundaries, you might:

» Share personal information appropriately (not too much or not too little)

» Understand your personal needs and wants and know how to communicate them

» Value your own opinions

» Accept when others tell you "no"

Many of us have a mix of boundaries depending on the situation. For example, you might have strict boundaries at work and more loose ones at home or with family and friends.

There might even be different boundaries based on a person's culture. For example, some cultures find that sharing personal information is not appropriate at any time, while in other cultures, sharing might be encouraged at all times.

HOW TO SET AND MAINTAIN GOOD BOUNDARIES

Not sure how to go about creating boundaries or effectively uphold existing ones? Here are some of the best approaches to try.

Reflect on the reasons for your boundaries

To successfully introduce and set boundaries, it's key to understand why they're each important to you and how they will benefit your emotional well-being.

Take some time to be a detective of your own psychology. So often stuff happens to people and they feel uncomfortable, but they're not sure why. The first step in having healthy boundaries in any situation is spending the time to explore what's happening to you.

Start with a few boundaries

If you don't have many boundaries in place already, the prospect of introducing more might seem overwhelming — so build them up slowly. Doing so allows you to take things at a more comfortable pace, and it provides time to reflect on whether it's heading in the right direction or if you need to make some tweaks.

Consider setting boundaries early on

Sometimes it can be really hard to start putting boundaries in, especially in pre-existing relationships. If you can put in boundaries straight away, it's a lot easier to work with.

By setting boundaries and expectations from the very beginning, everyone knows where they stand, and feelings of hurt, confusion, and frustration can be lessened.

Try to be consistent with your boundaries

Letting boundaries slide can lead to confusion and encourage new expectations and demands among those around you. Try keeping things consistent and steady. This helps to reinforce your original thresholds and beliefs, and it ensures those lines remain clearly established.

Carve out time for yourself

Vary depending on the type of relationship but if you find it helpful, there's no reason not to have a few basics in place that can be adapted accordingly. Consider getting an hour or two of alone time each weekend.

This boundary could apply whether you live with a partner, have a busy social schedule with friends, or are close with your family.

Don't be afraid to include extra boundaries

In some aspects of our lives, there are boundaries already in place — such as in the workplace. But consider these the minimum. Colleagues will likely have some of their own in place, and it's okay for you to add some too.

Set healthy boundaries on social media

These platforms allow for more communication than ever, but they've also encouraged some considerable boundary blurring.

If you deem a particular action as boundary-crossing in real life, your concerns are no less valid when it occurs digitally. You don't have to expose yourself to social media that's distressing you.

Communicate when your boundaries are crossed

Communication is critical in the world of boundaries, especially if someone consistently oversteps yours. While you might need to raise your concerns, these discussions need not be confrontational.

Practice self-love and engage in activities you enjoy

For boundaries to have a strong foundation, you need to show yourself a bit of love. If you've got a narrative in your head that says you're worthless and undeserving, then you're going to find it difficult to put boundaries in place that protect you. A lot of it comes down to self-worth and self-value.

It doesn't take much to start encouraging this mindset either. The more you engage in activities that release feel-good hormones, like singing, running, or whatever you want to do — things that feed your own heart — then that's going to help change your internal dialogue and make you feel more deserving.

Gain some perspective on your boundaries

Not having boundaries can be detrimental to our mental health, but going too far and over-thinking them can also impact our emotional well-being. Get a healthy level of thinking about boundaries. Have some but don't be dictated by them. Sometimes you've just got to go with your gut instinct. We can forget that we're actually quite good at navigating most things and are quite intuitive as human beings.

Setting boundaries and prioritizing self-care are powerful strategies for preventing burnout and maintaining well-being while pursuing your passions. Burnout often occurs when you push yourself beyond your limits and neglect your own needs in pursuit of your goals. By establishing clear boundaries and making self-care a priority, you can safeguard yourself against overwhelming stress and exhaustion.

One essential aspect of setting boundaries is learning to say no when necessary. It can be challenging to decline additional responsibilities or commitments, but saying yes to everything can lead to overextension and burnout. Being selective about what you take on and ensuring that your schedule allows for sufficient rest and self-care is crucial for maintaining balance.

Effective time management is also instrumental in preventing burnout. Prioritizing self-care activities and integrating them into your daily routine ensures that you make time for yourself amidst other responsibilities. Blocking out specific periods for self-care, whether for exercise, meditation, or leisure activities, creates a sense of structure and ensures that you prioritize your well-being.

Moreover, recognizing your limits and being self-compassionate is key. Acknowledging that it's okay to have bad days or to take breaks when needed allows you to be kinder to yourself and reduces the pressure to perform constantly. You can build resilience by accepting that setbacks are part of the journey and that taking care of yourself during challenging times is crucial for long-term success.

Besides setting personal boundaries, create boundaries in your work and social environments. Communicating your needs clearly to colleagues, friends, and family members can help them understand your limits and prevent unnecessary stress. By setting boundaries, you empower yourself to make self-care a priority and protect your physical and emotional well-being.

Ultimately, preventing burnout requires a proactive approach to self-care. By setting boundaries, managing time effectively, and practicing self-compassion, you create a foundation of well-being that enables you to pursue your passions with sustained energy, enthusiasm, and focus. Prioritizing self-care is not only beneficial for your personal life but also enhances your ability to excel in your endeavors and find fulfillment in the pursuit of your passions.

Recognizing the Signs of Burnout

In the pursuit of your passions, it's natural to encounter challenges, setbacks, and moments of exhaustion. Staying motivated and avoiding burnout are crucial for maintaining momentum and achieving long-term success. The ability to navigate through these obstacles with resilience and determination can significantly affect your journey toward finding and pursuing your passions.

Burnout is a serious condition that can result from too much stress unchecked over a prolonged period of time. Recovering from burnout, as discussed earlier in the chapter, can be time-consuming and arduous. Seeing the signs early to prevent burnout is by far better for your mental and physical health and for your stamina when pursuing your passion.

In this section, you will explore effective strategies to avoid burnout and cultivate sustained motivation, empowering you to stay on course and thrive in your passion pursuit. Being able to identify signs of burnout and its potential causes can ensure you take proactive steps to maintain your well-being and momentum.

Burnout can stem from a variety of factors, both personal and professional, that can accumulate over time and take a toll on your well-being. Understanding the causes of burnout is essential for taking proactive measures to prevent it from manifesting.

Following are some common causes of burnout and effective strategies to thwart its impact on your passion pursuit:

>> **Work overload:** One of the primary culprits of burnout is an overwhelming workload. Feeling constantly swamped with tasks and responsibilities can lead to physical and emotional exhaustion. To counter this, practice time management, and prioritize tasks based on importance and urgency. Learning to delegate when possible and setting realistic goals can alleviate the pressure and create a more balanced work environment.

>> **Lack of autonomy:** Feeling micromanaged or having little control over your work can drain your enthusiasm and motivation. Building autonomy in your endeavors can be empowering and invigorating. Seek opportunities to have a say in decision-making and take ownership of your projects. Embrace a growth mindset, and view challenges as opportunities for growth rather than burdens.

>> **Conflict and stressful relationships:** Interpersonal conflicts and a toxic work environment can contribute significantly to burnout. It's essential to address conflicts promptly and constructively. Communication is key. Express your concerns, seek resolutions, and, if needed, consider seeking guidance from HR or a supervisor to foster a healthier work environment.

>> **Neglected self-care:** Failure to prioritize self-care can exacerbate feelings of burnout. Make time for activities that bring you joy, relaxation, and fulfillment. Regular exercise, mindfulness practices, and hobbies can recharge your energy and prevent burnout.

>> **Lack of alignment with values and passions:** Pursuing endeavors that don't align with your values or passions can lead to burnout. Take time to reflect on what truly matters to you, and explore avenues that resonate with your interests and purpose.

>> **Inadequate support system:** Feeling isolated and unsupported in your passion pursuit can be draining. Surround yourself with a strong support system of friends, mentors, and like-minded individuals who can offer encouragement and guidance.

>> **Ignoring warning signs:** Sometimes you may ignore early signs of burnout, believing that pushing through will lead to success. Instead, it's essential to pay attention to these signals and address them promptly. Listen to your body and mind, and don't hesitate to take breaks or seek professional help if needed.

By proactively identifying the causes of burnout and taking necessary measures to address them, you can safeguard your well-being and maintain the enthusiasm you need to pursue your passions with determination and vitality. Remember, prevention is key, and making self-care a priority can contribute significantly to a sustainable and fulfilling passion-pursuit journey.

Recognizing the Importance of Rest and Rejuvenation in Sustaining Motivation

Recognizing the significance of rest and rejuvenation in sustaining motivation is crucial for maintaining long-term enthusiasm and drive in your passion pursuit. Often, in the pursuit of your goals, you may be tempted to overlook the value of rest, thinking that it will slow you down or impede your progress. However, the truth is that rest is an integral part of the journey toward success and fulfillment. Rest and rejuvenation contribute to sustaining motivation in several ways:

>> **Replenishing energy reserves:** Just like a car requires fuel to keep moving, your body and mind needs energy to stay motivated and focused. Rest and rejuvenation, such as getting adequate sleep, taking breaks, and engaging in leisure activities, replenish your energy reserves. When you're well rested, you can approach your passion projects with renewed vigor and creativity.

>> **Preventing burnout:** Sustained passion pursuit can be demanding, and without proper rest, you risk burnout. Overexertion can lead to exhaustion, diminish your passion, and even compromise your physical and mental health. Taking regular breaks and downtime allows you to recharge and reduce the risk of burnout.

- **Enhancing cognitive function:** Fatigue and stress can impair cognitive function, affecting your ability to think critically and creatively. Rest and relaxation support mental clarity and sharpen your problem-solving skills, enabling you to tackle challenges more effectively.

- **Boosting productivity:** Counterintuitive as it may seem, incorporating rest and rejuvenation into your routines enhances productivity. Quality rest improves focus and concentration, allowing you to accomplish tasks more efficiently.

- **Fostering mindfulness:** Restful moments are an opportunity to be present and mindful. By engaging in activities that promote relaxation, such as meditation, or spending time in nature, you can gain valuable insights and clarity about your passions and goals.

- **Preventing diminishing returns:** Continuously pushing yourself without adequate rest can lead to diminishing returns. The quality of your work may decline, and you may find yourself stuck in unproductive cycles. Taking breaks and allowing time for rejuvenation can lead to more sustainable and meaningful progress.

- **Balancing well-being:** Pursuing your passions is an essential aspect of a fulfilling life, but it's equally essential to maintain overall well-being. Rest and rejuvenation contribute to a balanced life, supporting not only your passion pursuits but also your personal happiness and satisfaction.

Incorporating rest and rejuvenation into your passion-pursuit journey isn't a sign of weakness but a testament to your commitment to long-term success and fulfillment. Embracing the value of rest and balancing it with your drive to achieve your goals is a powerful combination that can sustain motivation, creativity, and joy in your passion-filled endeavors.

SOURCES OF INSPIRATION AND MOTIVATION TO KEEP YOU GOING

Identifying sources of inspiration and motivation is fundamental for sustaining passion pursuit. Along the journey toward your goals, you may experience moments of uncertainty or challenges that can dampen your enthusiasm. In such times, having reliable sources of inspiration can reignite your drive and keep you moving forward.

By being mindful of these sources of inspiration and motivation, you can build a resilient mindset that sustains you throughout your passion pursuit. The fusion of these

(continued)

(continued)

factors keeps your enthusiasm alive and fuels your determination to bring your passions to life. Here are some valuable sources of inspiration and motivation to sustain passion pursuit.

- **Role models and mentors:** Learning from the experiences and wisdom of successful individuals who have achieved similar goals can be highly motivating. Their stories of overcoming obstacles and achieving greatness can inspire you to persevere in your own pursuit of passion.

- **Personal values and purpose:** Reflecting on your core values and the purpose behind your passion can offer intrinsic motivation. When you align your pursuits with what truly matters to you, the journey becomes more meaningful and fulfilling.

- **Positive feedback and support:** Receiving encouragement and support from friends, family, or a community of like-minded individuals can boost your confidence and motivation. Surrounding yourself with positive influences can fuel your determination to keep going.

- **Challenges and growth opportunities:** Embracing challenges as opportunities for growth and development can be a powerful source of motivation. When you view setbacks as learning experiences, you become more resilient and driven to achieve your goals.

- **Visualization and goal setting:** Creating a clear vision of your desired outcome and setting specific, achievable goals can keep you focused and motivated. Visualizing success can help you stay on track and committed to your passion pursuit.

- **Learning and curiosity:** Embracing a mindset of continuous learning and curiosity can be highly motivating. Exploring new ideas, acquiring new skills, and expanding your knowledge can reignite your passion and sense of wonder.

- **Moments of flow and peak performance:** Experiencing moments of "flow" or peak performance, where time seems to fly by, can remind you of the joy and fulfillment that comes from pursuing your passions.

- **Reminders of past achievements:** Reflecting on past achievements, no matter how small, can boost your confidence and remind you of your capabilities to succeed in your passion pursuit.

- **Purposeful breaks and self-care:** Taking intentional breaks and engaging in self-care practices can rejuvenate your mind and body, helping you maintain motivation and avoid burnout.

- **Connecting with like-minded communities:** Engaging with communities or groups that share similar passions can bring a sense of belonging and foster a supportive environment for sustained motivation.

5

The Part of Tens

IN THIS PART . . .

Fuel your passion and keep motivated.

Pursue other activities on your way.

Chapter **20**

Ten Ways to Fuel Your Passion

This book has taken you through various aspects of passion pursuit, from brainstorming ideas to focus on what you're passionate about to concrete steps to make your goals achievable.

To get going and keep yourself motivated, it helps to be reminded of the key ideas, summarized in this chapter, that can keep you focused and energized to successfully pursue your passion.

Set Goals and Create a Plan

In the pursuit of meaningful aspirations, setting clear goals and crafting a well-defined plan are foundational steps that lay the groundwork for success. Goals act as guiding stars, steering you toward your desired destination, while a thoughtfully constructed plan acts as the roadmap to navigate the complex terrain of turning dreams into reality.

Surround Yourself with Inspiration

Creating an environment that nurtures your passion is an essential aspect of your journey. Surrounding yourself with inspiration can ignite your creativity, boost your motivation, and propel you toward your goals. Curating your surroundings can have a profound impact on your passion pursuit, helping you stay focused and connected to what truly drives you.

Stay Curious and Keep Learning

In a world marked by rapid advancements and constant evolution, the significance of curiosity and continuous learning can't be overstated. The journey toward realizing your passions isn't just about reaching a destination; it's about engaging with a process that fuels your personal and professional growth. At the heart of this journey lies the insatiable thirst for knowledge, the commitment to staying curious, and the determination to keep learning.

Take Action and Practice Consistently

Imagine an orchestra without musicians or a canvas devoid of color — a vision, yet unfulfilled. Just as creative pursuits need action to come to life, your passion requires consistent practice to flourish.

Celebrate Your Progress and Successes

In the pursuit of passion, the journey is as important as the destination. As you navigate the path toward your dreams, taking moments to celebrate your progress and successes becomes a source of motivation, affirmation, and reflection. Acknowledge and commemorate your milestones, both big and small. Celebrating isn't just about the destination; it's about acknowledging the distance you've come, the obstacles you've conquered, and the growth you've achieved.

Find Balance and Prioritize Self-Care

In the pursuit of passion, it's easy to become consumed by the excitement and determination to achieve your goals. However, maintaining balance and prioritizing self-care is essential for your overall well-being and sustained success. Finding equilibrium between your passions and other aspects of your life ensures that you can continue your journey with vitality and enthusiasm.

Embrace Failure and Learn from Mistakes

In the pursuit of passion, failure isn't a dead end; it's a pathway to progress. The road to success is often paved with setbacks and mistakes, each offering valuable lessons that propel you forward. Embracing failure can lead to unparalleled growth and transformation.

Collaborate and Seek Feedback

In the journey of pursuing your passion, collaboration and seeking feedback can be potent forces that drive you forward. Although the notion of individual genius is celebrated, the reality is that the collective power of diverse minds often fuels remarkable accomplishments.

Visualize Success and Manifest Your Dreams

Visualizing success is more than just wishful thinking. It's a powerful technique that can help you transform your dreams into reality. By crafting a clear mental image of your desired outcomes, you set the stage for manifesting your aspirations.

Never Stop Exploring and Evolving

Life's journey is a boundless expedition, a tapestry woven with threads of discovery, growth, and transformation. In the realm of passion and purpose, the pursuit of exploration and evolution is the compass guiding you toward a deeper understanding and uncharted territories.

Chapter **21**

Ten Fun Things to Do While Trying to Find Your Passion

t can be difficult to keep yourself motivated when you hit a roadblock while pursuing your passion. Perhaps you're still searching for something to be passionate about, or you're having trouble keeping your level of inspiration up as you face setbacks or other low moments. This chapter offers some activities you can pursue to keep you energized and excited about finding your passion, help you network and connect with others, and recharge you.

Take a Cooking Class and Experiment with New Recipes and Ingredients

Embarking on a culinary adventure can be as exciting as it is fulfilling. Taking a cooking class and experimenting with new recipes and ingredients opens up a world of flavors, techniques, and creativity that can ignite your passion for cooking. Whether you're a beginner or an experienced home cook, this journey can be both educational and delightful, enriching your culinary skills and inspiring you to explore the art of gastronomy.

Attend a Music Festival and Discover New Artists and Genres of Music

Immersing yourself in the vibrant atmosphere of a music festival is more than just attending a concert. It's a journey of musical discovery and a celebration of diverse sounds and genres. From the rhythmic beats of hip-hop to the soulful melodies of jazz, music festivals supply a unique platform to broaden your musical horizons and connect with both established and emerging artists.

Try a New Sport or Fitness Activity

In the vast tapestry of life, few things have the power to ignite the human spirit as much as movement. For millennia, sport and fitness activities have been not only a testament to physical prowess but a reflection of cultures, communities, and personal identities. Within each leap, sprint, throw, or stretch lies an opportunity for self-discovery, growth, and boundless joy.

Travel to a New Place and Immerse Yourself in Its Culture

In the vast tapestry of human existence, every region, city, and village boasts its own unique stories, traditions, and ways of life. Travel isn't just about escaping the routine or seeking leisure; it's about diving deep into these narratives, embracing the unfamiliar, and expanding your horizons. When you step foot in a new place and truly immerse yourself in its culture, you don't just observe; you participate. You learn, evolve, and often discover aspects of yourself previously unexplored.

Attend a Comedy Show or Improv Class and Explore Your Sense of Humor

In the tapestry of human experiences, laughter holds a universal thread. It transcends languages, breaks down walls, and bridges gaps between cultures and generations. Your sense of humor is unique. By attending a comedy show or diving into an improv class, you're not just in for bouts of laughter; you're embarking on a journey to explore, understand, and perhaps even redefine what tickles your funny bone. Whether you're seeking a hearty laugh, looking to challenge your comedic boundaries, or eager to uncover latent comic talent, attending a comedy show or improv class promises a roller coaster of emotions and insights and might even offer a few belly laughs along the way.

Visit a Museum or Art Gallery and Explore Different Forms of Artistic Expression

The world of art is a boundless expanse, mirroring the depths and dimensions of human emotions, histories, and imaginations. By stepping into a museum or art gallery, you're not merely walking through rooms filled with paintings or sculptures, but journeying through time, cultures, and the intricate labyrinths of artists' minds. Whether you're an art aficionado or a casual observer, these spaces offer an opportunity to pause, reflect, and connect both with the world outside and the universe within.

Volunteer for a Cause That Resonates with You and Learn More about Social Issues

In an interconnected world, every act of kindness, every hour dedicated to service, ripples out, creating waves of positive change. Volunteering isn't just about lending a hand; it's an immersion into the heart of societal issues, offering a firsthand understanding and an opportunity to be part of the solution. As you stand on the threshold of this transformative journey, remember that this isn't merely about giving, but about growing — growing in empathy, in awareness, and in connection with the global community.

Attend a Book Club or Literary Event and Discover New Authors and Genres

In the sprawling tapestry of human expression, literature stands as a timeless testament to your dreams, struggles, joys, and reflections. Every book, every page, is a window to a different world, a fresh perspective. But in an age teeming with countless voices, how do you sift through the cacophony to find those tales that truly resonate? Enter the enchanting realm of book clubs and literary events! These spaces, dedicated to the celebration of words and stories, offer a curated exploration into the vast literary landscape. Whether you're a seasoned bibliophile or setting sail on your maiden literary voyage, these gatherings promise a treasure trove of discoveries.

Attend a TED Talk or Public Speaking Event and Explore New Ideas and Perspectives

In the symphony of human intellect are some moments that stand out — moments when an individual, armed with a unique idea or insight, steps onto a stage and captivates an audience, weaving a tapestry of thought that has the power to shift paradigms. TED Talks and public speaking events are such crucibles of innovation, where inspiration, knowledge, and transformative ideas converge. These platforms amplify voices that challenge the status quo, introduce groundbreaking perspectives, and inspire change. Whether you're seeking to fuel your curiosity, broaden your horizons, or simply engage with a community of thinkers, these gatherings are a beacon.

Start a New Hobby or Craft, and See Where It Takes You

In the bustling rhythm of everyday life, it's easy to find yourself ensnared in routines, adhering to a set pattern day in and day out. But every so often emerges a desire to break the monotony, to sprinkle your life with a dash of novelty and creativity. This is where hobbies and crafts come into play. These pursuits, driven not by necessity but by passion and curiosity, have the magical ability to transport you to new realms of exploration and self-expression. Whether it's the delicate art of pottery, the thrill of photography, or the rhythmic dance of knitting needles, embarking on a new hobby or craft is like opening a door to uncharted territories.

Index

bullet journals, 93

burnout. *See also* stress management

about, 135, 329–330

avoiding, 236

compared with stress, 330

impact of, 331–334

self-care for, 305–306

signs of, 340–342

business ideas

aligning your passion with, 151–153

developing, 145–146

business plans, developing, 146–149

C

calculated risks, 258–261

call-to-action (CTA), in storytelling, 208

career adaptability, as a role of training and professional development, 163

career advancement, as a role of training and professional development, 163

career counselors, 73

career opportunities, as an advantage of formal education, 162

careers

about, 72, 123–124

aligning with values and interests, 74

enhancing opportunities, 160

finding meaning and purpose in work, 124–127

identifying potential paths, 49–50

making work more fulfilling, 127–134

pursuing your passion within your, 74–75

researching, 72–73

transitioning to new, 134–138

catastrophizing, as an example of negative self-talk, 322

celebrating milestones, 91–97

certifications, 165–166

challenges

embracing, 61, 294–296

embracing as opportunities, 223

of fear, 253–254

of growth mindset, 217–218

navigating, 111

of starting a business, 141–143

taking on new, 129

time management, 238–239

change, fear of, 252

characteristics, of growth mindset, 214–217

Cheat Sheet (website), 3

check-ins, scheduling, 114

choices, informed, 35

clarity

with mentors and role models, 120

in storytelling, 207

classes, taking, 67

CliftonStrengths, 38

clubs, joining, 67

coaching, 182

cognitive benefits, passion and, 9

collaboration

about, 114, 131, 349

as an advantage of formal education, 162

embracing, 157

enriched, 31

opportunities for, 102–103

promoting, 161

collaborative projects, 273

colleagues, building relationships with, 132–134

comedy shows, 352–353

comfort zone, stepping outside your, 64

commitment, with mentors and role models, 120

communication

about, 131

effective, 110–112

enhancing skills of, 102

with mentors and role models, 121

self-care and, 308

community

finding, 71

growth-oriented, 232–234

involvement in, 107

comparison

as an example of negative self-talk, 322

with others, 219

competitive advantage, 178

conciseness, in personal story development, 209

confidence

building, 102, 116, 176, 263–264

effect of setbacks on, 285

lack of, 53–54

maintaining, 316–320

Google Sheets, 93
government programs
    for a business, 150
    scholarships and grants from, 171
Grandin, Temple, 60
grants, 150, 170–171
gratitude
    practicing, 312
    practicing in your work, 126–127
    towards mentors and role models, 121
groups, joining, 67
growth
    lack of, 135
    targeted, 31
growth mindset
    about, 129, 179, 180–181, 186, 213–214
    achieving successful outcomes, 223
    challenges of, 217–218
    characteristics of, 214–217
    cultivating a, 227–231, 307
    developing a, 56–57, 221–223, 294–296, 299
    developing a growth-oriented community, 232–234
    fixed mindset *versus*, 218–221
    impact of on perseverance, 226–227
    impact of on resilience, 225–226
    overcoming obstackes and taking risks, 222–223
    pursuing continuous learning and development, 224–227
    as a role of training and professional development, 164
    self-checklist for, 216–217
    tips for practicing self-awareness and self-reflection, 230–231
growth opportunities, identifying, 324–325
guidance
    access to, 102
    from mentors and role models, 121
    seeking, 168–169

H

habit trackers, 93
Habitica, 93
Habitify, 93
habits
    building to support continuous learning, 185–187
    building to support self-care, 312–313

happiness, passion and, 9, 17–18
heroes, in storytelling, 207
hobbies
    about, 68, 354
    benefits of, 69–70
    finding new, 66
    incorporating into your life, 70–71
    merging values with, 71
    for self-care, 304
    that align with values and interests, 68–70
    trying new, 67
horizons, broadening, 64–68
housing expenses, for educational paths, 172
humanity, 321

I

icons, explained, 3
impact
    positive, 131
    in storytelling, 207
improv classes, 352–353
improvement, areas for, 32–33
indecision, as an obstacle to finding passion, 52
in-depth knowledge, as an advantage of formal education, 161
industries
    about, 72
    requirements for educational paths, 169
    researching, 72–73
industry events, 114, 182
industry trends, benefits of staying up-to-date with, 178
industry-specific events/conferences, 106
industry-specific networking, 104
information sharing, networking and, 101
informational interviews, 73, 103
informed choices/direction, 35
informed decisions, about taking risks, 260–261
initiatives
    with mentors and role models, 121
    that align with interests/values, 130–132
innovation
    as a benefit of time management, 245
    embracing, 157
    growth mindset and, 181

online presence
  creating a strong, 201–206
  metrics for, 95
online research, on careers and industries, 73
opportunities
  access to, 102
  creating new, 177
  educational, 164–169
  embracing challenges as, 223
  exploring new, 71, 131
  finding hidden, 102
  for growth in your job, 128–130
  identifying for networking, 106–107
  identifying pathways to, 298–299
  leveraging, 112
  mapping skills to, 50
  turning setbacks into, 60–61, 293–300
opportunity costs, for educational paths, 172
organizations, scholarships and grants from, 171
outcome goals, 81, 82
outcomes, achieving successful, 223
overcoming
  fear and limitations, 64
  obstacles, 51–61
overcommitment, time management and, 238
overgeneralization, as an example of negative self-talk, 322
overwhelm
  as an obstacle to finding passion, 52
  as a benefit of time management, 245
ownership, promoting, 178

P

partnerships, establishing for your business, 156–157
passion
  about, 7–8
  defining in life and work, 10–13
  effect on general well-being of, 8–10
  identifying your, 19–20
  myths and misconceptions about, 15–18
  value of finding your, 13–14
past experiences, as an obstacle to finding passion, 52
peer networking, 104
peer support, role of, 273–279
people, in support system, 271–272

performance goals, 81, 82
perseverance
  benefits of, in overcoming setbacks and rejection, 288–289
  building, 299–300
  cultivating, 325–327
  fear and, 254
  impact of growth mindset on, 226–227
  practicing, 300
personal brand statement, creating, 197–201
personal branding
  about, 191
  creating a bio, 202–203
  creating a professional social media profile, 203–204
  creating personal brand statement and elevator pitch, 197–201
  creating strong online presence, 201–206
  defining values, strengths, and unique selling points, 193–197
  developing, 101, 103
  developing content strategy, 204–206
  engaging with your audience, 204–206
  establishing, 192–193
  importance of, 192–197
  importance of storytelling in, 206–209
personal connections, with mentors and role models, 120
personal development
  about, 130
  goals for, 81, 82–83
  growth mindset and, 181
personal growth
  about, 50, 113, 130, 160
  as an advantage of formal education, 162
  benefits of setbacks and rejection in, 287–288
  enhancing, 179–180
  fostering, 177, 268–269
  growth mindset and, 181
  passion as a catalyst for, 14
  value of networking in, 101–103
personal referrals/introductions, 107
personal relationships, self-care and, 308–309
personal story, developing your, 208–209
personality, assessing, 34–44
personality types
  about, 35–37
  identifying your own, 37–40

personalizing
  as an example of negative self-talk, 322
  interactions, 114
perspective
  gaining new, 64
  maintaining, 299
physical exercise, for self-care, 304
physical health
  as a benefit of hobbies, 69
  improving, 306
  passion and, 9
  self-care and, 311–312
plans
  for career transitions, 137–138
  creating to achieve goals, 84–91
  time management and, 238
podcasts, 182
portfolios, building to showcase expertise, 189–190
positive reinforcement, success and, 97
possibilities, expanding, 64
practice
  deliberate, 188
  power of in building skills, 48
presence, self-care and, 308
prioritizing
  hobbies, 71
  time management and, 238
proactiveness, 114
problem-solving abilities, enhancing, 179
process goals, 81, 82
processes, developing to maximize efficiency, 248
procrastination
  about, 90
  elimination of, 236
  time management and, 238
productivity
  as a benefit of time management, 245
  improving, 306–307
  passion for enhanced, 14
  time management and, 237
professional associations/organizations
  about, 106, 182
  scholarships and grants from, 171
professional circle, expansion of, 101
professional development, 50

professional growth
  about, 113
  benefits of setbacks and rejection in, 287–288
  enhancing, 179–180
  fostering, 268–269
  value of networking in, 101–103
professional networks
  about, 103, 129
  building, 137–138
  as a role of training and professional
    development, 163
professional relationships
  building and maintaining, 105–106
  self-care and, 308–309
professional training programs, 182
professionalism, maintaining, 133
progress
  acknolwedgement of, 96–97
  celebrating, 231, 348
  tracking, 91–97
project management metrics, 96
projects, that align with interests/values, 130–132
psychological well-being, passion and, 9
public speaking events, 354
public-funded programs, scholarships and grants
    from, 171

R

reckless risks, 258–261
recognition
  empowerment through, 27
  as a role of training and professional development, 164
reflection
  about, 129, 131, 231
  opportunities for, 237
reflection prompts, 231
reframing failures, 60–61
reinforcement, positive, success and, 97
rejection. See setbacks and rejection
rejuvenation, importance of, 342–344
relationships
  authentic, 28
  building with colleagues and supervisors, 132–134
  developing, 272–273
  enriched, 31

strategies

  for career transitions, 138

  for handling failure and mistakes, 320–325

  for managing rejection and setbacks, 289–293

  for managing stress and burnout, 334–340

  for overcoming fear and taking risks, 254–258

  for self-care, 309–313

strengths

  defining your, 193–197

  understanding your, 22, 25–28

stress management

  about, 59, 329–330

  as a benefit of hobbies, 69

  compared with burnout, 330

  impact of, 331–334

  passion and, 9

  self-care for, 305–306

stress reduction

  about, 307

  time management and, 237, 245

successes

  celebrating, 348

  fear of, 252

  visualizing, 300, 349

supervisors, building relationships with, 132–134

support

  lack of, 91

  from networks, 102

  seeking, 186, 300

  seeking from mentors and peers, 292

support system

  about, 265–266

  benefits of accountability, 274–275

  boosting motivation and well-being, 267–268

  creating a, 58

  developing, 269–273

  developing plan for accountability and peer support, 276–279

  developing relationships and networks, 272–273

  fostering personal and professional growth, 268–269

  identifying potential accountability partners and peer support groups, 275–276

  maintaining, 269–273

  people in, 271–272

  resources in, 271–272

  role of accountability partners and peer support, 273–279

  self-care and, 308

  value of social support, 266–269

systems, developing to maximize efficiency, 248

T

talents

  identifying potential career paths based on, 49–50

  identifying your natural, 45–50

  uncovering hidden, 64

targeted growth, 31

task automation, 244, 246–247

team-building, for your business, 156–157

technical requirements, of educational opportunities, 168

TED Talks, 354

testing values, 25

time, lack of, 90

time management

  about, 235–236

  developing systems and processes to maximize efficiency, 248

  effectiveness of, 239–242

  importance of, 236–239

  role of delegation and automation in, 242–247

timelines, creating for achieving goals, 86–88

Tip icon, 3

Todoist, 93

tools, for tracking progress towards goals, 93

tracking progress, 91–97

traditional roles, 50

training. *See* education and training

training and development programs, 129

traveling, 65, 66, 67

Trello, 93

trust-building, 112, 308

tuition, 172

U

uncertainty, fear of, 252

unique selling points (USPs)

  defining your, 193–197

  in personal story development, 208

uniqueness, in storytelling, 207

Acknowledgments

As I reflect upon the culmination of this Guide, profound gratitude wells within me for the many hands and hearts that contributed to its creation. To the individuals who generously shared their stories, insights, and expertise, you have added depth and authenticity to these pages. Your experiences serve as beacons for others.

A heartfelt appreciation extends to the countless mentors, teachers, and visionaries whose wisdom has been distilled into the essence of these words. Your teachings have been the guiding stars, offering direction in passion exploration.

To the tireless editorial team at Wiley who worked diligently to refine and elevate this Guide, your dedication has been invaluable. Your commitment to clarity and coherence has transformed ideas into a narrative that I hope will resonate with every reader.

Special thanks to the readers — the seekers, the curious, the bold — who embark on the journey outlined in these pages. Your willingness to explore the terrain of your passions is an act of courage. May you find in these words not just guidance but a mirror reflecting the limitless potential within you.

Finally, I express my deepest gratitude to the universal force that binds all of us. Whatever name we give to this cosmic energy — whether it's inspiration, the muse, or the divine — it is to this ineffable source that I bow in acknowledgment and appreciation for the creative impulse that flowed through the creation of this Guide.

In gratitude and appreciation,

Noeline Kirabo

Publisher's Acknowledgments

Acquisitions Editor: Jennifer Yee

Managing Editor: Kristie Pyles

Project Manager: Tracy Brown Hamilton

Copy Editor: Gill Editorial Services

Technical Editor: Rosalie Putman

Cover Image: Vladimir Vladimirov/ Getty Images

If you're a dreamer who has yet to embark on this odyssey, may these words be the spark that ignites the flame of curiosity within you.

Author Biography

Noeline Kirabo is a distinguished personal and business development coach/consultant, author, TED speaker, certified mentor, trainer, and life coach. With a doctorate in entrepreneurship management and more than 15 years of experience in the civil society sector, she is a recognized authority in the fields of personal and professional growth.

As a family therapist and social entrepreneur, Noeline has made a lasting impact on the lives of children, youth, women, and community initiatives. She has also served as a personal and business development consultant for numerous exceptional companies in the East African region and beyond.

Noeline is the founder and executive director of Kyusa, a for-impact organization committed to improving the quality of life for marginalized youth through entrepreneurship development. Her dedication to this cause has earned her a reputation as a transformative leader in the field of social entrepreneurship.

In addition to her extensive work in social entrepreneurship, Noeline is an accomplished author. She has published several self-help books, business workbooks, and personal development planners. Her writing style is engaging, practical, and informative, giving readers the tools they need to unlock their full potential.

Whether you're seeking a consultant to guide you on your personal or professional journey, a partner to coauthor a project, or an inspirational speaker for your next event, Noeline Kirabo is a name you can trust. Her expertise, dedication, and transformative leadership make her a powerful force in the world of personal and business development.

Dedication

If you're a seeker of purpose and architect of your destiny, this guide is dedicated to you: the dreamer, the adventurer, the one who dares to uncover the depths of your passions.

If you've navigated your passions and emerged with a sense of purpose, your stories have illuminated the way for others.